THE BERLIN MISSION

THE
BERLIN
MISSION

THE AMERICAN WHO RESISTED
NAZI GERMANY FROM WITHIN

RICHARD BREITMAN

PUBLICAFFAIRS
New York

PublicAffairs
Hachette Book Group
1290 Avenue of the Americas, New York, NY 10104
www.publicaffairsbooks.com
@Public_Affairs

Printed in the United States of America

First Edition: October 2019

Published by PublicAffairs, an imprint of Perseus Books, LLC, a subsidiary of Hachette Book Group, Inc. The PublicAffairs name and logo is a trademark of the Hachette Book Group.

The Hachette Speakers Bureau provides a wide range of authors for speaking events. To find out more, go to www.hachettespeakersbureau.com or call (866) 376-6591.

The publisher is not responsible for websites (or their content) that are not owned by the publisher.

Print book interior design by Trish Wilkinson.

Library of Congress Cataloging-in-Publication Data
Names: Breitman, Richard, 1947– author.
Title: The Berlin mission : the American who resisted Nazi Germany from within / Richard Breitman.
Description: First edition. | New York : Public Affairs, [2019] | Includes bibliographical references and index.
Identifiers: LCCN 2019019036| ISBN 9781541742161 (hardcover) | ISBN 9781541742178 (ebook)
Subjects: LCSH: Geist, Raymond Herman, 1885-1955. | Consuls—United States—Biography. | Jews—Germany—History—1933-1945. | Germany—Emigration and immigration—1933-1945. | United States—Foreign relations—Germany. | Germany—Foreign relations—United States.
Classification: LCC E748.G294 B74 2019 | DDC 943/.004924009043--dc23
LC record available at https://lccn.loc.gov/2019019036ISBNs: 978-1-5417-4216-1 (hardcover), 978-1-5417-6764-5 (e-book)

ISBNs: 978-1-5417-4216-1 (hardcover), 978-1-5417-6764-5 (e-book)

LSC-C

10 9 8 7 6 5 4 3 2 1

To Dr. Kenneth Davis, Dr. Myron Schwartz, and Dr. Sean McCance, who made this work possible.

Much of what Hitler did in the German Reich, the processes of dictatorial government which he invented and set in motion, are schemes which any group of politicians might seize upon here or anywhere else at any time! I . . . have seen them worked out to the utmost limit under Hitler; and I fear that we have those among us who would gladly sacrifice their liberties for the kind of precarious security which Hitler provided for his followers for all too brief a time.

FROM A 1940 ADDRESS BY RAYMOND GEIST

CONTENTS

Photo section appears after page 138

PROLOGUE

On the evening of January 30, 1939, Adolf Hitler spoke from the podium of the Kroll Opera House in Berlin to the nearly six hundred deputies of the German parliament. High Nazi officials sat on the stage behind him, and on the back wall above was a mounted casting of a huge eagle clutching a large swastika.

About halfway through, Hitler thundered this prophecy: if "international finance Jewry"—Jews inside and outside Europe—once again plunged the nations into a world war, they would regret it. Gesticulating with his right arm and right index finger, he exclaimed: "The result will not be the bolshevization of the earth and thereby the victory of Jewry, but the annihilation of the Jewish race in Europe." The Nazi deputies, all of them men, applauded wildly.[1]

Some foreign dignitaries were on hand. Prentiss Gilbert, the senior US diplomat in Germany on that day, had chosen not to attend, fearing embarrassment if Hitler in his speech attacked the United States and President Franklin Delano Roosevelt. Gilbert arranged instead to have "certain Embassy secretaries" get their impressions firsthand.[2] The longest serving of the six US embassy officials who held the title of secretary then was Raymond H. Geist; he had the best German language skills and he had lived in Berlin longer than the others. Hitler's words in the opera house were consistent with what Geist had anticipated more clearly, and for longer, than any other

American. He knew exactly what was foreshadowed and he brought this awareness to the heart of his mission: he was our man in Berlin during its darkest decade, and he would do far more than merely bear witness to it.

INTRODUCTION

A young man, five feet ten inches tall with thick, dark-brown hair, intense blue-gray eyes, and a ruddy complexion entered the office of Wilbur J. Carr, director of the US Consular Service on April 21, 1921. This was Raymond Herman Geist, living in Cambridge, Massachusetts, and lecturing at Harvard. He was soon hired as a vice consul, the lowest rung in the Consular Service. His long-shot job interview would later benefit Albert Einstein, Sigmund Freud, and tens of thousands of German Jews. Few of them ever learned just how he helped them.

During his long stay in Berlin from December 1929 to October 1939, Geist negotiated occasionally with Heinrich Himmler, Reinhard Heydrich, and Hermann Göring. Through his Nazi contacts, he accumulated vital information about the future course of the Nazi regime. His actions influenced not just President Franklin D. Roosevelt, but Adolf Hitler as well. But his unconventional life and work remained buried in obscure files, barely registering with historians.[1]

Geist was a central figure in gathering information about questions that resonate in the twenty-first century. How much did Hitler and other leading Nazis plan their course, and how much did they improvise? What might the West have done to limit or reduce the toll from Nazi persecution and mass murder before war broke out? Was it possible to strike any kind of bargain with Nazi Germany?

Unlike the Swedish activist Raoul Wallenberg, who undertook dangerous rescue activities late in the Holocaust, Geist was a loyal US Foreign Service officer who tried to help Jews and others get out of Germany before the Holocaust. Geist probed the outer limits of what was possible within the system. His aspirations and experiences are still relevant today.

Geist's efforts give us a better sense of what was possible in a time of demagoguery, mass murder, and dire threats to Western civilization. His story cautions us against simplistic solutions or partisan distortions retroactively imposed on history long after the events. Indiscriminate moral outrage and scapegoating do not help us learn to deal with our own problems, but the careful study of history might. History does not repeat itself, but sometimes it rhymes.

CHAPTER ONE

VISAS

When Raymond Herman Geist came for his fateful interview in 1921, he brought with him a letter of introduction written by an assistant to Herbert Hoover, who had just become secretary of commerce. Geist had worked on the successful presidential campaign of Warren Harding, who had taken office one month earlier, so he had some connections in the capital.[1] But the State Department had no familiarity with his work or credentials.

Geist liked the idea of becoming a diplomat,[2] but in the 1920s US diplomats were almost without exception wealthy men. On top of their duties dealing with the broad issues of foreign relations, negotiating with foreign government officials, and reporting to the State Department, they were expected to entertain frequently, largely at their own expense. Inevitably, most diplomats then came from private schools and Ivy League universities.[3]

Although Geist was lecturing at Harvard, he was a graduate of Oberlin and Western Reserve (now Case Western Reserve), and he had no money to speak of. Maybe for that reason, Wilbur Carr discouraged Geist from a diplomatic position during their interview, but he suggested Geist might manage quite well as a consul.[4] At that time the Consular Service was entirely separate from the Diplomatic Service, handling mostly visa matters and specific issues or problems of US citizens and American commercial interests abroad. Consuls were also commonly looked down upon by the diplomatic corps for their perceived lower class. One diplomat who later became undersecretary of state cattily observed that consuls had a fondness for YMCA standards and phraseology. Another waspishly compared a nervous, sweating person to "a consul at an embassy dinner."[5]

That would start to change three years later when Carr, among other key State Department officials, arranged the merger of the Consular and Diplomatic Services into a unified Foreign Service. The lines between diplomats and consuls began to blur as consuls were allowed and sometimes encouraged to write economic or political reports to the State Department, and a few crossed over to the diplomatic side. Social distinctions were harder to erase, but the consuls, to the extent they could, began to adopt the style and standards of the diplomats.

Carr noted after the interview that Geist had impressed him.[6] However, in the following months, as Geist took and passed the oral and written exams for the position, Carr became more cautious. Geist was a little old and academically overqualified to be taking a junior position. Nonetheless, in view of all the testimonials and Geist's references, which included letters from Admiral William Benson, the retired chief of naval operations, and Charles Haskins, dean of the Graduate School of Arts and Sciences at Harvard, he agreed to give Geist a trial run.[7]

A major part of a consul's work was the administration of the visa process and deciding the eligibility of visa applicants. Government officials, tourists, businessmen, and others who sought short-term stays in America applied for temporary visas good for up to six months. The consul had to determine that the applicant had a valid reason or purpose for entering the United States and intended to return to his or her native land. Those who sought long-term or permanent stays applied for immigration visas and had to show, at a minimum, that they met the physical, mental, and moral standards under US immigration laws to become productive residents, and that they had no police record. The burden of proof lay with the alien; the decision rested with the consul.

The visa system changed fundamentally in the 1920s. Only weeks after Geist's 1921 interview with Carr, Congress passed the Emergency Quota Act to reduce European immigration to the United States and to change its distribution. Each European country received an annual quota, and the size of its quota depended upon that nationality's share of the American population according to the census of 1910. This law favored countries of northern and western Europe, particularly Britain, and it reduced immigration from southern and eastern Europe, which had boomed in the decades before World War I.

The pseudoscientific doctrines of that age established a hierarchy of races and determined Jews to be a lower one. In his testimony before the House Immigration Committee, Carr himself had singled out eastern European Jews as "filthy un-American and often dangerous in their habits," economically and socially undesirable, "abnormally twisted," and "inclined to become agitators." There was no Jewish quota, because there was no religious or racial category in the law, but the 1921 bill reduced Jewish immigration through a new ceiling on total immigration and through low national quotas for eastern European countries with large Jewish populations. Carr, reflecting the pro-eugenic orientation of many Americans of that era, helped to push this law through. However, one country with a Jewish population of more than half a million was granted a large quota under the new law: Germany. Raymond Geist's grandparents had immigrated to the United States after the revolutionary upheavals of 1848 in the German states, as did hundreds of thousands of others, all of whom counted as German Americans in the 1910 census. The annual quota for Germany was set at fifty-one thousand.[8]

Three years after the immigration bill, the American public and Congress grew even more critical of the ramifications of US involvement in the Great War. They shunned postwar European problems, and they feared the spread of communist radicalism to American shores. President Calvin Coolidge and a Republican Congress made the national origins quotas permanent over the objections of Secretary of Commerce Herbert Hoover, who fretted over inaccuracies in the data and the "hardships" it would result in for American relatives of prospective immigrants. The bill that effected this change, the Immigration Act of 1924, also known as the Johnson-Reed Act, lasted until the 1950s. It reduced the maximum annual immigration from Europe to 153,774. Legislators also tinkered with the national quotas indirectly by using the outdated 1890 census as a basis for determining them.[9]

The effect of this change was that the annual quotas for Russia, Poland, Romania, Lithuania, Latvia, and Yugoslavia together *totaled* about ten thousand. Germany suffered too, with its quota sliced almost in half to 25,957. The law allowed for certain categories, such as children or spouses of US citizens, as well as ministers and professors, to qualify outside the quota, but the loopholes were modest. It also created some preferred groups within the quotas, especially relatives of US citizens. Initially, the State Department and the consuls controlled entry. The Bureau of Immigration and Naturalization in the Department of Labor took over jurisdiction only when visa holders reached American shores.[10]

In September 1930, amidst deteriorating economic conditions and a general climate of hysteria about foreigners, President Hoover asked his cabinet how to cut immigration radically without going back to Congress. State Department experts, led by Carr, now an assistant secretary of state, recommended a provision of the Immigration Act of 1917 barring anyone "likely to become a public charge." Originally aimed at individuals with physical or mental disabilities who would be unable to support themselves in the United States, the public charge regulation allowed Hoover to determine that, under prevailing conditions, only those bringing substantial wealth with them or whose close American relatives had sizable assets (and were willing to support them) could enter. Anyone else who would have had to work was considered likely to become a public charge. Issuing a press release, the White House indicated that consuls should apply this regulation and deny visas to those without substantial resources. The State Department duly sent revised instructions to consuls in Europe.[11]

From July 1, 1929, until June 30, 1930, the annual German immigration quota was filled and the monthly allotments of the annual quota were nearly used up for the next few months. But after the consuls received the new instructions in September, the monthly numbers dropped sharply. By the end of the fiscal year (June 1931), fewer than ten thousand visas had been issued, still too many for the Hoover administration.

Geist was sent to Berlin as a consul in 1929, and he quickly drew praise for his work. After just six months, his outgoing superior called him "a distinct credit to the Service" and a man of mature judgment who would have advanced further if he had entered at an earlier age.[12] In mid-1930, Geist was joined in Berlin by George S. Messersmith, a Pennsylvania-born descendant of Rhineland Germans who had come to the English colonies in the eighteenth century. Messersmith was an experienced consul general who had served in Belgium and Argentina, and as his superior, he became Raymond Geist's ally in Berlin.[13]

Messersmith tried to placate the Hoover administration's increasingly stringent immigration demands. He suggested that in the future he could hold visas to 10 percent of the quota, but that he did not want to do away with visas for applicants without US relatives as the administration suggested. He argued that some of these applicants would make good citizens and benefit the United States. The State Department's Visa Section responded that some of the regular visa recipients were nonetheless likely to become public charges. Messersmith bowed to the pressure, even as he held onto the principle that some nonrelatives were qualified. In the year ending in June 1932, only 2,068 individuals received immigration visas under the German quota; the majority of them had relatives already living in the United States.[14]

Reacting to the tense political mood in Washington, the Consulate General in Berlin reviewed its long waiting list for immigration visas. Most applicants were told they were now defined as potential public charges and advised to either to drop their applications or defer consideration of their cases until economic conditions in the United States improved. The waiting list shrank considerably as a result. In March 1931, Messersmith reported that it was down to nothing. Millions of Americans were destitute; the plight of foreigners was not viewed charitably. In such circumstances, the awarding of any kind of visa could become a charged and highly politicized act.

Geist, however, found a way to keep the hopes of would-be immigrants alive, allowing people to apply informally, without paying the application fee. These individuals were temporarily inadmissible, but their files would be activated once US unemployment declined substantially. In effect, he converted an active waiting list to an inactive list, without jeopardizing the immediate cutback.[15]

With the issuing of immigration visas effectively shut down, State Department officials worried that some temporary visitors would intentionally overstay their visas. They called on consuls to submit information sheets on each individual visitor, and Messersmith and Geist complied.[16]

In this charged atmosphere, a world-renowned physicist sought to come to the United States. The case of Albert and Elsa Einstein raised political issues on both sides of the Atlantic, and it landed on the desk of Raymond Geist. Before Hitler came to power, the Nazi Party had excoriated Einstein as a Jew, a leftist radical, and a pacifist—and they didn't like his theory of relativity either. Although Albert and Elsa had invested most of their savings in their house near Potsdam, in 1932 they tentatively agreed on a new academic base at what was to be the Institute for Advanced Study at Princeton. Albert also accepted for the third time a short visiting professorship at the California Institute of Technology.[17] He needed a temporary visa, but there was a good chance he would stay permanently if allowed.

The German government had sponsored Einstein's earlier visits to the United States, giving him a courtesy diplomatic passport. Getting a temporary visa for the United States was routine, and the shipping line had handled it. But in December 1932 Einstein was a private citizen who might, one way or another, become an immigrant. Getting a new visa would be much more complicated. While Einstein had other options for a new home and base of scientific research, he did not have all that much time to get out of Germany. The rising tide of anti-Semitism was worrying.[18]

Reports of Einstein's impending trip to the United States mobilized the Woman Patriot Corporation, a fading bastion of upper-class, right-wing American prejudice with a history of fulminating against perceived radicals at home. Mrs. Randolph Frothingham, widow of a former Massachusetts congressman and chair of the corporation, denounced Einstein at length to the State Department and various congressmen as an atheist, anarchist, and communist and declared him inadmissible under several different provisions of immigration law. She also contacted the press.[19]

The Seventh Circuit Court of Appeals recently had ruled any member of a communist organization inadmissible into the United States. As a result, despite the fact that Einstein was the most famous scientist in the world and obviously a huge intellectual asset to any country he lived in, Carr wanted strict examination of the Einsteins' possible communist connections. He instructed the Berlin Consulate General that if the Einsteins should apply for any kind of visa anywhere in Germany, the consul would have to ensure they had no links to the Communist International (Comintern). Beyond that, he would have to check with Washington before he granted them visas.[20]

In late November, the shipping line that would take Einstein to the United States, the Hamburg-American Shipping Line (Hapag), asked the Consulate General in Berlin if the Einsteins had to appear in person to apply for visas. The response was yes, unless they held diplomatic passports. On December 2, the Consulate General warned Hapag that time was getting short if the Einsteins expected to make their booked departure the following week.[21]

With their personal interviews looming, the Einsteins decided that they too would use the media to swing the ruling in their favor. They gave an interview to the lead Associated Press correspondent in Berlin, Louis P. Lochner, whom they knew well. Directing his fire at the Woman Patriots, Albert Einstein declared satirically that the fair sex had never before rebuffed him so sharply, and that, as a pacifist, he was opposed to all war except the inevitable one with his own wife. In a letter written days afterward, Lochner reveled in the humor and called it one of the finest scoops he ever had.[22]

Albert and Elsa showed up visibly nervous at the Berlin Consulate General on December 5 to meet with Geist. Messersmith had a previous commitment to inspect the US consulate in Breslau; despite the high-profile nature of the scheduled Berlin visitors, he did not change it. Afterward, he explained that he normally did not conduct visa interviews anyway, and he knew Geist to be courteous and discreet.[23] Messersmith either did not want to alter his schedule to accommodate the eccentric physicist, or he tried to duck what he saw as a no-win situation.

Elsa insisted on doing most of the talking, and Geist struggled to pose questions directly to her husband. Both Einsteins said they regarded it as humiliating to have to appear in person to get a visa. Unable to explain his constraints, Geist assured them that they simply had to fill out certain forms at the consulate and that he wanted to help them. Both Einsteins repeatedly rose from their seats as if to leave during the course of the interview. Geist, with some difficulty, persuaded them to stay put while he filled out the forms with their answers.[24]

He asked about Albert's membership in nonscientific organizations. Albert said he belonged to none, but Elsa corrected him: there were some social and political organizations. Asked if he belonged to any anarchist organizations opposed to government, Einstein replied that he belonged to only pacifist organizations. His affiliation was loose; he did not know if he really supported them. Both he and Elsa denied an alleged connection with the World Congress against Imperialist War, an organization nominally protesting Japanese aggression in Manchuria. It had a communist organizer, and Albert had written a friendly greeting for its August 1932 meeting.[25] Elsa said she alone knew which organizations her husband belonged to, because she handled all their correspondence. Geist had the Einsteins read the relevant provisions of the Immigration Act of 1917, and Albert said he considered himself admissible under those provisions. He pursued his pacifism through peaceful and legal means and took no part in (radical) politics. Messersmith, in contact by phone with Geist during the day, wrote afterward that the Einsteins were anxious that some of Albert's political affiliations might jeopardize their visas.

It wasn't just Messersmith who eagerly watched the proceedings from afar. During this interview, Lochner called Geist to get his side of the issue, but Geist could not talk.[26] (He could not have commented on the record in any case.) When the Einsteins finally finished the paperwork, Geist told them he would let them know as soon as possible, and that he would return their passports with proper visas. The Einsteins had wanted an immediate decision, but they left the office amicably.

Elsa telephoned later with a correction that her husband was a member of Workers' International Relief, affiliated with the communist movement. But now that he knew how this would affect his visa application, he would leave the organization. She also added that unless they received visas by noon the next day, they would withdraw their applications and hold the Consulate General responsible for breaking their contract in the United States. Geist expressed regret for any inconvenience and said that he would get a decision as quickly as possible.

In spite of his faultlessly polite demeanor, he sprang into action immediately after his conversation with Elsa. He telegraphed both the State Department and Messersmith, declaring that the Einsteins qualified for temporary visas. Meanwhile the Einsteins continued to pursue their campaign in the press, not only through the AP, but with the *New York Times* and others. Elsa denounced the "Consul General" (Messersmith) for his rudeness—even though he had not even been present at the interview. A front-page article on the December 6 edition of the *Times* blared: "Professor Albert Einstein was so angered by forty-five minutes of questioning at the United States Consulate General as to his fitness to visit America that he refused to submit to further interrogation and returned home."

Einstein did indeed get a visa shortly afterward, but the subsequent *Times* headline, "Einstein's Ultimatum Brings a Quick Visa," was misleading. Washington had responded on the morning of the sixth with their approval after Geist had speedily prepared a telegram to the State Department, hours after his interview with Elsa and Albert Einstein. Their public ultimatum had nothing to do with it.[27]

The publicity about the Einsteins' visas had its own repercussions. Walter Lippmann, the prominent columnist, demanded Messersmith's recall over the affront to the Einsteins. Unbeknownst to the public, Messersmith had in fact pleaded with the State Department to support

Geist and the Foreign Service. On hearing about the events in the Berlin Consulate General, the outgoing secretary of state, Henry Stimson, was incredulous that Carr had sent instructions to question Einstein. He held a background press breakfast in Washington on December 10 to clarify the situation that was being badly misunderstood by the public. Touching lightly on the stupidity of the proceedings, he compared those who demanded scrutiny of Einstein to those who insisted on draping nude statues. In any case, Stimson told the attendees that the consul—he did not remember Geist's name—had treated the Einsteins with the utmost courtesy. He completely exonerated the Consulate General. Carr then bowed to higher authority and telegraphed the State Department's appreciation for the visa work in Berlin.[28]

The American Chamber of Commerce in Berlin, the American Women's Club of Berlin, and the American Club of Berlin protested what they called grossly exaggerated US press descriptions of the Einsteins' visa interview. Sigrid Schultz, a Berlin reporter for the *Chicago Tribune*, called earlier press reports shoddy because they blamed the absent Messersmith. She also complimented Geist.[29]

Messersmith privately explained again and again that the Einsteins received their visas within twenty-four hours of their appearance at the Consulate General and that in questioning them Geist had done only what Washington and regulations required. In fact, Messersmith felt it was the Einsteins who had subjected Geist to an "ordeal," and he deserved a gold medal for his tact and skill.[30] In effect, Geist had brought about the best result and as quickly as possible; he understood the rules under which he was obliged to operate, managed them deftly, and secured the result in the best interests of natural justice and the United States. He knew the Einsteins were far better off in the United States, and he must have known the United States was better off for admitting them. It was a textbook example of discreet diplomacy. The consul's touch was almost impossible to discern, but somehow the right result was achieved with the minimum of disruption. It was a signature quality of Raymond Geist's tenure. He had become not just "our man in Berlin" but to many Germans in peril he was theirs as well.

Arriving in California in January 1933, Einstein was obligated to give a lecture at Caltech with the goal of improving German-American relations—one of the terms of a grant the university had obtained. Three weeks later, Adolf Hitler was appointed chancellor of Germany. Two months after that, Einstein renounced his German citizenship. In May, Nazi storm troopers ransacked the Einsteins' Potsdam home. In November 1933, the Gestapo announced it had confiscated the Einsteins' property under laws directed against communists and enemies of the state.[31]

Einstein was unique, but other Jewish and non-Jewish immigrants from Nazi Germany contributed greatly to the well-being of the United States. Operating under serious political and legal constraints, Geist helped many to get in. He failed with others. His efforts, his successes, his failures are in part their story.

CHAPTER TWO

THE RISE OF THE NAZIS

Geist's public service began with what his generation called the Great War. He was eager to serve his country after the United States declared war on Germany in 1917, but he ran into obstacles when he tried to enter what later became the Foreign Service.

Germany had stoked American paranoia about German Americans. Americans changed German names of towns, streets, and individuals; the government interned German aliens; a mob even lynched one pro-German speaker in Illinois.[1]

Someone who called himself an "American citizen" described Geist as a rabid pro-German, the son of Germans, and one whose past remarks would suggest he was an enemy of the United States. In his anonymous letter to the secretary of state, the citizen claimed that the president of Western Reserve University—now Case Western Reserve—had written the private secretary of Secretary of War Newton D. Baker, hoping to secure Geist an appointment as attaché in the American Legation in Copenhagen. Other sources suggest Geist sought a position abroad as a translator. The complaining self-styled patriot thought any such foreign assignment outrageous.[2]

William Bullitt, an up-and-coming State Department figure who later came to be known for his personal feuds and political antagonisms, interviewed Geist and found him to be very capable intellectually and apparently loyal. But State Department investigators had turned up some criticism of Geist's character, including the anonymous letter, and one of his references did not check out. So Bullitt stalled any appointment to a position abroad.[3]

Instead, Geist enlisted in the navy and was appointed yeoman second class in the naval reserve. Once the navy learned that he had command of multiple foreign languages, in June 1918 he was assigned chief translator in the naval office of the cable censor in New York under Lieutenant Commander George Barr Baker. During Geist's tenure as chief translator, Admiral William Benson, chief of naval operations, also got to know Geist. Benson, who became naval adviser to the US delegation to the Paris Peace Conference, soon appointed Geist to his own staff.[4]

Thus in December, Geist was able to finally serve his country abroad when he went to Paris with the US peace delegation. He translated German, French, Italian, and Spanish documents for the naval censor's office, and he prepared a daily digest of world news for the heads of the US delegation. When President Woodrow Wilson arrived in Paris in January 1919, Geist was among those who went to tea at the president's hotel.[5]

In mid-January, part of the delegation toured battlefronts in eastern France. Geist salvaged some battlefield souvenirs, such as a large red tassel from the rubble of the cathedral at Soissons. He was horrified to find the Reims Cathedral, one of the most beautiful in the world, horribly mutilated. In a letter home he asked his sisters to imagine nine hundred thousand rounds of ammunition fired daily for four years into Reims. He jumped into a German trench so deep that it was black as night. Lighting a match, he found and liberated a German helmet, an axe, and an alarm bell.[6]

In April, the peace negotiations effectively concluded, Admiral Benson deactivated Geist so that he could join Hoover's private organization called the American Relief Administration, to supply food and clothing to distressed areas of Europe.[7] Geist went to Vienna, no longer the capital of a large multinational Austro-Hungarian Empire, but of a shrunken, politically divided, and insecure new republic.[8] The city and the country desperately needed outside help. During 1918 the domestic harvest had fallen by 50 percent, and food imports from Romania and Hungary, which usually covered more than half of Vienna's needs, slowed to a trickle. Hunger and devastation were widespread, and only those who had recourse to the black market could manage to rise above subsistence level.[9] Under the Allied naval blockade, which continued after the armistice, food supplies in Europe still were desperately short.

Austrians found the terms of the 1919 peace settlement very harsh: despite its largely Germanic population, the country was barred from merging with Germany, and it had to pay reparations for war damages. Budget deficits and trade deficits grew uncontrollably. Middle- and upper-class Austrians feared a communist revolution like the one that had shaken neighboring Hungary. An uneasy and inexperienced coalition government of Social Democrats, Christian Socials, and right-wing nationalists responded by printing money, which accelerated inflation. Rationing and price controls were in force.

With the title of food commissioner for Vienna and lower Austria, Geist concentrated first on establishing municipal facilities to prepare and supply meals to more than one hundred thousand malnourished children, many suffering from rickets. The initial feeding effort quickly generated publicity. Lines of children began to form hours before the kitchens opened.[10] The scene made an impression on Geist. Months after he'd moved on to other endeavors, he still talked about those Viennese children and tried to raise money for them. He donated money himself.[11]

Geist's academic credentials, fluent German, and commitment impressed Viennese officials. The Austrian government telegraphed Hoover, asking him to lend Geist to them. American Relief Administration officials in London agreed.[12] Once they had received approval from Geist's superiors, the Austrians gave him an impossible job—management of soup kitchens for adults and of the general food-rationing system. He became, in a term that his backers meant positively, the American food "dictator," because the state and the city were too weak to do the job.[13]

Geist drew up a plan to feed a million people in open public kitchens through the winter of 1919.[14] Viennese Social Democratic officials praised Geist publicly and in the press. Municipal Councilor

Hugo Breitner, the leading financial expert of the Austrian Social Democrats, announced that under Geist one million people would soon enjoy meals distributed by the city. The mayor announced that it was impossible to exaggerate the city's gratitude to the Hoover mission for lending Geist to Vienna. It appears that Geist had the backing of Austrian chancellor Karl Renner as well. The Austrian government apparently hoped that Geist, with his Hoover connections, would add to the meager food supplies in ways that the Austrians themselves could not. A cartoon in an illustrated newspaper showed Geist wearing a chef's hat and swinging a spoon as a scepter.[15]

But it wasn't all praise and gratitude for Geist. Captain Claire M. Torrey, the nominal head of the Hoover team in Vienna, resented him. Torrey felt Geist acted independently of his authority. Some other Hooverites felt that Geist's publicity contravened their strategy of taking a low-key role to underscore their idealism. Geist responded that—for better or for worse—he had become a figure of interest to journalists. He had no control over the attention he was receiving, but he might have reasonably argued that publicity could mobilize additional people and resources.[16]

Despite his achievements, in November 1919 he was ordered by the Hoover organization to withdraw. At the time, Geist claimed that his kitchens were already supplying fifty thousand adults with food and he expected that the number would rise to one hundred thousand by the end of the year. He wrote passionately: "My duty to humanity and a starving city only too clearly teaches me what to do. I cannot carry out this order as I am morally bound before God to fulfill the task I have been officially and providentially appointed to do."[17] The Austrians by this time had given him their Salvator Mundi Medal for humanitarian achievement.[18]

Baseless and bigoted rumors were swirling around Geist. The Christian Social press complained about the abolition of the wartime Christian Women's soup kitchens, and took umbrage at the fact that Geist, to whom they referred as "an American Jew," managed their municipal successors.[19] Some Austrian rightists associated Jewishness with humanitarian work performed by outsiders. In fact, although

Geist was progressive in some ways, he was no socialist, and he had no Jewish ancestors.

In the winter of 1920, *Collier's* ran an extremely favorable feature on Geist, depicting him as the most striking case study of American "pep" doing battle with Old World bureaucracy. According to the article, Geist tore around the streets in a car with a big American flag streaming from the windshield, and no one hated him because he was so good-natured. But by the time the article appeared, Geist was gone from Vienna, and not by choice. By January 1920, he was forced to leave both the Hoover organization and his Austrian position.[20] It was a short-lived food dictatorship.

Although he had been unable to complete his mission, from his months in Vienna Geist must have gained confidence that he could connect personally (as well as politically) with Europeans of different walks of life and social standing. He also witnessed firsthand that despite inflammatory reports, Social Democrats in central Europe were committed democrats, not wild-eyed revolutionaries. He faced pressure and political fire without flinching: his withdrawal came not because of the Europeans with whom he negotiated and worked, but because of the jealousies and turf rivalries of his fellow Americans. It was a hard lesson but one he learned well.

His first ten years in what became the Foreign Service were a long slog. His individualistic impulses notwithstanding, he had to get accustomed to working with two bureaucracies—the State Department in Washington and the local US institutions at each post. In the larger or more important countries, the United States had an embassy headed by an ambassador; elsewhere it had a legation run by a minister. Almost everywhere it had consulates or consulates general (at more important sites). Geist was immediately subordinate to the local head of the consular operations, but an ambitious or energetic ambassador could exercise authority over the consulate, too. He had a lot of superiors in different capacities, and as vice consul and then a junior consul, he had little scope for initiative.

In the years that followed, Geist had a miserable post in Buenos Aires because of an obnoxious superior. He did better in Montevideo,

Uruguay, because he had freer rein. He seems to have been little challenged (and perhaps bored) in a long stretch in Alexandria, Egypt, where his elder sister Anna accompanied him. His work generated praise and criticism in roughly equal measure. Geist nearly resigned twice.[21] He never encountered the intensity and the challenges—the sense that he had a unique opportunity to help change the world—of his Vienna months until he and Anna arrived in Berlin at the end of 1929.

Geist and his sister found an apartment in Wilmersdorf, a pleasant neighborhood southwest of the city center with some private houses, nice apartment complexes, and parks.[22] The Consulate General building at 5 Bellevuestrasse, a street known for its art galleries, was a couple of miles away. That was very close to the Tiergarten and German government buildings, in the city center. Geist could ride his bicycle there from Wilmersdorf, or, when he preferred, he could use the city's rapid transit underground system. American diplomats, journalists, and businessmen stationed in Berlin and their families made up a sizable group of Americans for the Geists to meet.

A couple of months after the Geists arrived, the United States announced the selection of Frederic M. Sackett as ambassador. Born to wealth in Providence, Rhode Island, Sackett married into an even wealthier Louisville family. After getting a law degree, he managed his wife's family's mines, banks, and real estate for several decades. During this time, he also met Herbert Hoover. In midlife, he dove into Republican politics and won election as senator from Tennessee. But looking toward reelection in 1930, he faced a tough Republican primary battle. The Depression also limited his prospect for winning the votes of Kentucky's Democrat-leaning coal miners in the general election. His old friend, Herbert Hoover, was now president and wanted a smart businessman in Berlin attuned to his own policies. Sackett agreed to shift to diplomacy.[23]

The State Department chose George A. Gordon, an experienced diplomat, as Sackett's counselor of embassy, the top career post in Berlin. Gordon was a prickly character. He did not think it proper for the ambassador to mix with private German citizens. He loathed journalists, and he did not think American consuls were much better.

According to Martha Dodd, daughter of Sackett's successor, Gordon would no sooner consort with consuls than be seen in public in his underwear. In official meetings Gordon could be abrupt to the point of rudeness.[24] Sackett also drew on First Secretary John Cooper Wiley, a wealthy diplomat who had wider German contacts. When Gordon went home to tend to an ailing wife, Wiley stepped into the top post. Later, another veteran diplomat, Alfred Klieforth, supplemented Wiley. It was a rapid rotation of diplomats. Geist quietly outlasted them all. The longer he stayed, the better he grasped the political forces and the key people.

Messersmith, who arrived a few months after Sackett, was of much greater significance for Geist's ascent. The new German American consul general had attended college in Delaware but failed to complete the work for his degree. He had worked his way up through the consular ranks nonetheless. He had a passion for administration and memo writing the way some today have a passion for tweeting. He resented diplomatic snobbery, and he sought contacts across German society. Urging the new ambassador to travel to major cities and to meet businessmen, bankers, and academics, Messersmith was the antithesis of Gordon.

One former subordinate said that Messersmith couldn't resist talking to subordinates as if they were naughty students who had not done their homework. If that was the case, he treated Geist like his star pupil. Only two years apart in age, Geist and Messersmith had a good deal in common: German roots, command of the German language, interest in commerce, and a willingness to get to know Germany and Germans. Messersmith chose Geist as his executive assistant, and Geist learned how to cut budgets during the Depression with a minimum of fuss. Messersmith's working group often continued after hours and would conclude over dinner at his home. Geist learned from him how to report to Washington formally and informally, although luckily he did not imitate Messersmith's writing style, which was often dreadful.[25]

The American colony in Berlin was a large network. After embassy and consular officials noticed a substantial number of destitute

Americans in Berlin, the American Women's Club, the American Chamber of Commerce, and the American Club formed a committee to raise funds for emergency support. Sackett, honorary chair, and Messersmith, honorary vice chair, were the first donors. Anna Geist, Raymond's sister, had joined the American Women's Club when they moved to Berlin. She was one of five committee members who ran the appeal and the program.[26] The Geists were part of a group, even a real team, of American officials in Berlin.

Messersmith used the Rotary Club of Berlin to connect with influential Germans in private. Resentment of Germany's World War I role delayed Rotary International's authorization of German chapters until 1927, but Rotary arrived in Berlin in 1929.[27] Berliners already had a plethora of formal and informal clubs, but to join Rotary was to make a statement: its German members wanted to rejoin the international community, promote German exports, and demonstrate their humanistic values. Seeking camaraderie, they shed their formal German mannerisms: "Herr Doktor" was out; members addressed each other with "Rotarian" plus their last names. Rotary was inclusive, with Protestants, Catholics, and Jews.[28] It met weekly for lunch at the Hotel Kaiserhof, Berlin's first luxury hotel, on the Wilhelmplatz, located next to the Reich Chancellery. Messersmith kept contact with businessmen and professionals there whom he might not see otherwise.[29]

In this period, Messersmith and Geist did not need to submit political reports like those done by consuls in other German cities because the two took part in almost daily discussions about German politics with Sackett, likely at the ambassador's initiation.[30] Consequently, Geist's views of the rise of the Nazis in this period are hard to trace. He did submit two voluntary political reports during 1931, but they apparently went only to the Embassy, not to Washington.[31] And most embassy records were destroyed during World War II.

Although Geist was a junior member of a team of American officials in Berlin, his experience in Vienna allowed him to grasp the seriousness of German political and economic problems. Despite its isolationist mood in the 1920s, the United States had committed itself to stabilizing Germany economically in the belief that a successful democracy was unlikely to start another war. American interests were at stake, too. As secretary of commerce, Herbert Hoover had created a special unit to alert Americans to trade and financial opportunities in Germany. Between 1925 and 1930, private American investors had lent nearly $3 billion to Germany.[32] However, the Depression disturbed the relationship between the United States and Germany, affecting the consul's traditional role of promoting American exports.

A provision of the Treaty of Versailles made Germany liable for reparation payments to France, Great Britain, and Belgium. In 1930, the German government proposed to take out an American loan to help meet reparations. It would have made American investors directly liable for Germany's political stability. Moody's Investors Service reassured banks and investors that no German party would wish to default on such a loan.[33] American bankers failed to grasp the volatility of Germany's political scene.

The German republic established by a revolution in November 1918 informally went by the name of Weimar, the town where its Constituent Assembly met a few months later. Weimar had been a focal point of eighteenth-century German culture, but parliament chose to meet there in 1919 because left-wing and right-wing extremists made Berlin too dangerous. Weimar Germany had multiple political parties and deep political divisions. The German National People's Party (Nationalists), the closest thing to a party of big business, favored restoration of the monarchy and an aggressive nationalism. The Nationalists detested the working-class Social Democratic Party, associated with postwar international conciliation. The Center Party looked to secure the position of the Catholic Church and its Catholic constituents. Smaller parties of the middle and right filled out coalition governments, but the Depression exacerbated Germany's political and social fault lines, weakening the center.

Growing poverty and social discontent benefited extremists. In theory, the German Communist Party worked toward proletarian revolution in Europe. They did not care to make democratic systems work as a means to their ends. German Communists promoted

Soviet foreign policy and tried to stymie the German Social Democrats, from whom they had split. Initially independent, the German Communists soon fell under the control of the Soviet Union and the Moscow-dominated Comintern.[34]

To the German middle classes in 1930, the communists seemed more dangerous than the Nazis. At the time, Nazis did not seem like credible national actors. Hitler's Beer Hall Putsch in 1923 failed even to take control of Munich, let alone the country. Hitler received sympathetic treatment from the judges at his trial for treason, and a light prison sentence, but his reorganized National Socialist Party failed for years to achieve electoral success. In the 1928 national parliamentary elections, the Nazis received about 3 percent of the vote.

A political standoff developed in 1930, when a special government-run unemployment insurance fund ran dry. Corporate leaders wanted to reduce government spending and the tax burden on industry and commerce, not replenish the fund. The Social Democrats wanted to raise worker and employer contributions to the fund in order to maintain benefits for the unemployed. Business-oriented parties in the coalition government opposed compromise, thinking they would be better off without the Social Democrats sharing power.[35]

At the end of March, the broad coalition government under Social Democratic chancellor Hermann Müller collapsed. Heinrich Brüning, an economist by training and member of the Center Party, received the backing of President Paul von Hindenburg to form a new minority government without the Social Democrats. It turned out to be the first move toward legislative paralysis and unchecked executive authority.

George F. Kennan, one day to be the foreign policy expert credited with the post–World War II doctrine of containment of the Soviet Union, came to Berlin in 1931 to learn German. While Geist took a leave, Kennan filled his post as consul.[36] On June 1, Kennan asked a dinner companion whether they were now witnessing the crisis of capitalism.[37] He and other observers feared that the Great Depression was dragging down liberal democracies and that Germany was particularly vulnerable.

American diplomats reported early and often about Hitler and the Nazis during their rise to power. John Wiley filed the first detailed report even before Brüning took office. Calling them Hitlerites and German fascists, Wiley correctly noted that one part of their political strategy was to harp on the danger of a communist uprising. He also perceived that their gains came at the expense of the Nationalists. Initially, Ambassador Sackett was confident that the Social Democrats were strong enough to prevent excessive growth of the extremists. In fact, both Sackett and Wiley described the Social Democrats as the main support of the republic.[38]

In 1931, the executive director of the Council on Foreign Relations in New York asked if Geist could supply more accurate and up-to-date information about the goals of each of the many German parties, after noting increasingly unstable political conditions there. Geist contacted the editor of a publication in Germany, got the page proofs with the official platforms of each major German party, and laboriously set about translating them during his vacations, because he had all too much to do during regular hours. He also sent a copy to the State Department, since this basic information about Germany's major parties was not available in English in Washington.[39]

Geist's personal experiences also afforded him additional insight into the political landscape of Germany. During his time in Vienna, he had had close ties with the Austrian Social Democrats. The German Social Democrats shared a similar ideology and traditions with the Austrians: they were more democrats than they were socialists. So Geist probably encouraged his embassy colleagues to take a favorable view of the Social Democrats, not a natural stance for wealthy (and in Sackett's case, anti-union) American diplomats. But he likely was preaching to the converted: it did not take inside knowledge to reach the conclusion that the German Social Democrats were the strongest supporters of the democratic republic.

Sackett and Messersmith also expressed optimism about Heinrich Brüning's minority government, and they hoped and believed that the new chancellor was seeking to rebuild a parliamentary majority and to avoid new elections during the Depression.[40] In the short run,

Brüning was comfortable using the president's emergency powers to issue laws by decree. But he was determined to dissolve parliament and hold new elections rather than cave in to challenges to his deflationary economic and financial measures. Thus, when one of his financial decrees failed in July 1930, in part due to the efforts of the Social Democrats, Brüning called for new elections.

Brüning had no sense of timing. In September 1930, German voters spurned conventional parties. The Social Democrats, still the strongest party, dropped about five percentage points. Some of those voters deserted to the German Communists, who topped 13 percent for the first time. The Nationalists saw their support sliced in half, with many of those voters moving to the Nazis. A flood of previous nonvoters also selected the Nazis. The Austrian-born Hitler, not yet a German citizen, now led the second-strongest party, with about 18 percent of the seats in parliament. From this point on, both the German Communists and the Nazis worked to thwart legislation. The Weimar Republic had become a candle burning at both ends. Nazi campaigners gradually became the most energetic and effective critics of the status quo.[41]

Geist began to see the threat of fascism spring up in daily life. One example was the church he attended with Anna. He found that the pastor at the American Church in Berlin, Reverend Ewart E. Turner "had the tendency to turn his pulpit into a political forum and gave Nazi sympathizers a chance to use the American pulpit in Berlin as a means of furthering Hitler doctrine." He noted further that the clergyman "aroused the animosity of conscientious people who believed in upholding the American traditions."[42]

Ambassador Sackett recognized other ominous signs: in the segmented world of German politics, the Nazis had broader social appeal than most parties. The Nazis were primarily responsible for political riots in the streets of major cities, and the breakdown of law and order only added to pessimism about the political system. But at times, Sackett undercut his own reports of the Nazi danger by stressing the more familiar communist threat.[43]

Sackett became Brüning's confidant and advocate. The ambassador tried to give the chancellor greater leverage in Berlin and greater clout in Washington, especially in thorny negotiations over reducing reparations during late 1930 and 1931. Brüning was a difficult ally, aiming to use the economic crisis to obtain a moratorium on reparations payments. He secretly wanted to eliminate reparations entirely and ultimately hoped to restore the monarchy. President Hoover could only do so much for Brüning—a one-year moratorium on reparations payments. Sackett became Brüning's favorite diplomat, but it was not enough to alter political dynamics. Brüning remained heavily dependent on the goodwill and the emergency powers of President Hindenburg, as well as the toleration of the Social Democrats. Although a member of the Center Party, Brüning's heart was to the right. When push came to shove, he would not rely on democracy.[44]

In the fall of 1931, the politically right-wing association of disabled war veterans arranged for a national memorial service for the German soldiers who died during the Great War. The United States, alone among Germany's wartime foes, was invited to send a speaker for a ceremony broadcast nationally on radio.

Perhaps Ambassador Sackett chose Geist because he had the best command of German among the Americans, but he was also capable of balancing political crosscurrents at a time of rising nationalism. Sackett read and approved Geist's text in advance. Using generous doses of rhetoric to avoid difficulties over specifics, Geist managed to turn the service of the fallen and disabled Germans toward the cause of peace:

> Their names are recorded in history and engraved on monuments . . . but not because they have been able to deliver deadly and awful battle, not because they have dared to perform heroic deeds, but because in all their panoplies and liveries of war they were the instruments and symbols of the defenders of the peace of their country. In honoring them we honor them in all their greatness, and in honoring them we do not honor war, but honor peace.[45]

He expressed Western hopes for peace and disarmament after the horrendous bloodletting of the First World War. But his words could not alter the prevailing mood in the country.

In a late 1931 speech in Mainz, Chancellor Brüning gave a friendly nod to the Nazis, trying to set up possible negotiations for a Center-Nazi coalition government in the state, depending upon the outcome of the state elections. Brüning now hoped to "tame" the Nazis. He thought getting them to support or tolerate his government might work better—and might be more acceptable to President Hindenburg—than leaning on the Social Democrats.[46] But Hitler was not much interested in being tamed.

Instead, the Nationalists and the Nazi Party joined forces with the veterans association called the Stahlhelm, the Agrarian League, and the Pan-German League. Meeting in the spa town of Bad Harzburg, media magnate and Nationalist leader Alfred Hugenberg and Hitler suggested that they were prepared to join in a right-wing coalition. The Nazis and the Nationalists had worked together once before— in a referendum campaign against the Young Plan for reparations in 1929–1930. Both had used reparations as a symbol of the humiliating peace settlement that they and many of Germany's voters hated. They attacked the pro-republican parties that had agreed to the Treaty of Versailles under duress. They refused to believe that Germany had lost the war militarily, and they had many of the same enemies on the left. The two parties and the three associations called their alliance the Harzburg Front. Hitler created the impression that he was willing to cooperate to a limited degree with establishment conservatives. Their availability offered him the first realistic path to power working through the political system.

In November 1931, the Nazis obtained about 37 percent of the vote in the state elections in Hesse, making them the strongest party there. Ambassador Sackett reported to Washington that the voter turnout reached 90 percent and that these results were a good indicator of the strength of the parties throughout the Reich and in Prussia, the largest and most powerful German state.[47] That was not what Washington wanted to hear.

American diplomats in Berlin now needed a better sense of Nazi leaders and their goals. A high official of the Deutsche Bank invited Ambassador Sackett and Alfred Klieforth to a Saturday afternoon tea at his home with a small group of Nazi officials and a certain "Herr Wolff." When "Wolff" turned out to be Hitler, Sackett was not really surprised. He had had some previous hints that high Nazi officials would like to meet with him.[48]

Hitler gave a long harangue as if he were speaking to a large audience. Klieforth translated. Hitler blamed Germany's economic plight on its loss of territory and colonies in the peace settlement and political "tribute" (reparations). His paramilitary forces were for domestic purposes—keeping order and suppressing communism. If France were to invade Germany, Germany would have to repudiate all its private debts. Hitler did not pose questions to Sackett, and the ambassador made only perfunctory comments. Sackett thought it telling that Hitler did not even look him in the eye. It seemed to indicate a man putting on an act.[49]

Sackett called Hitler a fanatical crusader whose forcefulness and intensity attracted the uncritical. His methods were those of the opportunist. Those who weighed the content of his speeches, however, would not be impressed. Any intellectuals or professionals who supported Hitler had to be desperate. Sackett did not believe Hitler capable of handling power; a Nazi government would soon go "on the rocks."[50]

A regular reader of the German press and a man with many contacts in Berlin, Geist was an asset to Sackett, who recognized that. The State Department's Division of Western European Affairs had fallen into disarray in the early 1930s. It lacked anyone who had served in Germany or even spoke German.[51] Sackett later responded to the new chief of western European affairs that Raymond Geist could easily fill that gap in Washington. Discussions with Messersmith and Geist had apparently convinced Sackett that Geist had a particularly good grasp of German political currents. Sackett added, however, that Geist was especially valuable to Messersmith and would be hard to replace in Berlin.[52] It became a refrain that others would repeat over the next seven years.

Brüning prevailed upon eighty-four-year-old President Hindenburg to run for reelection in April 1932. The Harzburg Front split apart. Hitler, having just gained German citizenship through a back-door maneuver in the state of Thuringia, ran as the Nazi candidate, and Theodor Duesterberg, head of the Stahlhelm, as the Nationalist candidate. The German Communists ran their working-class leader Ernst Thälmann. Hitler rented an airplane, flew from stop to stop, and gave forty-six speeches amidst a massive display of organized effort. A Nazi propaganda book of photographs bore a cover with an airplane superimposed on a map of Germany: it was entitled *Hitler over Germany*. Wiley filed a diplomatic report to Washington noting that the constant Nazi appeals to the passions of the Germans were unhealthy; Germans had shown themselves susceptible to nationalist appeals.[53]

Joseph Goebbels, Nazi Party leader for the Berlin district, had correctly predicted that none of the four presidential candidates would get a majority in the first round; a plurality would suffice in the runoff. Goebbels had a system to gauge the Nazi vote by taking a multiple of the size of its party membership, and he projected that Hitler would receive 13.5 million votes in the first round. This turned out to be too high by a couple of million: Hitler's share of the initial vote was about 30 percent. Goebbels had underestimated Hindenburg's 49.6 percent share. When the Nationalist candidate, Duesterberg, withdrew after the first round, his party backed Hitler, in the process wounding Hindenburg's feelings. A monarchist at heart, the elderly president did not think of himself as the candidate of the Social Democrats and the Center. Goebbels had forecast that Hitler would win the runoff, with about 18 million votes. Actually, Hindenburg got 19.3 million votes, about 53 percent; Hitler's more than 13 million votes constituted 37 percent. The Communist Thälmann fell to 10 percent. The results were more than enough to give the impression that the Nazis were the strongest single political force. But they were not enough to bring Hitler to power.[54]

The campaign failed to answer questions about Nazi strategy or intentions. In contacts with foreigners, some Nazi officials had seemed more moderate in 1932 than Hitler's earlier speeches suggested. At lunch with Wiley, Goebbels, for example, disclaimed any intention of harming German Jews. A Nazi government would simply treat them as foreigners, tax them heavily, and deport Russian and Polish Jews to the east. But Wiley must have known that other Nazis had voiced much sharper threats. In a September 1930 trial of several junior army officers who had distributed Nazi propaganda in the army, Hitler himself had testified that after a Nazi victory the heads of the "November criminals"—those responsible for the revolution of November 1918—would roll in the sand.[55]

While Brüning remained chancellor, American diplomats in Berlin had good access to the government and a little leverage with it. But in the six months following the presidential election, the barriers to a Nazi-Nationalist government fell one after another. And Germany's future became opaque to Sackett and the State Department.

Brüning was the first to go. On May 30, 1932, Brüning told Sackett that he had lost the president's confidence and would resign at noon.[56] Hindenburg appointed his old friend Franz von Papen, a Catholic landed aristocrat, as the new chancellor. Papen's prior connection with the United States was a disaster. Serving as military attaché to the United States during World War I, he had spied there and been caught. Declared persona non grata, he was expelled. The new chancellor had once belonged to the Center Party, but he quarreled there in 1925, and he resigned from its parliamentary delegation. Closest to the Nationalists in 1932, Papen was an authoritarian who sought to restore traditional social hierarchy. His cabinet consisted mostly of aristocrats and men of wealth without political experience; observers called it a cabinet of barons. He had little likelihood of getting political support in parliament unless he could win over Hitler. He and his defense minister, the shadowy intriguer General Kurt von Schleicher, decided to lift the ban on Nazi paramilitary forces. Papen also had Hindenburg's approval for dissolution of parliament and for new elections to be held at the end of July.[57]

On July 20, three days after a bloody clash in Hamburg between communist and Nazi paramilitaries, Papen used presidential emergency powers to oust the Social Democrat–led government from the state of Prussia, claiming that it had lost the ability to maintain law and order. Army troops took over the streets of Berlin. Papen appointed himself to take over the affairs of Prussia. Prussia had the largest police force in the country, and it had served as a bulwark of the republic.

After Papen's coup from above, the July 31 national elections shredded what little remained of the democratic system. The Nazis more than doubled their vote in the September 1930 elections to 37.4 percent, getting 230 seats in parliament. The Social Democrats fell to second with 133 seats, and the German Communists obtained 89, about 14 percent. The Nationalists fell to 37 seats. The net result was that the two extremist parties—Nazis and Communists—constituted a negative majority in parliament: together they could block anything. The Nazis, meanwhile, had almost conquered the political right. How long the Papen government could last without Nazi support was an open question.

Sackett took comfort in the fact that the Nazis only slightly exceeded Hitler's vote in the April 1932 presidential election; the ambassador thought they might be peaking. But continuing violence soon led him to speculate that Hindenburg might dismiss Papen and appoint Hitler as chancellor. President Hoover expressed alarm at this prospect. The State Department told Sackett to send more frequent and more complete reports on events, along with more analysis of their significance.[58]

Hitler met with Hindenburg, Papen, and Schleicher on August 13, but they refused his demand to be named chancellor in a predominantly Nazi government. Sackett reported that the most likely outcome of this stalemate was another round of elections and a maze of uncertainties in the meanwhile. He called Hitler "one of the biggest show-men since P.T. Barnum." He complained that those who read only the Nazi press got a daily dose of constant Nazi successes. If Hitler came to power, he would be able to suppress all non-Nazi publications and control perceptions even more. The Nazis were targeting even German youth, he noted.[59]

Geist followed Papen's efforts very closely, reporting officially on the chancellor's desperate efforts to revive the economy. Geist seems to have calculated that if Papen succeeded economically he would figure out a way to stay in power, constitutional or not. Papen's emergency decrees offered businesses tax rebates and subsidies for hiring new workers; at the same time, they cut wage levels and gave the government powers to reduce all the social insurance programs for which Germany had become famous. Government spending programs were supposed to stimulate growth. The *Frankfurter Zeitung* worried that the effect of tax cuts and spending increases would create a huge deficit to burden future taxpayers. Geist's final report on Papen's economic-financial program, submitted in May 1933, after Hitler had become chancellor, pronounced it a failure.[60]

State Department officials praised the reporting of the staff of the Consulate General. Economic adviser Herbert Feis, the only Jew among high State Department officials, commented that Washington had received a better, more thorough picture of economic and financial events in Germany than in France or Britain.[61] Geist played a substantial role in that reporting.

Geist's public role involved constant visa work and assistance to American firms to export their products to Germany. After he delivered one long report to Robinson Fire Apparatus Manufacturing of St. Louis, a company executive responded: "It was beyond our comprehension that the Consular Service would go to the detail it did in giving us such a report, which left nothing to the imagination, and you have no idea how helpful this is and how it answers our questions so readily."[62]

When the newly elected parliament assembled in September 1932, Papen raced to dissolve it while the deputies overwhelmingly voted no confidence in Papen's government. The result either way was another round of elections in early November. But with some voters tired of constant electioneering, the novelty of Nazi propaganda wore off. Nazi Party coffers were exhausted. Hitler's increasingly bitter attacks on Papen scared off some conservative voters. The Nazis lost nearly two million votes, although they remained the largest party, with about a third of the vote. The Communists rose to about 17 percent, so that the two extremes held almost exactly half of the popular vote and the seats. Papen hoped to simply dismiss the Reichstag, but Schleicher objected, denying him the support of the military. Papen resigned, and negotiations for a new government took place behind a curtain of secrecy.[63]

As Defense Minister Schleicher began to emerge as an alternative to Papen as chancellor, Papen, sensing betrayal, rethought his options with Hitler. After President Hindenburg nominated Schleicher, the new chancellor quickly began to unravel the unpopular anti-labor measures of his predecessor and to draft plans for putting unemployed Germans to work on government projects. The Reichstag adjourned voluntarily, giving Schleicher a breathing spell until at least mid-January 1933.[64]

Schleicher tried to exploit the political and financial strains of the Nazis. He offered Gregor Strasser, a prominent member of the anti-capitalist, pro-union Nazi faction, the vice chancellorship in his cabinet, as well as the top post in the Prussian government. Strasser then pleaded with Hitler and other party leaders to give Schleicher time to operate. Hitler continued to demand full power as chancellor or nothing. Lacking an organized faction among the party elite, Strasser could not withstand Hitler's counterattack. When Strasser resigned from his party positions in early December 1932, no one followed him.[65]

A month later, Hitler met with Franz von Papen at the Cologne home of a German banker who was a belated supporter of Hitler—the first step in a complicated dance toward an alliance.[66] Papen was close to Nationalist leader Alfred Hugenberg, and, even more important, Papen had President Hindenburg's confidence. The press sniffed out the January 4, 1933, meeting at the banker's home, and a photographer captured Papen stepping out of a taxi upon his arrival.[67] Hitler escaped detection by entering through the back door, symbolizing future events that gave him the post of chancellor. President Hindenburg appointed Hitler without his ever having received close to a majority in free elections.

Looking back years later, Geist explained that the Weimar Republic rested on a working alliance of the Social Democrats and the

Catholic Center Party, something that, if it had lasted, might have led the German people to appreciate democracy.[68] Brüning wrecked that alignment at the national level, and then Papen illegally removed the Social Democrat–Center coalition government in Prussia. In the process, they opened the way for Hitler.

CHAPTER THREE

AMERICANS ENCOUNTER THE NAZI REVOLUTION

A t the start of 1933, Raymond Geist decided to write a series of reports on Germany's past economic policies and practices. It was an alarming moment in America. The economy was so buffeted by the Depression that people openly speculated about the collapse of American democracy. The United States had more than 12.8 million unemployed, just under 25 percent of its work force. Franklin D. Roosevelt's inauguration was on March 4, and it was widely expected that, in contrast to his predecessor Herbert Hoover, he would vigorously attack unemployment. Geist believed that a review of past German experiences and economic policies might be helpful in this American effort, even if they did not yield any magic solutions. The State Department rated one of Geist's reports on German workers' councils excellent in view of its relevance to the unemployment problem in the United States.[1] By the time he completed the last of several detailed reports in March, however, history's guidance was overwhelmed by crises immediate.

At 11 a.m. on Monday, January 30, 1933, eighty-five-year-old President Paul von Hindenburg formally named Adolf Hitler as chancellor and Franz von Papen as vice chancellor in a minority coalition government. American diplomats explained to Washington that Hitler's January 1933 meetings with Papen had restored the Harzburg

Front of Nazis and Nationalists, and that Papen had then smoothed the way for Hitler with a previously resistant Hindenburg.

Senior US diplomat Alfred Klieforth reported that Papen and Nationalist leader Alfred Hugenberg believed that they had limited Hitler's influence by giving the Nazis only two ministries in the new cabinet. Klieforth predicted that a Nazi-Nationalist cabinet under Hitler would first attack the German Communists and Social Democrats—the "Marxist" parties Hitler considered enemies of the German people. Indeed, the afternoon of the first cabinet meeting, Hitler raised the idea of banning the Communists, but non-Nazi foreign minister Konstantin von Neurath spoke against it.[2] Ambassador Sackett still believed Nazi officials incapable of running the economy.[3] Both US diplomats thought that Hitler's reign would be short-lived.

Demonstrations and spectacles gave Berliners a sense that this changeover differed from all the previous ones. Bella Fromm, the German Jewish gossip columnist for the liberal newspaper *Vossische Zeitung*, wrote that the Nazi paramilitaries used the password "Grandmother is dead" on the evening of January 30 to launch a torchlight parade of SA and SS men through the center of the city, including the Tiergarten, past the US Consulate General.[4] Joseph Goebbels, soon to become minister of a new government agency called the Ministry of People's Enlightenment and Propaganda, grasped the reins of state-run radio to broadcast his commentary on the march, including his estimate of a million participants. The Nazi press afterward claimed five hundred thousand to seven hundred thousand people participated. A sympathetic but realistic newspaper reported about eighteen thousand SA and SS men, another three thousand from the Stahlhelm, and perhaps an additional forty thousand civilians. The procession circled around from 7 p.m. until midnight on a brisk winter night, creating the sense of a much larger number of marchers. One sharp observer noticed the same faces pass by again and again; he called it a con.[5] Fromm put the number of marchers at twenty thousand, but even she described it as an endless sea of brown uniforms.[6]

The march was visible from Geist's office near the corner of Bellevuestrasse and Tiergartenstrasse and from his apartment as well. He and Anna had by this time moved from Wilmersdorf to an apartment building called Bellevue Park nearer the center of the city, and he had a balcony that allowed him to enjoy the view, but this occasion was no pleasure.[7]

Messersmith downplayed the significance of the unfolding political events. The political situation was so complicated, he wrote, that any predictions were hazardous, but whether the Hitler government lasted for only a few months or a longer period, it was only a phase toward stable political conditions. Nothing in Germany's internal situation would interrupt the improvement in world economic conditions, he declared.[8] Like embassy diplomats who had previously underestimated Hitler, the consul general fell victim to the illusion that practical economic factors would ultimately shape political conditions and decisions. In a private letter, Messersmith called the Hitler-Hugenberg government an impossible combination, and despite extreme uncertainties, Messersmith thought neither the Nazis nor the Nationalists were strong enough to "fasten" themselves on the German people.[9]

Hitler moved to lock in his power by quickly requesting an emergency measure allegedly aimed at communist acts of terror. The February 4, 1933, presidential "Decree for the Protection of the German People" allowed the new Nazi interior minister, Wilhelm Frick, to work with local police to prohibit public meetings and to suppress publications deemed "dangerous" to public security and order. Frick's ministry and police authorities had the power to ban strikes in vital areas. They also were granted expanded powers of arrest. They could even arrest individuals who knew about forbidden activities but failed to inform the authorities. This decree allowed the government to round up German Communist candidates and to cripple anti-government campaign activities in the weeks leading up to the March 5 elections.[10]

On February 27, an emotionally disturbed young Dutch communist turned anarchist, Marinus van der Lubbe, set the Reichstag building afire. Geist saw the red glow of the flames from the balcony of his apartment. He later aptly called it "the funeral pyre on which the short-lived liberties of the German people were extinguished."[11]

Nazi officials used the arson to denounce an attempted communist coup. Their minds wrapped in conspiracies, some may even have believed this. The police arrested van der Lubbe on the spot and then four thousand communists across the city. Göring wanted them shot, but Rudolf Diels, a high official in the police section of the Ministry of the Interior who was not a member of the Nazi Party, refrained.[12]

Interior Minister Frick drafted an emergency decree suspending constitutional protection of free speech, freedom of the press, the right to free assembly and association, and the right of privacy in mail and telephone communication. Police gained broad power to search houses and confiscate property, and the government was empowered to hold individuals without trial. This "Reichstag fire" decree also enabled the national government to assume the powers of the state governments to keep order. The federal system, with its constitutional checks upon the national government, was eviscerated. Hindenburg signed the measure on February 28, giving the Nazis an even bigger club to wield against political opponents and other perceived enemies. (It remained in force until the fall of the Third Reich in May 1945.) Geist explained years later that it legally mutilated the constitution and confiscated all the liberties of the people. It was the biggest single legal-political step toward dictatorship.[13]

Hitler was not yet secure enough to proclaim a one-party state. But he unleashed the SA against "Marxists" and assorted enemies. Police and prosecutors accepted the notion that thousands of communists had committed criminal acts.[14] As a result, the election of March 5 was unlike any previous one in the Weimar Republic. The state and the intimidating forces of the SS and the SA arrested and beat up communists, swayed voters, censored or shut down the opposition presses, and reduced the turnout of opponents. The voting results were mixed. Despite all the distorting factors, Nazi candidates received just shy of 44 percent, and the Nationalists 8 percent, a bare majority for the coalition. The German Communists, with most of their candidates under arrest or in hiding, still received more than 12 percent, and the Social Democrats, who also had some members arrested, declined slightly to 18.3 percent. The Center Party held steady at about 11 percent, with smaller parties sharing the remainder. By this time, it was clear that Papen and Hugenberg could not seriously restrain Hitler.

Geist later wrote that the day after this election was the day Hitler came to power as supreme chancellor and "it was as though hell had broken loose. . . . Political enemies and private enemies were rounded up for days and the reign of terror continued unabated." He intentionally compared the violence to the worst period of the French Revolution.[15] SA men attacked anyone who offended them for whatever reason. Any Jew in the streets of major cities—or anyone who "looked Jewish"—was a potential target, and the police offered no protection.

Amidst this new wave of violence in Germany, the Roosevelt administration lost Ambassador Sackett. Depressed by the disastrous turn in German politics, he resigned to let a new administration choose its own ambassador. Sackett still hoped that wise treatment of Europe's economic problems would somehow restore sound German politics.[16] Counselor of Embassy George Gordon, who was the acting head of the Embassy, reported the closure of Jewish-owned department stores and chain stores and the beginning of a Nazi campaign to purge Jews from public life and the professions. But he foresaw physical violence diminishing amidst a struggle between Nazi storm troopers and more pragmatic party officials.[17] During the next stage of the Nazi revolution, the Embassy was leaderless and disinclined to do anything too pointed. Gordon was a competent observer and analyst, but he had no access to German officials.

Messersmith and Geist raised their profiles and expanded their roles in this vacuum. They could not legally intervene in cases involving Nazi brutality against German citizens. But they worked hard on many pressing cases of American Jews (and some non-Jews) who suffered from the wave of violent attacks and damages to property or trade. Under a 1923 treaty, any US citizen arrested in Germany had the right to meet with an American consul.[18] So under the postelection reign of terror, Geist and Messersmith gained a new and difficult job—to rescue Americans from the hands of the SA, the SS, or the police—and to seek arrest and punishment of those who had assaulted or robbed them.

In late March, SA men seized three Americans and took them to an empty warehouse converted into an improvised prison. They were stripped and forced to sleep on the floor. The next morning, they were beaten and dumped on the sidewalk. At Messersmith's request, these victims signed affidavits describing their mistreatment. The American Embassy complained to the German Foreign Office, and Messersmith took the documents to Berlin police headquarters. Berlin police officials expressed regret, but said they were powerless to act against the perpetrators because the German government had issued an amnesty covering all cases during the weeks after the Reichstag fire.[19]

At about 5 a.m. on March 29, three SA men and a companion attacked Julian Fuhs, an American Jew married to another American citizen who was the owner of a restaurant-nightclub on the Nürnberger Strasse. They also shot up Mrs. Fuhs's nightclub. She filed a complaint at the Consulate General. Messersmith and Geist reached the number two man in Berlin police headquarters that evening. Messersmith pointed out that this was not the first, but the second SA attack upon Fuhs; the SA also had attacked at the nightclub on March 11. A young Nazi policeman tried to write off the incident as a private grudge. Messersmith called the incident inherently political because it involved uniformed members of the Nazi movement. Regardless of motive, the treaty between the United States and Germany guaranteed the life and property of US nationals. If the police refused to act against the SA men, Messersmith pointed out, American newspaper correspondents would certainly exploit the story. After investigating, the police concluded that two SA men had only indirectly participated in the attack: their commander simply reprimanded them. The SA man who shot up the club was to be given a summary trial in the police station. A civilian with them, Oskar Joost, deemed the main instigator, was arrested. Messersmith regarded the outcome as a symbolic victory in that SA men had previously been entirely beyond the reach of police and prosecutors.[20]

Geist attended Joost's trial. The chief judge asked leading questions designed to put Fuhs in a poor light. The judge asked whether Joost knew that Fuhs was a Jew. Joost said it was common knowledge that Fuhs was an American Jew, but this had nothing to do with the incident. The judge asked Joost about his own religion, which was Evangelical (Lutheran). Geist, observing the exchange, wrote that the judge seemed to be emphasizing the religious difference between plaintiff and defendant. The SA men who had accompanied Joost to the club were not present in court. The employees of the nightclub, who were called up as witnesses, were too intimidated to give incriminating testimony. One called the attack a mild altercation. The prosecutor went through the motions, recommending one month in prison. The chief judge made a brief statement and announced a 50 mark fine and no prison for Joost.[21]

In early April 1933, Messersmith held a wide-ranging, "unofficial" conversation with Hermann Göring, who had become minister-president and minister of the interior of Prussia in March. Göring launched a tirade against anti-German propaganda in the United States, by which he meant American newspaper articles critical of Nazi Germany. Messersmith explained the concept of a free press, but Göring thought that any government unable to control the press was weak. Messersmith defended the accuracy of stories sent out by American correspondents in Berlin. Blocked from harping on press distortions, Göring warned against overemphasizing individual cases. Later, he exclaimed: "We don't make a fuss in Germany every time a gangster shoots down innocent people in the streets of Chicago." Göring said that Germany had had an unprecedented revolution with relatively little bloodshed. If some Americans had suffered, he said, he regretted it, but it was unavoidable. He then denounced the role of Jews in German life, and he pointed to anti-Semitism in the United States. Conceding that anti-Semitism existed, Messersmith denied the analogy: it was nothing like the wholesale breakdown of equal rights visible in Germany. Messersmith was able to dent Göring's wall of self-confident prejudice only when he raised the possibility that American businesses and investors might lose confidence in Germany and withdraw, affecting German investors as well.[22]

In the short run, Göring's creation of a political police force in Prussia known as the Gestapo improved prospects for Messersmith and

Geist to deal with individual abuses, because one of Göring's goals was to build a force powerful enough to restrain the notoriously violent SA.[23] This tension between the storm troopers and the police was only one example of a more general feature of the Nazi regime: the Nazi Party and the Nazi-controlled state remained separate organizations with overlapping functions. They competed as much as they cooperated.

That spring and summer, Geist pursued his cases with extraordinary tenacity. In May, an American in Karlsruhe was arrested and imprisoned for unknown reasons, and an American student at the University of Heidelberg was accused of disseminating atrocity stories, that is, reporting Nazi violence that put Germany in a poor light. The American consul general in Stuttgart could make no headway with local or state officials, so the cases were brought to Berlin. Geist met with a high Interior Ministry official, who assured him that both men would be released immediately in the absence of definite evidence against them.[24]

In late June, Geist brought Messersmith personally into the case of a native-born Jewish American citizen who had been living and studying medicine in Germany for years, and in private practice in Berlin for at least six months. Dr. Joseph Schachno sometimes described himself as Bavarian, so the Nazis may have had some doubt about his nationality. When Schachno came to the Consulate General, Geist found him in distress and took him to the public health officer who normally examined applicants for visas for their medical fitness to immigrate. Then Geist brought Messersmith into the examination room. Schachno's backside from neck to heels was a mass of raw flesh.

Geist told Messersmith the story: SA men, responding to an anonymous denunciation of Schachno as an enemy of the state, had seized Schachno from his home in a Berlin suburb, taken him to a converted tavern serving as their headquarters, and whipped him nearly to death. Somehow, he had made his way home and, once recovered enough, days later, to the Consulate General. The two officials arranged for him a new US passport. Messersmith notified one of Göring's aides, and Geist contacted Gestapo chief Rudolf Diels. Both expressed regret. Messersmith insisted on the arrest of the two SA officers who had whipped Schachno, and he was told this had occurred. Schachno fled to Sweden, and soon returned to the United States, from where he tried to sue the German government.[25]

Daniel Mulvihill, a chest surgeon taking postgraduate training with a world-famous German surgeon, Ferdinand Sauerbruch, stopped to watch an SA band on its march along Unter den Linden in August 1933. An SA man separated himself from the procession and assaulted Mulvihill, because he had failed to raise his hand in a "Heil Hitler" salute. Mulvihill complained to the Consulate General. Geist then intervened with both the Interior Ministry and the Gestapo, who arrested the assailant. Geist also pressed hard for a public statement by the government that foreigners were not expected to "Heil Hitler." But a high official of the Prussian Ministry of Justice was evasive about the date of the trial, leading Geist to conclude that the SA probably had succeeded in obtaining the assailant's release.[26]

Geist and Messersmith's most difficult early case was that of Walter Orloff, a twenty-nine-year-old Brooklyn native and graduate of the University of Pennsylvania who was studying medicine at the University of Greifswald. In early July, police had arrested Orloff for membership in the German Communist Party and participation in its reorganization. Orloff's Penn classmates and the American Jewish Committee vouched for him and thought the charges completely trumped up. After Messersmith got no response from local authorities regarding Orloff's arrest, he decided to send Geist to Greifswald, a town in Mecklenburg–West Pomerania on the Baltic Sea, where they suspected Orloff was being held.[27]

Once there, Geist learned that Orloff had associated with a group of communist students and had written a letter expressing interest in their activities. Geist wondered aloud whether Orloff realized that a US citizen should not be taking part in the politics of another country, let alone illegal activities.

The police had already beaten Orloff badly and extracted admissions from him by the time Geist arrived. Geist asked the Greifswald police why Orloff had not been given an attorney, and the police said no attorney in Greifswald would defend a communist. They simply arrested communists and gave them the third degree.

Geist persuaded Diels to get Orloff transferred to Berlin.[28] The next day, Messersmith warned Göring that the American public would never understand how German authorities could charge a university student with treason based on trivial evidence, and then beat him in prison. The best solution for both countries, Messersmith suggested, was to release and deport Orloff immediately. Göring retorted that the Nazi government had to root out communists, some of whom had been found within Nazi organizations. He could not just release a communist because some diplomat asked him to. But he appeared to be concerned about negative publicity impairing Germany's relations with the United States.

On August 3, Diels told Geist that Orloff had withdrawn his claim of mistreatment by the Greifswald police. But Geist, in a second interview with Orloff, learned that he had recanted only after being beaten again in Berlin. Unhappy that evidence of additional mistreatment had surfaced, Diels summoned officials in the national and state ministries of justice for a serious discussion of the case.

On August 4, Messersmith and Geist met with Diels and high ministry officials at Gestapo headquarters. The German authorities read from Orloff's letter to the communist group. Messersmith deemed the evidence of banned political activity a "secondary issue." He emphasized police misconduct, denial of a US citizen's access to American consular officials, and the political effects of the case in the United States. Diels asked whether, if Orloff were deported to the United States, he would spread anti-Nazi propaganda there. Messersmith cleverly pointed out that there would be far more critical publicity if he were put on trial in Germany for treason. This argument seemed to be decisive, and Göring signed an order stopping the proceedings against Orloff. The German authorities arranged for his quick departure, giving American newspaper correspondents no opportunity to interview him, and Orloff refused to give interviews once back in the United States as well. The State Department commended Messersmith and Geist for their handling of the case. For once, they could celebrate a victory against the odds.[29]

At a mid-August cabinet meeting, President Roosevelt asked Undersecretary of State William Phillips about the number of cases of assault or mistreatment of American citizens in Germany. Intentionally or not, Phillips understated the problem, reporting back that there were twelve cases involving Germans wearing Nazi uniforms, and there may have been others not yet brought to the State Department. Of the twelve victims, all but one had likely Jewish names.[30] In fact, there were closer to thirty-two such attacks by the end of the summer.[31]

The pro-German CBS radio commentator H. V. Kaltenborn had told Messersmith that the American press had exaggerated violence in Germany. But on September 1, when he and his wife and sixteen-year-old son were out shopping in Berlin, they encountered a march of SA troops. One of the SA men, seeing that they did not give the Hitler salute, asked why. Kaltenborn, in German, explained that they were Americans. The man then attacked his son. Kaltenborn asked for Messersmith's protection. Messersmith, enjoying the irony, found himself too busy to help, but Geist arranged the safe departure of the Kaltenborns from Germany.[32] The German chargé d'affaires in Washington apologized, and a German Foreign Office senior official expressed regret. Afterward, German foreign minister Neurath expressed his unhappiness to the newly arrived American ambassador and pledged to do his best to prevent such attacks in the future.[33] His words were not worth much.

The attacks extended into the fall of 1933, despite US protests, because it was still unclear who had effective authority in the Nazi dictatorship. Beyond that, Nazi racial ideology transcended the principle of nationality, and Hitler had no intention of seriously punishing Nazi activists who took it upon themselves to translate ideology into action. Geist interceded on behalf of an American sailor who talked loosely in a bar about Hitler, which provoked a brawl. The consul helped an American veteran of the Spanish-American War living in Silesia for reasons of health after the veteran's anti-Nazi stories published abroad led local Nazi elements to attack him.[34] Messersmith informed various high German officials that the United States government might have to issue an official warning to Americans planning to go to Germany that they were not safe there. This finally prompted

Interior Minister Wilhelm Frick to order regional and local officials, as well as police authorities, to prevent such damaging incidents.[35] Nazi officials still feared the unknowable consequences of completely alienating the United States, and this was the power that Messersmith and Geist wielded.

The two Americans had more detailed information about the Nazi system than the Embassy—or any other foreigner—had. They became familiar with German officials, some of whom became more prominent over the next few years. Others, like Diels, lost influence but became useful sources. While Messersmith and Geist rescued Americans from the paramilitaries or the police, the two Americans built up their contacts with police, prosecutors, Interior Ministry, and Gestapo officials. They found many conservative bureaucrats uncomfortable about the direction of events.

Nazi Party officials were far from it. By the second half of 1933, Hitler and other Nazi high officials were almost giddy with success. During the months following his appointment, Hitler not only established a dictatorship; he gained broad popular support. Unemployment declined. All the excesses against Americans and an even larger array of brutal attacks and new discriminatory measures against German Jews apparently mattered little politically, as the Nazi government attacked mostly unpopular targets. A substantial majority of Germans were swept up in a current of national and racial pride.[36]

During their takeover, a kind of revolution by stages, the Nazis practiced what they called *Gleichschaltung* (coordination), synchronizing all other levels of government with their dominant position in the Reich government, either through managed elections or simply by force majeure. Then Nazi officials began to spread this process to private activities and organizations. In late August 1933, Geist began to report on the coordination of nongovernmental activities. He described a battle still in progress over the Protestant Church: some Protestant pastors in the big parishes in Berlin (in the districts of Steglitz, Friedenau, and Charlottenburg) had denounced Nazi radicalism, and some storm troopers had disturbed their services. A so-called German Christian faction was helping the Nazis to take control of church elections and church organization. The forced creation of a unified national Protestant church ruptured the bonds of four hundred years of state churches, Geist noted. The Nazis saw control of religion necessary because they wanted to instill Nazi ideals in the youth. Since Nazism was itself a kind of religion, there was grave danger that the regime, rather than strengthen Protestantism through centralization, would try to supplant all real religion, degrading Protestantism to a kind of pan-Nordic mysticism, Geist observed.[37] It must have been painful for Geist, a religious man proud of his Lutheran heritage, to witness this process firsthand.

Geist wrote with great insight that the Nazis had borrowed from Italian Fascism the idea of the "total state," a state that heavily influenced or fully controlled all areas of life. The Nazis regarded the nation as a living body: the press, radio, theater, industry, and trade were but limbs of the body that must function harmoniously with it. He described Joseph Goebbels's Propaganda Ministry's step-by-step maneuvers to exclude hostile or even non-Nazi influences from all branches of culture, with particular attention to radio, the press, and cinema. The ministry's ultimate goal was to mold a unified public opinion.[38] That might have seemed far-fetched to Americans used to the concept of a private sphere, but the Nazis had accumulated enough control to influence the majority of Germans.

Geist got a personal look at one dimension of the Propaganda Ministry's efforts through his onetime Harvard professor Friedrich Schönemann, who had come back to Germany to teach at the University of Berlin. In his first few years as consul in Berlin, Geist saw a good deal of Schönemann, but things changed quickly after Hitler came to power. Schönemann threw himself "into the lap of the National Socialists," Geist wrote: "His conduct during the early months of the Nazi regime when the Jewish persecutions and other excesses had shocked all decent people, was . . . disgusting to us Americans who frequently met Schönemann."

Schönemann became a confidential agent of the Propaganda Ministry, giving pro-Nazi lectures during tours in the United States. At a lecture at Vassar in late October 1933, Schönemann compared

Hitler's takeover to the American Revolution and urged students to keep an open mind about the Nazi regime. He claimed that Germans understood and used the word "propaganda" not as an indicator of distortion but as a means to mass education and solidarity. German émigré historian Alfred Vagts, speaking at Vassar a week later, found it strange that Schönemann, a philologist, should confuse the words "democrat" and "demagogue." Geist was both alarmed and saddened when he learned how Schönemann had tried to mislead Americans about the new Germany. It moved Geist to recommend stronger US regulation of suspected Nazi agents.[39]

In his December 1933 report on the Nazi takeover of all labor organizations, Geist observed that the Nazis had moved closer to realization of the "totalitarian ideal."[40] Mussolini's term "totalitarianism" has lasted, with ups and downs, to the present day as a label for the aspirations of Nazism and Stalinism.

The school system, also a key to molding future generations, was part of government and nominally easier for Nazi officials to control. Geist analyzed new guidelines released by Prussian minister of education Bernhard Rust, not yet fully implemented.[41] They included the teaching of ancient and modern history from the point of view of Nordic superiority, the dropping of Goethe from the teaching of literature because of his liberal and internationalist views, and the complete banning of all Jewish authors. Biology classes had to include teaching of Nazi racial doctrines and a survey of eugenics.

Geist researched and wrote extensively on what a later age would call soft-power targets; his report on Nazi culture was forty-one pages long.[42] It was clear from his writing that Geist understood that the regime could prove durable, and that raised questions about his own future.

It was normal for a Foreign Service officer to transfer to a new post after a few years, often with added responsibilities or a promotion. At the end of 1933, Messersmith, hoping to receive a transfer and promotion to another post, took an extended leave in the United States.[43] This left unresolved the question of what Geist would do next. Berlin was not only stressful: the Nazis had either wrecked or distorted much of what earlier must have attracted him to Germany. But if or when Messersmith left Berlin for good, it would establish Geist as *the* Foreign Service expert on Nazi Germany. In the meantime, he was acting head at the Consulate General.

Political reporting had become vital even for a consul, and Geist already was saving lives threatened by the totalitarian system. Whether he could influence the Nazi regime beyond individual cases depended more on the balance of forces in Berlin and in Washington than on his own abilities, but if he stayed in the German capital he would have the opportunity to try.

CHAPTER FOUR

VERY PRIVATE LIVES

A curious book entitled *Berlin Embassy* was published by E. P. Dutton & Co. in 1940. Author William Russell, a low-level clerk in the Consulate General, described the activities of Americans in the eponymous American Embassy. The publisher billed the book as containing "the inside story of the American Embassy in Berlin," and it sported an endorsement by the famed journalist William L. Shirer.[1]

Russell's superior in the book was a "Richard Stratton." No one by that name ever served in the Consulate General or Embassy. "Stratton" is a composite character. But there are clues that Russell used Geist, who hired him, as part of the composite. The physical description of Stratton matches Geist well. Another similarity is that Stratton is very successful at ferreting out information from Nazi officials. And generous in approving visa applications.[2]

According to Russell, Berlin beauties used to telephone Stratton because he was a fascinating person who played harder, attended more parties, had more hangovers, and nonetheless got more work done than any other "consul" in the Embassy.[3] If this description is based on Geist, it was a fiction or a cover for a more complex reality in his private life.

In early September 1933, Geist took accumulated leave to travel around Germany and into the Swiss Alps with his sister Anna. Anna, three years older than Raymond, pursued her own social activities

with the American Women's Club of Berlin and other local organizations. She ran his household, helped him entertain, and generally
helped and guided her brother.[4] She served as a substitute wife. But
she was also a serious diabetic, and all too often Raymond had to care
for her. Their trip was part therapy.

They began their itinerary in Eisenach, where they stayed at a de-
luxe hotel just outside Wartburg Castle, the historic site where Martin
Luther translated the Bible into German. Next, they went to Wiesbaden, famous for its spas. At that time, many people believed that
natural spas were beneficial for a wide range of ailments. Several years
later, Heinrich Himmler went to the Wiesbaden spa for treatment
of his chronic stomach problems.[5] For the Geists, the spas at least
helped them decompress from the constant demands of work against
Nazi abuses.

Raymond and Anna next went to Baden-Baden, in the southwest
corner of Germany, on the edge of the Black Forest. Napoleon III
and Queen Victoria each had sampled its spas, and Dostoevsky used
the resort there as the setting for his novella *The Gambler*.[6] Both
Raymond and Anna wrote postcards to their sister Eugenia (Jennie)
and her young children in Cleveland. (One of Jennie's children was
named Raymond, after Geist.) On one postcard from Baden-Baden,
Anna signed another name besides hers and Geist's—Erich. This was
for Erich Mainz: Geist's lover.[7]

Mainz was born in 1908 in Düsseldorf into a religious, farm-
owning Catholic family, and he served as an altar boy and attended
primary school until roughly age fourteen.[8] Mainz moved to Berlin,
probably by 1931, when he was twenty-three years old. It is at least
possible that he entered the practice of physical therapy in his early
Berlin days; he did so decades later. He was an uncommonly handsome youth with dark hair, good muscles, fine facial features, and a
vibrant expression. He, like Geist was, five feet ten inches. He posed
as a boxer and a javelin thrower, at least for photographs.

Someone who knew Mainz decades later described him as a person
who had a facility for striking up conversations with strangers. He also
enjoyed going to the beach.[9] The most popular and stylish beach in

Berlin was an artificial one on the shore of the beautiful Wannsee, the sand having been brought in from the Baltic. Geist and Mainz were photographed together in a motorboat with a US flag waving behind it, possibly in Wannsee.[10] Although it is not known when and how they met, if Mainz was close enough to Geist to be included on post-cards to Cleveland relatives in the fall of 1933, their relationship was already well established.

An undated photo, probably from Baden-Baden in September 1933, shows Anna in a dress resting in a chaise lounge, Mainz standing behind her, smoking a cigarette and carrying a parasol, Geist to Mainz's left, and a fourth unknown woman in front of Geist in another chaise next to Anna. Mainz, well chiseled, wore modern-style swim trunks; he could have posed as a swimsuit model. Geist, showing signs of a middle-age spread, had on the more conservative style of the day, with thin shoulder straps.[11]

The two men knew they were taking a risk. Homosexual behavior, if very common in Berlin, was a crime even in pre-Nazi Germany. The Nazi regime began an "educational" campaign against homosexuality in February 1933 and closed a number of homosexual bars in Berlin. Over time, it turned toward much more severe measures, eventually sending many male homosexuals to concentration camps.[12]

Although Geist was protected by the mantle of American sovereignty, exposure would at least have compromised his career. The decriminalization of homosexuality in the United States did not begin until 1962 in Illinois. The Nazis might have tried to blackmail him. Mainz was more vulnerable still. But many Germans who were not political and not perceived as a racial threat carried on their private lives independent of the law and party propaganda. The early police state was not so large or efficient that it could threaten all people, especially in their private lives.

From Baden-Baden, Anna, her brother, and his lover crossed the Swiss border and went to St. Moritz, almost six thousand feet above sea level. Its mineral springs had been discovered thousands of years earlier. The town, which had hosted the 1928 Winter Olympics, was known for attracting the athletic, the rich, and the famous. Surviving photos show Geist and Mainz climbing one of the many mountain trails. The two men posed on a mountain ledge for an unknown photographer.[13] It apparently was the last stop on their vacation; at least there are no photos from additional sites.

Teenage photos show Mainz with attractive girls, and much, much later in life, he married.[14] We may conclude that he was bisexual. But from at least 1932 on, he remained personally ensconced with Raymond Geist in Berlin, who also grew up bisexual. That was only the most striking element setting Geist apart from his Foreign Service colleagues.

Geist had scrambled to make his way in the world. His very modest family background immunized him against diplomatic snobbery. Even more important, he had experience as a professional actor and lecturer. He knew how to assume different roles at different times, and he was sensitive to the reactions of others. These unusual skills helped him communicate with Germans of all classes and operate effectively in Nazi Germany.

Geist's father, Philip Charles Geist, the son of German immigrants, at age twelve became operator of a printing press at the *Cleveland Leader*, a local newspaper. In 1881 he married Lena Emmert, also the daughter of German immigrants. They had three daughters: Anna Katherine, born in 1882; Clara Ida, born in 1884; and Eugenia (Jennie) Hart, who arrived in 1898. Raymond Herman, the only son, was born on August 19, 1885.[15]

Of necessity, the Geist children stuck together. Philip was an alcoholic. A loving mother, Lena was diabetic and was frequently confined to bed.[16] The family often scraped by. Raymond excelled in school and skipped fourth grade, but he dropped out of high school to support his family. He became an office boy for the *Cleveland Leader*. Then he landed a job at the Grasselli Chemical Company. Originally a family firm, Grasselli was a highly successful national company with nearly thirty plants. Geist later wrote that he was promoted to be the car accountant for the American Tank Line, a division of Grasselli, which had six hundred tank cars.[17]

Geist's first known homosexual relationship was with another Grasselli employee. Looking back at that time, Geist writes with some ambiguity in his diary about the "peculiar" relationship he had with a man named Will Mills: "It appears that our hearts are our mast and that no age or state of development exempts us from its tyranny." "The sovereign will of the heart" always prevails over the guidance of reason.[18]

The Cleveland YMCA ran an adult education program in the evening.[19] Geist joined the Cleveland Y very early, and he seems to have made quite an impression. Shortly after he turned twenty, he moved to New York City to become social secretary of the YMCA there.[20] Geist also joined the Broadway Tabernacle, originally an antislavery Presbyterian Church that turned Congregationalist, becoming one of the most prominent and socially progressive churches in the country. Pastor Charles Jefferson, known for his speaking ability, took an interest in Geist, who did some preaching of his own.[21]

Geist wrote home frequently and sent money when he could.[22] His father had lost his job, Clara had a job but was not a reliable source of support for the family, and Jennie was just beginning school. Anna, now twenty-three, was the one who ran the household. She cautioned him, "Don't fly too high."[23]

Geist's mother, Lena, died in March 1906. Two years later, on the anniversary of her death, he wrote, "There are no thoughts deep enough to express my meditations about her. . . . She lives in my heart—in my prayers. All the beauty of this world points back to the time when I had a mother."[24]

Rapidly completing his remaining high school work in New York, Geist passed an entrance exam and was admitted to Oberlin College as a freshman in the fall of 1906. But he had little money, even to pay tuition. He was forced to take out a $40 loan from the Oberlin College Fund, which just covered a semester's courses.[25]

The oldest coeducational college in the country, Oberlin had admitted African Americans early as well. The progressive school had women's dormitories, but most men lived in boarding houses in groups of four or five.[26] Raymond found a vacancy a block away from the center of town in a large house on South Professor Street, partly a residence, partly a boarding house, owned by Frederick Webster, an attorney, and managed by his wife.[27]

Through one means or another Geist acquired a roommate, Henry Edze Langeland Jr., the son of Norwegian immigrants who had settled in Muskegon, Michigan. Langeland was unusually handsome. As their friendship deepened, the two Oberlin roommates became lovers.

Using his YMCA connections as well as his Oberlin status, Geist gave dramatic readings from Shakespeare or sermons in small towns in Ohio and neighboring states. He performed extensively during his sophomore and junior years.[28] His readings earned him his campus nickname "Shakespeare."[29] They helped him pay his way through Oberlin, but they also got him into trouble with college officials who thought him insufficiently qualified to be paid to interpret Shakespeare.[30]

Geist obviously hoped that college would bring a clearer sense of his own identity and sexuality, and with it, happiness. He frequently pondered the tug of war between his reason and emotions. But more often than not, he was unhappy, and he had to ask himself whether the diary that he began to keep (after three semesters) had become "a shrine for sorrows."[31] He enjoyed attending college events with nineteen-year-old Sarah Webster, the daughter of his landlord, and he noted it glumly when she went out with another male student. But his interest in Sarah fell short of his intense attachment to Henry Langeland. In his diary, Geist declared that he loved his roommate more than any girl in Oberlin.[32] It was not a durable friendship, however, and ended by the conclusion of Geist's junior year, with Geist declaring melodramatically that he had "parted roads with a 'traitor.'"[33]

Geist transferred to Western Reserve after his junior year.[34] He still resented Oberlin's treatment of him. A dean had chastised him for his lectures, and he believed he received an unfairly low grade in English. So he declined to repay the loan he had taken out from the college fund. Oberlin kept reminding him, and five years later he paid $25 back.[35] A century later, when Geist's great-niece went to Oberlin to do research on him, college officials asked her if she wished to repay the remaining $15. She laughed.[36]

At Western Reserve, Geist performed well. He continued to study German, took some Spanish, and did his best work in philosophy. He joined the Beta Theta Pi fraternity and impressed Western Reserve's president, who later wrote recommendations for him. He graduated at age twenty-five in 1910.[37]

College graduates of that era generally had some sense of what they wanted to do with their career and their life. Geist was hoping for an acting career, despite knowing that there was a substantial risk of failure. He lacked a clear backup plan but was confident that he would be able to demonstrate his abilities in the world of the arts somehow. He could live with uncertainty.

Geist became a staff member of the New York Superintendent of Public Lectures, which put on costumed performances of the principal scenes of *Julius Caesar*. After moving to New York he also enrolled in an MA program at Columbia, but he completed only one course before dropping out.[38] Meanwhile, a well-known physician named George Biggs took a shine to him. Probably in 1911, Geist moved into the Biggs residence at 133 West 71st Street with Mr. and Mrs. Biggs and their son.[39]

In 1911, with some assistance from Biggs, the Geist siblings acquired and occupied a sizable building at 39 College Place in Oberlin, Ohio, where Geist's sisters Anna, Clara, and Jennie opened a popular and lucrative tea room. They served sandwiches and more, as well as tea in different rooms, each assigned a color. A flier described the Cozy Tea Rooms at Oberlin College as a "refined eating place for particular people, serving dainty, delicious, homemade things to eat." With Anna in charge, it became a campus hangout.[40]

The substantially profitable tea room boosted the Geist family well into the middle class. Raymond formally became Jennie's guardian, and Jennie soon entered Oberlin. The Geists then purchased a summer home in the Villa Beach section of Cleveland in 1915. A wealthy family named Baker lived there, and Geist already had become friends with their son Julian, a few years younger than he.[41] The family house at Villa Beach served as his formal address in the United States for decades.

The theater still beckoned to Geist. A Shakespearean company headed by actor-producer John Kellerd, which regularly performed at the Garden Theater in New York, gave him an opportunity. In late November 1911, Geist went on stage in New Haven as Portia's servant Balthazar in *The Merchant of Venice*. In Hartford he reprised Balthazar in a matinee, and that evening he played Rosencrantz in *Hamlet*.[42]

During the troupe's eastern tour, Geist managed to work in some lectures at high schools, as well as visits with friends and nature walks wherever the troupe traveled. In his diary at the time, he pondered whether the stage would permit him a conventional marriage and family.

In 1911, Geist began a serious heterosexual romance with Norma Reinhart, also a child of German immigrants who had settled in Cleveland.[43] Just how they met remains murky. He was about the right age to settle down, but he was too conflicted to do so. Geist blamed his actor's lifestyle, as he wrote in his diary, but he was being a little coy:

> The important thing of the day [December 8, 1911] was my letter to Norma Reinhart, which I have contemplated so long and have so hesitated to write. Ah! Who can tell how grieved she will be to know I have added so materially to the life struggles which have so long separated us. How can we help from being serious and sad when love conflicts with ambition—not as a matter of choice, or any measure of volition, but as a necessity—the law of happiness. . . . I fear she will not dare to hope for me in the actor's profession. I must not write more of this, it pains me to think how lonely I make my own life, by choosing to fight for fortune, and for fame.

Geist was not *that* lonely. Days later, he wrote to a younger male friend, John Kenneth Tilton, a Princeton undergraduate with a common interest in the theater: "You are those same eternal qualities of godlike beauty, incorporated in the human soul which call me by the same spirit and by the same light to love and adore." He rarely used such enthusiastic language when writing about his female friends.

The Kellerd tour lasted nearly two months, with appearances as far north as Massachusetts, as far south as Florida, and as far west as Tennessee. The results of Geist's acting experiment were at best mixed, but he shifted rapidly into a series of dramatic readings in the greater Boston area and elsewhere in New England. There he clearly regained his confidence as he performed major Shakespearean roles. He earned the largest fee of his career for his performance of *Macbeth* at Everett High School. He drew an audience of one thousand and received a long ovation at Haverhill High School. Everyone was spellbound at Gloucester High School. He drew about five hundred people at New Britain High School, and a local newspaper wrote a story about him. He began to envision himself eventually leading his own troupe.[44]

In the fall of 1912, another actor-director-business-manager, Robert Mantell, invited Geist to join his Shakespearean troupe, which launched *Romeo and Juliet* in Montreal and toured widely across the United States until the spring of 1913. The Scottish-born Mantell was the great-uncle of Angela Lansbury. One of the younger performers in Mantell's troupe was a tall, slim twenty-year-old, David Noel Tearle, who used Noel Tearle as his stage name. Born to an acting family in Birmingham, England, Tearle would later acquire fame on Broadway. Geist noted matter-of-factly that he and Tearle became intimate in Indianapolis, "staying at the same hotel, etc." They lived together at the Jefferson Hotel in St. Louis and at an unnamed hotel in Rochester, New York. But when they reached Boston, Tearle decided to live separately in Cambridge, because his reputation was at risk.[45]

After Mantell's national tour ended, Geist took off on a mini grand tour of Europe in the spring and summer of 1913. He sent enthusiastic postcards to his sisters from Prague, the Swiss Alps, the Austrian Tyrol, Monte Carlo, Amsterdam, and elsewhere. He visited numerous German cities, too.[46]

Geist disliked the climate of Pan-Germanism and militarism he found in Germany during the reign of Kaiser Wilhelm II; it was the complete opposite of eighteenth-century German culture centered at the court of Weimar, which he had studied.[47] He could not have imagined then that he would encounter a far more militaristic climate twenty years later under Hitler.

Geist returned home to rejoin the Mantell troupe, which toured the American and Canadian northwest. But after three months in Europe, Geist found little to enjoy in his supporting roles on stage. Unhappy with the management of the company, on March 28, 1914, he resigned from Mantell and returned to Oberlin, Ohio.[48]

Knocked off course, Geist decided to purchase a farm outside Oberlin with a notion of converting it into a chicken farm. But farm life was not for him, and he quickly sold it. He went into a brief funk, adopted Nietzsche as his next reading and studying craze, and then attended a lecture by novelist and activist Charlotte Gilman (author of *Herland*) on feminism. He was far from a convert to either Nietzsche or Gilman's views, but he appreciated other audacious spirits. Gilman also happened to be known as bisexual. It was probably not a coincidence that Geist thought her interesting.

Geist reactivated an earlier plan of getting his doctorate in modern languages at Harvard. He registered there in September 1915. He might have been able to pay his own way, but financial backing from Biggs made his course easier.[49] He received As and Bs. His interests shifted some, he learned Middle English, and he later wrote his dissertation on a narrative history of England by a twelfth-century English priest.[50]

One of Geist's professors was a star. George L. Kittredge, a specialist on Shakespeare and Chaucer, is still known for having produced a major scholarly edition of Shakespeare's works. His endorsement of Geist was unreserved and worth a great deal in the outside world: "He has a clear head, a steady and logical mind, and a good deal of initiative. He is quiet, but energetic—no fuss about him. He is an excellent scholar and has a practical knowledge of foreign languages. Personally I like him very much, and I believe him to be a man of high character and sound ideals."[51] Anyone who read this recommendation could not doubt Geist's intellectual ability. Another professor commented on his remarkable linguistic ability and impressive social qualities.[52] At this time, Geist met Friedrich Schönemann, a lecturer in the German department, who later showed up in Hitler's Berlin.[53]

Meanwhile, Geist's sister Clara was diagnosed with a serious heart condition and took to bed to recover. Jennie started a romance with a Cleveland man, Waldo Billenstein, who was seven years her senior. Billenstein, who was of Jewish origins, soon changed his name to Billens.[54] Geist seems to have approved of their relationship, and he later encouraged her to marry him, which she did in 1919.[55]

On January 11, 1918, Clara died. Geist's father, who had not been seen for years, showed up for the funeral, "emaciated to the last degree." He died later that year. Geist's diary ends shortly afterward, with its last entry about his application for foreign service.[56]

A biographer needs a mental photograph of his or her subject, even if it cannot be found in documents. In this sense, Geist's youthful diary is extraordinary helpful. Projection from Geist's youth to middle age is necessary because there are few comparable personal sources during his time in Berlin.

The forty-four-year-old man who came to Berlin with his eldest sister generally thought of himself as the smartest person in a room, but tried not to show that, except when it became necessary for a specific purpose. He abided by rules and regulations except when they offended his common sense or moral sense. He had learned to control his strong emotions. He had accepted his sexual identity and concluded that he could make it work even in the Foreign Service fishbowl. Self-satisfaction became more important to him than audience appreciation. He really cared about what he did. We don't know where his patriotism came from, but it was strong and enduring. He saw the United States as the modern and more powerful version of ancient Athens, blending culture and nature. He wanted to defend the United States against the Nazi threat. He saw no contradiction between his patriotism and his humanitarian impulses. His ability, honed on the stage and on the lecture circuit, to play different roles and make a strong impression turned out to be unusually useful where so many foreigners seemed bewildered by the totalitarian system or intimidated by Hitler's successes. Geist's acting skills allowed him to charm and to please while concealing his thoughts and motives. The traditional diplomat who kept his cards close to his vest was all too often boring and ineffective, and Geist was anything but boring.

Geist's background and career show that he believed in the value of education to offer moral direction. His golden age was built on a foundation of individualism, not collective emotions or strict observance of social and political norms. One line from Goethe's *Faust*, which he copied into his diary, might have demonstrated why he was a fundamental critic in Hitler's Berlin: "Nature does not produce Nations, only men."[57] Hitler could not have disagreed more.

If Messersmith knew about Geist's homosexual relationship with Mainz, it mattered little to him. After Messersmith left Berlin to become American minister to Austria in mid-1934, he wrote the State Department about Geist's unusual qualities. He concluded, "I have never had an officer associated with me whose collaboration was more loyal, more unselfish and more efficient, and whose interest in the Service is deeper and his devotion to it more real." Pierrepont Moffat, head of the Western European Affairs Division, wrote a note for Geist's file, expressing his hope that Geist would remain in Berlin.[58]

Geist became a combination consul, diplomat, self-directed intelligence analyst, and moral critic. He found it intellectually and emotionally impossible to accept the guiding ideological principles of the Nazi regime or to respond only weakly to its injustices. His fundamental opposition was grounded in what he saw as the highlights of Western civilization and Christianity. All the same, when he sat across the table from Himmler, Heydrich, or their SS subordinates, he must also have considered the fact that, if he were a German citizen, his sexual identity and behavior would have put his own life at risk. By virtue of who he was and how much he observed, Geist was more sensitive than most to the wide range of victims of Nazi persecution. He was an exception to the pattern in the Foreign Service and in the State Department.

CHAPTER FIVE

PROBING THE NEW STATE

Shortly after Hitler became chancellor, Nazi storm troopers vandalized synagogues, smashed windows of Jewish-affiliated shops, and beat and humiliated individual Jews in towns and cities across Germany. It was as if an avalanche had hit the German Jewish community.[1] Geist had enough Jewish friends and acquaintances to get some sense of their shock. On March 31, 1933, Messersmith told James G. McDonald, chair of the US Foreign Policy Association, who was visiting Berlin, that the Nazi paramilitary forces, the SA and the SS, were out of control.[2]

In addition, the Nazis were using public anti-Nazi protests and threats to boycott German exports in the United States as an excuse for their own boycott of Jewish businesses in Germany. Hitler told his cabinet that an economic boycott was an alternative to popular violence against German Jews.[3] On April 1, the Nazi Party crippled or simply shut down Jewish-owned businesses for one day. Then the government declared victory but threatened to resume the boycott if "atrocity agitation" abroad became a problem. George Gordon in the US Embassy thought German businessmen and financiers had urged Hitler to limit the duration of the boycott to avoid economic damage.[4]

Hitler and other leading Nazi officials began to shift their strategy, preferring organized action and discriminatory decrees to street violence.[5] The April 7 Law for the Restoration of the Professional

Civil Service, for example, enabled government agencies to dismiss their non-Aryan employees. Through police measures, the Nazis also sought to weaken Jewish influence. In May, Berlin police arrested Otto Schick, the editor of the Berlin bureau of the Jewish Telegraphic Agency (JTA), an American firm running an international Jewish news service. The JTA's lawyers in New York asked the State Department and the Embassy to intercede. When Boris Smolar, European director of the JTA, arrived in Berlin, he could get no information whatsoever from the police.

Geist was able to make more headway through his connection with Gestapo chief Rudolf Diels. He learned that the police had arrested Schick after he had wired a story about a police raid in Berlin, which created the impression that the police had raided a synagogue to enrich themselves. This was "atrocity propaganda," according to Diels. Geist called Schick's telegram ambiguous, and if Diels failed to resolve the situation, the diplomats in the American Embassy would have to raise this matter formally with the German Foreign Office. Deciding to avoid complications, Diels talked to Schick, then released him on June 7.[6]

The persecution of the JTA did not stop. In a July raid the police confiscated the furniture in the JTA's Berlin office and suspended its publication. The Gestapo insisted on the removal of the editor of another JTA publication called the *Jewish Daily Bulletin*. Geist complained that the 1923 treaty between the United States and Germany protected commercial activity, including reporting the news. Geist told Nazi authorities that they could expel individuals but not ban a US organization simply because it was Jewish. The Gestapo concurred, and Messersmith praised Geist for the settlement.[7] Schick, who took over the *Bulletin* after the raid, pledged not to write "propaganda."

This did not stop Nazi officials from trying again and again to restrict the US press. They put especially heavy pressure on Edgar Mowrer, the *Chicago Daily News* Berlin correspondent who, before Hitler came to power, had written a Pulitzer Prize–winning book critical of the Nazis. A government official told Mowrer that Hitler disliked his book, and Mowrer retorted that he felt the same way about *Mein*

Kampf. Hitler's foreign press secretary Ernst Hanfstaengl retaliated by putting out word that Mowrer was a secret Jew.[8]

Though nervous and angry, Mowrer remained determined to write and send out accurate stories regardless of what German government officials wished. Privately, he referred to Nazi leaders as thugs, perverts, and sadists.[9] Nazi officials began to make life difficult for all the American correspondents and suggested that Mowrer be removed from his post as the Berlin head of the Foreign Press Association, but the FPA refused to depose him.[10] In July, Mowrer began to receive anonymous death threats. Gestapo chief Diels warned the Embassy that "some fanatic" might try to kill Mowrer, so he had to assign some policemen to "keep track" of Mowrer and his family. The German ambassador to the United States said that the government could not guarantee Mowrer's safety. Frank Knox, owner of the *Chicago Daily News*, decided to transfer Mowrer to Tokyo, but Mowrer resisted pressure to leave Berlin immediately. Eventually, Messersmith, with tears in his eyes, persuaded him to leave for his own good.[11]

The Nazi regime also made life difficult for the Associated Press. Louis Lochner, who headed the AP office in Berlin, came under pressure to dismiss three Jewish employees from its photographic bureau, a German subsidiary subject to German law. At first, calling the men efficient, splendid, honest, and versatile, he refused to do so. Then the government expelled one of the AP photographers, who was Austrian, from the country.[12]

Lochner appealed to Geist, saying that the removal of its experienced employees would effectively end the AP's photographic business. After months of negotiations with Propaganda Ministry officials, in February 1934 Geist achieved a breakthrough. "Non-Aryan" photographers could apply for permission to join the Reich Press Chamber, a membership required of all German journalists, by filling out a special questionnaire, and Propaganda Ministry officials would decide case by case. They left the three Jewish employees alone temporarily. Geist hoped it would be a precedent.[13]

The wave of violence and discriminatory laws led a small minority of German Jews to try to emigrate during the first months of the

Nazi regime. Those vulnerable because of their past political records and individuals specifically targeted by Nazi paramilitary forces had reason to act swiftly. But most German Jews felt that they could not abandon their relatives, community, and country.

Many Jews, however, fled temporarily. The American consul general in Stuttgart reported in early April that about three thousand Jews from the state of Baden had entered Switzerland through nearby Basel. At that time, Switzerland had few restrictions on visitors, but it did bar from permanent residence refugees fleeing racial persecution.[14] Other German Jews went to France. An estimated thirty-seven thousand Jews left Germany by the end of 1933.[15] Few had the resources and skills to turn their stay abroad into permanent new homes at a time when most countries were hostile to Jewish immigration. The vast majority had little choice but to stay in Germany or to return to it once the violence substantially diminished.

The United States had few diplomatic or legal options to diminish Nazi persecution. President Roosevelt had talked to his new ambassador, William E. Dodd, about the plight of German Jews. FDR called Germany's treatment of the Jews shameful, American Jews were stirred up about it, but it was not a governmental affair, except when Nazis attacked Americans. (At least, this is the Dodd family's account of that conversation.) FDR urged Dodd to use his unofficial and personal influence to help moderate the situation of German Jews. Before he left to take his post in Germany, Dodd also met in New York with an American Jewish group led by judges Julian W. Mack and Irving Lehman, both close to the president. They pressed him for strong intervention.[16]

Dodd, who had long before studied in Germany, had fond memories of the country. A successful professor of history at the University of Chicago, he was a specialist in the American South, and he did not know much about the Nazis. Secretary of Commerce Daniel Roper persuaded him in April 1933 to make himself available for the post of ambassador to Germany. Dodd told Roper that he had grave doubts about the benefits of any diplomacy in Germany, and that he would "greatly dislike" talking with Hitler. But if it seemed his appointment might yield real benefits, he said he might accept, and he did.[17]

In mid-July, Dodd arrived in Berlin with his wife and daughter; his son, William Jr., arrived slightly later with the family Chevrolet.[18] Conversations with Foreign Minister Neurath and other conservatives still in government quickly convinced him that the Nazi regime was becoming more moderate. He did not want to jeopardize that process.[19] Knowing that an ambassador had to appear formidable, Messersmith temporarily put the Dodds up in the royal suite of a well-located luxury hotel, the Esplanade, a short walk from the Embassy and across the street from the Consulate General. Its previous guests included Greta Garbo and Charlie Chaplin. Dodd complained about the luxury but relented when he heard the cost. He had been unaware that the United States had received a discount.[20]

Shunning the mold of upper-class diplomats, Dodd hoped to make do on his salary as ambassador, even though life in Berlin was expensive and his family began to entertain more than occasionally. A thin and slightly frail man, he did not make a forceful impression. He was not hardened enough to shrug off Nazi hostility toward the United States. And, despite his ambivalence toward the Nazi regime, he was an anti-Semite.[21] In combination, these handicaps crippled him.

The American military attaché learned that Alfred Panofsky, a German Jewish private banker, was willing to rent out most of his four-story, stone, L-shaped mansion on the Tiergartenstrasse built for Ferdinand Warburg, a member of the famed Warburg banking family. Panofsky needed protection against Nazi radicals and against the government. He offered the Dodds the first three furnished floors for six hundred reichsmarks per month for one year. It was beyond a bargain-basement price: Geist later said Panofsky could have charged many times that rate. Yet Dodd complained that Panofsky and his mother retained the top floor. By the time the lease expired in August 1934, Panofsky felt safer and wanted his entire house back. Ambassador and Mrs. Dodd declined to move. Geist located other suitable properties and urged the Dodds to accept one of them; they refused. Finally, Geist went back to Panofsky to plead for an extension at a higher rate. Panofsky offered 1,000 marks a month, but the Dodds rejected it. They compromised on 800 marks, but the Dodds insisted on getting more rooms and furniture than they had originally. On a later visit to Washington, Geist told Wilbur Carr that the whole affair had almost become a scandal in Berlin.[22] Dodd's determination to live modestly came at the expense of his German Jewish landlord.

Dodd disliked a clerk-receptionist at the Embassy, a fifty-eight-year-old Jewish American widow named Julia Swope Lewin, also known as Dolly Levine.[23] She was a longtime resident of Germany with excellent German-language skills. Lewin was also well connected. One brother, Herbert Bayard Swope, was a three-time Pulitzer Prize–winning journalist for the *New York World*. Her other brother, Gerald Swope, an engineer by training, became CEO of General Electric and has been called one of the most talented business executives of his age.[24] Geist described Lewin as refined and cultured.[25]

Dodd decided that Lewin was ill-suited to run the reception room in the Embassy, calling her "very anti-German."[26] An outsider with the State Department, Dodd lacked the leverage to oust her, but he kept trying. In February 1934, Dodd asked James G. McDonald, who had become League of Nations High Commissioner for Refugees from Germany, whether there was room on his staff for Mrs. Lewin. Dodd stressed her excellent qualifications, adding that her brothers might help McDonald raise needed funds. But McDonald perceived that Dodd wanted to get rid of her because she was obviously Jewish and anti-Nazi.[27]

Dodd later suggested to the State Department that Lewin was perhaps too close to the Nazis, certainly a creative twist. When Geist went to Washington in June 1935, Carr asked him specifically about Dodd's complaints. Geist endorsed Lewin without reservation. Then he wrote a personal letter to Dodd, describing how he had met with high State Department officials. After flattering Dodd as much as he could, he added: "I wanted to mention that I heard in the Department that you were asking for Mrs. Levine's transfer. My friendship and loyalty to you prompts me to suggest that you allow this matter to rest for the time being."[28] Geist was confident that in this case he had more leverage than Dodd did.

This came to be Geist's tactic for dealing with Dodd: he flattered Dodd but maneuvered around him as often as he could. Quite apart from Dodd's eccentricities and fragile health, his family also caused problems. Geist could not tell how much information Dodd shared with his family, but he noted that Dodd's daughter, Martha, associated widely with members of the Nazi regime, gave wild parties lasting well into the early morning hours, and was particularly taken with Rudolf Diels, Geist's connection at the Gestapo, who was a married man. Martha Dodd counted the handsome, scarred Gestapo chief among her suitors. They went about town together.[29] Messersmith later told Undersecretary William Phillips that the Dodd children were a problem: "Too much inclined to running around to night clubs with certain Germans of not particularly good standing and with the press."[30] Later still, Messersmith, who saw himself as a potential replacement for Dodd, had even more serious complaints about Dodd himself.[31]

Dodd concluded, partly based on a rumor launched by Hitler's foreign press secretary Ernst Hanfstaengl, that Messersmith himself was Jewish. He wrote to Secretary Hull, "I am no race antagonist, but we have a large number [of Jews] here, and it affects the service [of the Embassy] and adds to my load."[32]

In his memoirs, Chicago journalist Mowrer described how he tried to explain what was happening in Germany to Dodd over dinner one night, but Dodd thought he knew better and said he did not wish to mix in Germany's affairs. American correspondents who had difficulties with the regime, Mowrer wrote, had only Messersmith, Geist, and commercial attaché Douglas Miller to rely on.[33]

On July 28, 1933, Germany's foremost chemist Fritz Haber came to see Dodd. Haber was carrying a letter of introduction from Henry Morgenthau Jr., FDR's friend and neighbor, soon to become secretary of the treasury. The sixty-five-year-old Haber had converted to Protestantism, but the Nazis considered him non-Aryan. The regime had offered him an exception as a war veteran so that, despite his Jewish descent, he could remain director of the Kaiser Wilhelm Institute for Physical Chemistry. Refusing to preside over the dismissal of his Jewish colleagues, Haber resigned anyway.

Haber asked Dodd about the possibility of emigrating to the United States. Claiming that the immigration quota was filled, Dodd promised to write the Department of Labor to see if there were any options. Dodd did write Labor, only to find out that his statement about the quota was quite inaccurate. By that time, Haber had managed to emigrate to Britain instead. He struggled there and died six months later in Basel, Switzerland, having aggravated a preexisting heart condition.[34]

Dodd failed to refer Haber to Messersmith and Geist, the men who determined which Germans qualified for visas in Berlin. They would have told Haber that he was not likely to become a public charge and could get an immigration visa, and that there was a special provision under immigration law for professors outside the quota. A Nobel Prize–winning chemist, the former head of Germany's most prestigious research institute, might just qualify! Dodd's treatment of Haber was both ignorant and negligent.

One reverberation of the Haber case reached Geist. The American journal *Chemical Engineering* published an editorial eulogy that included the statement, "The closing days of a life that probably contributed more to the practical advance of German science, agriculture and industry than any other, must be spent in exile while a flamboyant corporal struts his hour upon the German stage." A German subscriber complained to the Nazi government, which banned distribution of the journal. *Chemical Engineering* was unhappy at the loss of German customers, saying it never meant to insult Hitler. Geist contacted an official in the Interior Ministry to inquire about remedies, only to learn that the publisher, Houghton Mifflin, needed to apologize and promise never to offend Germany again. The German bureaucrat made it plain that he did not agree with this stance, but if he had not imposed a ban, he would have lost his job. Geist, Messersmith, and an embassy official all thought Houghton Mifflin could not humiliate itself with such an apology, so German readers went without *Chemical Engineering*.[35]

Nazi persecution of German Jews went through fits and starts. In October 1933, Hitler wanted to impress the outside world with German strength and solidarity. He withdrew from the long-running Disarmament Conference in Geneva, allegedly because the Western powers continued to discriminate against Germany by maintaining the limits on German armed forces set out in the Treaty of Versailles. The Führer formally took Germany out of the League of Nations. The government scheduled a November 12 plebiscite on these moves. Hitler also dissolved the Reichstag elected in March 1933; the newly elected one consisted only of handpicked Nazi candidates.[36] Geist observed that during this period Hitler did not want more violence against German Jews, and he issued a secret order to that effect. Hitler also wanted to avoid foreign press articles critical of Germany. Nazi officials in Berlin told local German authorities not to allow anti-Jewish demonstrations.[37]

More than 95 percent of German voters approved the plebiscite. Professor Victor Klemperer, of Jewish descent, voted no, but wrote in his diary that the authorities probably did not tamper with the results; it was enough that the public thought they might do so. Even so, he was depressed by the evidence of strong public support for Hitler's moves.[38]

After the plebiscite, Geist reported, Nazi authorities in Berlin launched another anti-Jewish campaign. Minister of the Interior Wilhelm Frick created a new division to stimulate racial pride among Germans and to convince them that Jews constituted a threat to racial purity. Frick pointed to American immigration laws as an example of how other countries excluded undesirable races. Government health insurance refused to pay German Jewish physicians for treating patients.[39]

Geist reported that the police in the Bavarian city of Augsburg confiscated the sizable bank account of the B'nai B'rith chapter there, while their counterparts in Würzburg, also in Bavaria, seized a house owned by B'nai B'rith, turning it over to the Hitler Youth organization. The authorities termed this Jewish organization an enemy of the German people and state. Other properties belonging to Jewish welfare organizations outside Bavaria also were seized. Geist reported that conservative minister of commerce Kurt Schmitt continued to battle Nazi Party forces over anti-Jewish moves.[40] Both Messersmith and Geist wrote and spoke frequently and harshly about Nazi anti-Semitic measures.[41]

In September 1933, many of the German Jewish organizations had joined to form an umbrella organization called the Reich Representation of Jews in Germany, or the Reichsvertretung, to help defend their community against ongoing Nazi assaults.[42] One official of this body had a confidential relationship with Geist, whom he trusted implicitly. Geist never revealed the informant's identity, but, decades later in the United States, Dr. Friedrich Brodnitz described himself as having been the Reichsvertretung's liaison to the press and to foreign diplomats. In fact, Brodnitz told oral history interviewers that he used to sit in one of the back rooms of the US Consulate General writing reports about Nazi persecution of German Jews; Messersmith and Geist sent the reports on to Washington. Many years after World War II, covering for another physician in New York, he encountered Messersmith. His memory prodded, Messersmith called him "our famous informant."[43]

In late January 1934, it probably was Brodnitz who showed Geist a small bound volume containing a list of all the Nazi laws and regulations discriminating against Jews, as well as police ordinances and local orders. This was a damning compilation of the evidence from government and party officials themselves. The volume reprinted anti-Jewish cartoons from the Nazi press and insulting photographs. It constituted "complete evidence taken from authentic sources, illustrating the scope and destructive force of the measures that have been taken in this country against the Jews." At the end, the editors of the collection issued an appeal for German Jews to regain the same rights as other German citizens, they called upon the government to reopen all professions and trades to Jews, they asked the government to rationalize the process of emigration and cease interference with Jewish organizations assisting would-be emigrants, and they urged the government to prevent the defamation of Jews.[44]

The Gestapo had approved the publication of thirty-five numbered copies of this astonishing volume. Someone allegedly gave it to Hitler on January 17, 1934, and it also was sent to every member of his cabinet. If the government failed to respond, Geist's informant said, Nazi persecution would continue unabated. He urged Geist, in communication with the State Department, to take extra precautions against any leaks. Only the recipients, the Gestapo, and the members of the Reichsvertretung knew of this initiative. The Jews in this body would certainly suffer from any publicity.[45] Their move did not leak out, but it generated no response from Hitler. A subordinate official in the Foreign Office called the ideas in the brochure reasonable, but said an answer was hardly necessary.[46]

Persecution kept steadily mounting. On March 3, 1934, two different people told Geist that the SS had taken Dr. Benno Walter, vice president of B'nai B'rith in Germany, into what the government called protective custody. Walter had given a speech in January to a group of influential Jews in Munich-Gladbach in which he urged German Jews to continue to defend their rights. How the authorities learned of his speech was unclear. But SS men carted Walter off to Columbia-Haus, the small SS concentration camp in the Tempelhof area of Berlin.[47]

Two days later, Ambassador Dodd told Geist that German authorities had spoken to him sharply about a mock trial of Hitler that a group led by the American Jewish Congress was about to stage in New York.[48] They apparently feared that an enraged Hitler might set off some sort of retaliation. Geist told Dodd about the arrest and confinement of Walter. The Jewish Telegraph Agency had learned of the arrest, and Geist was sure that as soon as they published their story, it would aggravate anti-Nazi sentiment in the United States. If the guards at Columbia-Haus were to injure Walter, the situation would become even worse, Geist warned.

Played into a corner, Dodd contacted the German foreign minister about the B'nai B'rith vice president's imprisonment. Neurath disclaimed any knowledge of Columbia-Haus. Dodd told him he could get information about it from Geist. Walter was released unharmed after two weeks.[49]

A month earlier, Secretary of State Cordell Hull had asked Dodd to complain to Hitler about Nazi propaganda targeted at German Americans. Two prominent non-Nazi conservatives in Hitler's government had also urged Dodd to criticize such propaganda and to stress the need for better relations between the United States and Germany. As a result, Hitler's foreign press secretary Hanfstaengl arranged for Dodd to meet with Hitler on March 7. He asked Dodd to keep this delicate meeting secret.[50]

Foreign Minister Neurath greeted Dodd as he entered Hitler's large office about 1 p.m. The minister and Dodd shook hands, and Neurath wished him well. Neurath then left through a door next to Hitler's office, because Hitler wanted what Germans sometimes call a meeting "under four eyes." In his diary Dodd wrote that Neurath was peeved about his exclusion.

Dodd politely asked Hitler if he had any message to send to President Roosevelt. Hitler was apparently caught off guard; the thought had never entered his mind. He asked for time to think about it. Dodd talked about a pending commission and improvement of commercial relations in spite of the fact that Germany had reneged on its debts to the United States, but Hitler was uninterested. Eventually, Dodd raised the subject of Nazi propaganda in the United States directed toward German Americans. Hitler remarkably attributed that to the Jews.

Hitler went on to blame the Jews for all ill feeling among Americans toward Germany. Not venturing to bring up the mock trial of Hitler in New York, Dodd decided instead to offer the chancellor some alternatives for dealing with Jewish problems. Dodd explained to Hitler that the State Department was cooperating unofficially with the League of Nations High Commission for Refugees from Germany. Dodd said that the body had "some millions of dollars" to assist German Jews to leave the country without too much suffering so that over eight or ten years the problem might be solved in a humane way. Hitler retorted that nothing would come of this effort regardless of its resources. The Jews inside and outside Germany would use the organization to attack Germany and to make trouble.

Dodd tried to balance a warning that some Jews held influence in the United States, especially in New York and Illinois, with a description of limits and boundaries on the number of American Jews in high positions. But Hitler only became more agitated, asserting that Jews held 59 percent of all offices in Russia, where, he said, they had ruined the country. His last words on this subject were that they now intended to ruin Germany, and if they continued "we shall make a complete end to all of them." Dodd shifted the subject, observing that Americans had the feeling that Germany was eager for war. Hitler said Germany wanted peace but insisted on equality of armaments. He blamed the Jews for the perception abroad that Germany was warlike. Dodd concluded by urging more cooperation between US and German universities, but Hitler was not much interested in this exchange.

Hitler had issued dire rhetorical threats against German Jews before;[51] no one quite knew how serious he was. But instead of following up, Dodd changed course and moved on to another topic. Their meeting ended politely. Hitler, who had found Dodd difficult to understand, afterward made fun of his enunciation. Ten years later, Hanfstaengl recalled that Dodd, a "trivial, pedantic professor," had missed the opportunity to impress Hitler with the vast power of the United States. Instead, the Führer concluded that he had nothing to fear there.[52]

Dodd apparently recognized that this meeting did not go well. He failed to notify the State Department officially about Hitler's comments. Instead, he wrote a six-page account of the meeting, marked strictly confidential, on very flimsy paper for Secretary Hull.[53] Then he avoided any further meetings with Hitler for the remainder of his time in Germany.

Dodd failed to observe that the Nazi regime was encountering rising internal tension. The focal point of behind-the-scenes conflict was Ernst Röhm, a onetime Bavarian Army officer who had become prominent in radical right-wing circles after the war. Röhm helped Hitler gain military contacts and support in the years before the 1923 Beer Hall Putsch. Afterward, despite some clashes with Hitler and a stretch living in Bolivia, Röhm mounted a political comeback and ended up head of the SA. He was one of Hitler's oldest allies, but he had independent ambitions.

By early 1934, Röhm's SA had three million men, partly through a forced takeover of the Stahlhelm, a paramilitary group that numbered over half a million members. Many others, including former communists, joined the SA out of opportunism. Cynics described the ex-communists as beefsteaks—brown on the outside, red on the inside.

Röhm hoped to establish his force as a people's militia, which would have rivaled the army, limited by treaty to one hundred thousand men. But Hitler, in a February 1934 speech to senior army officers, confirmed that the Reichswehr would remain the only regular armed force. Army leaders intensely disliked the SA and shunned Röhm personally, his private life having been exposed by the 1932 publication of his extremely explicit letters to a male lover.

Meanwhile, Himmler was vying for control of all the state police forces to add them to his existing stronghold in the SS. Prussia had the largest police force, and the Gestapo was its political nucleus—the perfect complement to the elite SS force. Göring was willing to cede control of the Gestapo to Himmler's men if it meant ending the threat from the SA. He decided to appoint Himmler as inspector—in effect, acting director of the Gestapo—with Himmler's right-hand man, Reinhard Heydrich, taking over practical control of it. Göring held enough other government positions to maintain his influence even without the Gestapo. Himmler, Heydrich, and Göring came to represent the heart of a coalition against Röhm, whom they considered a threat to stability and to good relations with the military.[54] Reichswehr officers viewed the SA as a threat to their own standing, and they believed that any combination of army and SA would besmirch the army's proud traditions and ethos.

Although unaware of this behind-the-scenes alliance, Geist did sense a crisis. Unemployment had declined but was still high. German workers were unhappy with part-time jobs and wage declines. Formerly, workers who had been Social Democrats or German Communists fought against SA men in the factories, but now the SA men were unhappy too, and the workers were shifting toward communism. Geist heard rumors of an impending coup by the Reichswehr directed at the SA, but he did not believe them.[55]

In April 1934, Messersmith believed that Germany's economic problems would unseat the regime. Geist, however, had recently gone to some remote villages, where he walked and bicycled around, talking to a great many people. The villagers considered Hitler a god and would not utter a word of criticism of him. All the problems came from his subordinates, they said. Geist predicted that stronger government controls would be used to whip the Jews and that Hitler would endure.[56]

In a June 1934 letter to Pierrepont Moffat, Geist laid out two possibilities. If Nazi Germany were to suffer a severe economic contraction, it might launch an attack on one or more neighboring countries out of desperation. But, he added:

> I cannot sufficiently emphasize what would happen if the present regime were able to create a strong Germany. This country under such conditions would certainly rearm and definitely prepare to wage a war against Europe in general which would change the course of history, if not of civilization, beyond what we even dream, if their supreme effort would be successful. The Germans are absolutely confident of their destiny; and they will make the attempt to establish a hegemony (or rather an empire similar to that maintained by the Caesars) in Europe unless forces beyond their control hinder the attempt. This regime will fall only if it fails to carry out the national destiny; if it shows signs of being able to succeed, it will endure.[57]

Moffat circulated this astonishingly prescient letter to others at State, and it reached Secretary Cordell Hull.[58] Geist was likely the only US official who, in June 1934, regarded Nazi Germany as a threat to the entirety of Western civilization.

Even the best-informed people, Geist wrote, knew very little. Logic suggested that the regime could not last. But Geist believed that it would, and the German people would come to terms with whatever shortages developed.[59] His careful observations in Berlin and his travels through German cities, towns, and villages had given him a feel for the dynamics of a totalitarian system. He understood that Nazi radicals were serious about translating rhetoric into action.

The final catalyst for an internal shake-up came on June 17. Franz von Papen, still vice chancellor but lacking political influence, agreed to give a speech at the University of Marburg. In preparation, Papen's press secretary Herbert von Bose had contacted a number of generals critical of the regime. Knowing that President Hindenburg was seriously ill, they hoped to take advantage of widespread discontent with the SA and economic problems to restore the Hohenzollern monarchy and install some checks on Hitler. Edgar Jung, a right-wing intellectual who worked under Papen, drafted the speech, and Papen received it only as he left for the university. It called for a stable state as opposed to the rule of a party. It warned against a second Nazi revolution and against the creation of a false cult of personality. Nobody had publicly uttered such sentiments since Hitler had taken power.[60]

The *Frankfurter Zeitung*, a newspaper that was not yet fully Nazified, printed extracts of the speech, and the Swiss *Basler Nachrichten* published the full text. Geist was on top of events. He translated the speech and sent it on to Washington, noting that it was so critical of Nazi policies that the authorities made all possible efforts to suppress stories about it.[61]

Papen's speech did not galvanize a conservative coup against Hitler. Instead, Hitler decided to act against the SA leaders, recalcitrant conservatives, and assorted enemies after Reinhard Heydrich gathered an amount of dubious evidence that Röhm was planning a coup. He did not need solid evidence to convince the Führer, only suspicion. Stringing together a vast conspiracy ranging from the French ambassador to Röhm and Schleicher, Hitler decided to confront Röhm personally at Bad Wiessee, where the SA chief and his associates were sleeping off a night of heavy drinking during a vacation.[62] This was the reality behind the so-called Röhm Putsch, sometimes called the Night of the Long Knives.

SS squads murdered approximately one hundred assorted enemies Hitler and key subordinates had accumulated over the years, not just the top SA men or conservatives close to Papen. Hitler authorized the killing without any pretense of a trial. Although former general and chancellor Kurt von Schleicher and his wife were among those killed, army leaders raised no objections because the executioners also neutralized their rival, the SA. Göring personally ordered the killing of Schleicher. He spared Papen, likely because of his tie with President Hindenburg.[63]

Anyone who had blamed the SA for all the early violence in Nazi Germany should now have realized otherwise. This was no longer an outburst by irresponsible thugs; this was murder ordered by Hitler and carried out by an obedient force. Messersmith told Undersecretary of State Phillips that the purge showed the outside world what barbarities the Nazis were capable of. Messersmith tried to analyze the various forces behind the bloodletting, which he condemned in forthright terms, but he had no solution other than for the United States to refrain from giving any moral or material support to Germany. Later, he described these events as without parallel in the history of modern Europe.[64]

Geist possibly may have contributed to Dodd's twelve-page embassy despatch with blow-by-blow coverage of the Röhm Putsch, but Geist certainly did not agree with all of the sentiments it contained. In Dodd's telling, Hitler had forestalled Röhm's coup.[65] This was in fact a bit of propaganda that Goebbels had created for Germans and gullible outsiders.

The narrative put forth was that Röhm and the SA leaders were not only traitors, but morally depraved; the SA was permeated with homosexuals. Hitler had told SA men to be leaders, not "abominable apes."[66] The purge was framed as a cleansing of dangerous and degenerate elements from the movement.[67]

Geist knew better than to believe Goebbels's propaganda. He followed up embassy reports with some of his own comments about the consequences of the Röhm purge. Beyond the killings, thousands of SA men had been arrested and thrown into concentration camps or prisons, with SS men as their jailers. The two organizations now openly hated each other. Public confidence in the Nazi movement had fallen, partly because of the SA's discontent. But there was no opposition to Hitler to speak of, only whispered criticism. The nation accepted whatever the government did in the hope of larger opportunities outside Germany, Geist concluded. He meant that the hope of an expanded German empire placated the German public and silenced critics of domestic conditions.[68]

The real victor in the Röhm purge was not the army but Himmler's SS. Himmler often came across as dull, pedantic, and colorless. But one of his later intimates described another man within: "His ways were the ophidian ways of the coward, weak, insincere, and immeasurably cruel. . . . Himmler's mind was not a twentieth-century mind. His character was medieval, feudalistic, machiavellian, evil."[69]

Geist was able to form his own impression of Himmler after another attack on an American citizen. On August 14, 1934, Albert Lepawsky, returning from a public speech by Joseph Goebbels, stopped to watch a parade of uniformed National Socialists through the streets of Berlin. Lepawsky failed to salute the flag when it passed, and one of the marchers attacked him. He complained to Geist.

Geist went to the stark and forbidding five-story building at Prinz-Albrecht-Strasse 8, only a few blocks from the luxurious Hotel Adlon. Once an art school, this structure had become Gestapo headquarters, with its own small prison.[70] Upon Geist's arrival at Gestapo headquarters, Himmler agreed to see him.

Himmler expressed his regret about the attack on Lepawsky and explained that the authorities had done everything possible to convince the public and party organizations that foreigners did not need to salute the flag. He promised to find the assailant. Geist also took the occasion to warn Himmler that Goebbels's escalating attacks on foreign correspondents' coverage of recent events might prompt enthusiastic party members to assault reporters. Himmler, who strongly disliked Goebbels, agreed with Geist that Goebbels's behavior was reckless and threatened further to harm Germany's image abroad. The meeting gave Geist the impression that, at least for the moment, Himmler was eager to maintain good relations with the United States, which was further reinforced when he learned the next morning that someone had been arrested for the assault.[71]

All in all, it was a surprisingly mild encounter with a mass executioner on his way to becoming the second most powerful figure in the Nazi regime. Himmler was a racial ideologue, a true Nazi believer.

Geist was of German descent, which gave him some standing in Hitler's Berlin. Himmler would not have gone out of his way to meet Geist, but if Himmler welcomed contact with an American official, Geist was the best available. With his acting skills and his familiarity with German culture, Geist made a very different impression than Dodd had with Hitler. He had presence.

Even if Geist could not reach Himmler directly in the future, he could make use of this August 1934 face-to-face meeting to gain access to Himmler's subordinates. When Himmler agreed to meet Geist, he rendered Geist an acceptable counterpart for Gestapo officials.

In late August, journalist Dorothy Thompson, wife of novelist Sinclair Lewis, arrived in Berlin from Austria. In 1931 Thompson had conducted a hostile interview of Hitler for *Cosmopolitan* magazine; she had Hitler blaming all Germany's problems on the Jews at a time when Hitler was starting to play anti-Semitism down for electoral reasons. Then she had published a book about Hitler that questioned his manhood, breeding, and mental status.[72] In the restaurant of the Hotel Adlon, despite the possibility of being overheard by Gestapo informants, she talked to a friend openly about trying to smuggle the wife of anti-Nazi journalist Carl von Ossietzky out of the country. Ossietzky, a nominee for the Nobel Peace Prize, was being held in a concentration camp. On August 25, the Gestapo arrived at Thompson's hotel room with an expulsion order: she had twenty-four hours to leave the country.

Using his new Gestapo connections, Geist viewed her police dossier, which revealed two grounds for her expulsion: her interview of Hitler in 1931, and the series of articles critical of Nazi Germany she had written for the Jewish Telegraphic Agency in 1933. After Geist gave her the results of his inquiry, she noted that Nazi officials particularly resented a non-Jew with an international reputation writing for a Jewish news service. Expulsion turned her into an international celebrity, a valiant warrior against the Third Reich. Her fame briefly eclipsed that of her husband.[73]

In the end, the hope Himmler expressed to Geist for better relations with the United States was either entirely empty rhetoric or insufficient grounds to prevent the Gestapo from restricting foreign press coverage of Nazi mistreatment of German Jews. Geist knew how to connect recent events: SS ascendancy after the Röhm purge meant, first, greater control of the press and, second, escalating persecution of German Jews. When essential Nazi principles or interests were at stake, Hitler would no longer worry very much about foreign reaction, only about immediate repercussions.

CHAPTER SIX

IMMIGRATION AND EMIGRATION

In April 1933, Hitler observed that the United States had shut its doors to German Jews. American immigration barriers reinforced his belief that many others besides the Germans hated Jews. The *Neue Breslauer Zeitung* courageously responded that the United States had cut immigration out of concern that immigrants would aggravate its widespread unemployment.[1] This exchange oversimplified a complicated tug of war in Washington that carried on for years.

In 1930, the Hoover administration had sharply cut immigration through executive action. In 1933, the Roosevelt administration debated whether to relax existing administrative barriers to immigration from Germany, and if so, how. The State Department blocked any real loosening during 1933, and Washington's politically charged conflicts over immigration carried over to Berlin. Geist was criticized for doing too little and for doing too much.

Key State Department officials initially believed that American Jews organized demonstrations against Nazi Germany primarily to force a breach in existing US immigration barriers, not because Nazis represented a special threat to the Jewish people. State Department officials discounted reports of widespread Nazi violence against German Jews, at least partly because acknowledging them would weaken State's defense of tight regulations.[2] Secretary of Labor Frances Perkins was the only cabinet member who spoke out clearly in favor of admitting a substantial number of Germans and German Jews suffering from Nazi persecution. Recognizing a humanitarian crisis, she called for a response in keeping with American traditions of generosity.

The White House referred legal disputes over State Department–Labor Department jurisdiction to the attorney general, whose deputy ruled in favor of Labor. In theory, after this ruling Americans would be able to post bonds with the Department of Labor on behalf of individuals applying for visas. Such bonds would prevent consuls abroad from rejecting these applicants as likely public charges. But the State Department officials feared that this ruling would set off an avalanche of German Jewish immigration and, with it, rising American anti-Semitism. So, they turned to restrictionist allies in Congress who sought to cut the quotas. Labor Department officials began to fret over the political backlash if they were to authorize the use of these public charge bonds.[3]

Boris Smolar told Geist that the New York Jewish Telegraphic Agency office had reported a more lenient State Department instruction to consuls. Geist called Vice Consul Archer Woodford in to join them. Woodford, handling much day-to-day visa work, had a habit of referring to applicants of "Jewish blood."[4] It was an insensitive and inaccurate term, but it was an age of racism (and the Nazi designation "non-Aryan" for those of Jewish descent was not any better). Woodford said he knew nothing about any press report. He said existing State Department instructions were to give full and sympathetic consideration to all evidence that an applicant would not become a public charge. Geist told Smolar that he could not comment officially. But off the record, he noted that the German quota was only 10 percent filled last year. The main reason was that prospective immigrants could not pay for transportation or lacked financial support in the United States. Many could not get German government permission to take their assets out of the country. The consuls were not at fault, Geist said. Smolar raised the possibility of American Jews formally adopting visa applicants. Woodford responded that adoption would not confer any preference under the law, but that consuls would have to consider evidence of the financial resources of the adoptive parents. Telephoning his story to the JTA office in London, Smolar complimented Geist and Woodford for the sympathetic way they carried out their duties.[5]

Two JTA stories distributed to Jewish newspapers over the next few days misrepresented this discussion, stating that Geist had been ordered to be more liberal in his handling of visa applications from German Jews, and that Vice Consul Woodford was carrying out this policy. Geist allegedly called attention to the fact that Americans could adopt German Jews, establishing a close family relationship and strengthening the case that they would provide support.[6] Geist never would have gone this far with a journalist. Recognizing that Geist offered useful information about making greater use of the quota, Smolar at the very least exaggerated in his article.

Smolar's pro-immigration stories enraged anti-immigration lobbyists. Francis Kinnicutt, president of the Allied Patriotic Societies, protested to the State Department against any weakening of the Immigration Act of 1924 and the public charge clause. Assistant Secretary of State Wilbur Carr told John B. Trevor, another "patriotic" anti-immigration activist, that the article was incorrect in every particular.[7]

Geist chided Smolar for his haphazard work, and Smolar apologized: he said he mentioned Geist and Woodford only because he had wanted to show his gratitude. Geist added in his report to Washington that he thought Reichsvertretung officials interested in getting children to the United States had persuaded Smolar to use the JTA to reach out to potential adoptive parents.[8]

If Smolar portrayed Geist as liberal on immigration, other critics called the Consulate General too strict. In late January 1934, journalist Edwin Mims Jr. denounced the State Department and American consuls for their hostility to immigration from Germany. Raymond Moley, initially part of President Roosevelt's "brain trust," wrote an accompanying editorial calling the State Department and the Foreign Service short on human understanding and out of touch with FDR's New Deal. Geist defended himself and fellow consuls against Mims's article, too. Some of what Geist wrote must be discounted as self-serving. Still, in arguing against the need for public charge bonds, he illuminated the attitudes and difficulties of German Jews.[9]

The large majority of German Jews, Geist wrote, could not manage to immigrate; financial difficulties were the reason. German authorities and pre-1933 laws barred Germans from taking substantial financial resources or property out of the country, and, as a result, German Jews could not live off assets that they otherwise might have transferred to a foreign country. New obstacles, which Geist did not list, may be summarized as follows: departing German Jews had to dispose of property at a fraction of its value, had to pay a "flight tax" equivalent to 25 percent of the proceeds, had to pay ship passage, and faced a government-imposed ceiling on the remaining funds that could leave the country. Proceeds above the ceiling remained in blocked accounts in Germany. Over time, the government reduced the ceiling for removable assets—in June 1934 down to 2,000 reichsmarks (about $770), except in cases where individuals could make special arrangements with Nazi authorities.

Geist wrote that some German Jewish families would make sacrifices to enable their children to emigrate to the United States, but the cost of passage and support after arrival remained out of reach for many. The adults who applied for visas at the Consulate General usually had assets they could bring with them or friends or relatives in the United States willing to support them. They did not need the still-unavailable public charge bonds, because they, their friends, or their relatives could simply supply evidence of their assets.

Geist's case against public charge bonds was more a weapon for the State Department to use in a bureaucratic battle than an impartial analysis. He did not mention the fact that the real demand for American immigration visas was far higher than the number of people filing formal applications. In July 1933, Messersmith had written Carr that fifty or sixty people a day (Monday through Friday) came to the Consulate General in Berlin, at least 80 percent of them Jewish. Annualized, that number yields more than 13,000 people and about 10,500 Jews seeking visas in Berlin alone. The other two consulates issuing immigration visas, Hamburg and Stuttgart, also saw heavy interest. Messersmith did not expect future decreases; the Nazi pressure on Jewish lawyers, doctors, and professionals was likely to continue for years.[10]

In the fiscal year from July 1, 1933, to June 30, 1934, 891 people got US immigration visas in Berlin. This means that somewhere around twelve thousand people were either formally rejected or, more commonly, placed on the informal and inactive waiting list. If one counts dropouts and wait-listed applicants as rejections, Berlin's rejection rate was about 93 percent. Some of those wait-listed would never be able to surmount the public charge barrier.[11]

Adoption of German Jewish children by Americans would eliminate any doubt about the tie between visa applicant and American sponsor. Geist also mentioned, probably not by accident, that an organization could also place children and arrange for their support by specific American families. None of this required the public charge bonds that the State Department fought. A limited number of children would not adversely affect the labor market, and the benefits in human terms would be large. Children looked to be an area of possible compromise among bitterly quarreling parties.

Commissioner of Immigration and Naturalization Daniel Mac-Cormack backed away from the use of public charge bonds shortly thereafter. The Labor Department and the State Department agreed that a new organization, German Jewish Children's Aid, would arrange for the support of about 250 emigrant children, coordinating with an existing German organization in Berlin, German Jewish Aid Association (the Hilfsverein).[12] The issues with the flight tax and cost of immigrating were circumvented. German Jewish Children's Aid accepted a moral obligation to place each child in a private home and cover his or her travel expenses from a fund raised from individual donations. Children's Aid would submit lists of individual children to Labor, which would send them to State, which would send them to the Consulate General in Berlin. The first list of twenty-one children emerged in late September 1934.[13]

The procedure would be normal in the sense that consuls in Berlin would still have to examine each child individually and would make final decisions case by case. Even though these children were barred from working until they reached age sixteen, the consuls still were required to examine their predictable fitness to work once they were of age. Those with serious disabilities would be rejected. That put Geist in charge, as long as he oversaw the visa work of the Berlin Consulate General.

In October 1934, Douglas Jenkins became the new consul general in Berlin, filling the post Messersmith had left vacant. A fifty-four-year-old South Carolinian graduate of a military academy, Jenkins had little background on Germany and could not compete with Geist intellectually. He had seniority and rank but apparently felt insecure. Jenkins quickly complained about inconsistencies in the immigration work of the Jewish organizations.[14] Geist managed to overcome Jenkins's objections to the children's program.

A potentially bigger problem arose when the German police, suspicious of the Hilfsverein and of any agreement to send groups of Jews out of the country, appeared at the Consulate General. Jenkins sent them to Geist. The policemen asked Geist how many children there were; was the Hilfsverein paying for the passage of the children; were they traveling in a group or individually; if all the children were poor; and what was the purpose of their stay in the United States? Geist politely but firmly declined to answer a range of such specific questions. He said that he considered each individual case on its merits. Jenkins, too, thought the police questions inappropriate. Assistant Secretary Carr and Visa Division chief John Farr Simmons sent Jenkins a commendation for his handling of the matter, and the program continued.[15]

Still more trouble emerged in the United States shortly after. John B. Trevor, head of the Coalition of Patriotic Societies, was incredulous when he read press reports of the agreement to admit 250 children. Carr and Simmons told each other that the State Department had a limited role and that the admission of Jewish children was "not primarily our problem." The agreement ultimately was extended to cover at least 350 children who applied at the Berlin, Hamburg, and Stuttgart consulates up through the summer of 1938. Geist made the process work.[16]

In mid-November 1934, the *Jewish Daily Bulletin* called for American Jewish groups to press to fill the German quota, describing the Labor Department as willing, the State Department as liberal, and granting visas as without difficulty. Simmons called the editorial completely inaccurate on the facts but revealing as to American Jewish goals. Reviewing the data, he saw that 1933 fiscal year quota immigration from Germany had been 1,241, while it rose to 4,052 for the period ending June 1934. The first months of the 1935 fiscal year suggested that there would be another increase to an annual rate of more than 5,100.[17]

Proponents of increased Jewish immigration saw a reasonably large quota (25,957) still mostly unused. They recognized a general threat to a German Jewish community of nearly six hundred thousand, even if most proponents did not anticipate the severity of the threat. They hoped for some sort of rescue program for the persecuted. State Department officials defended a system of laws and regulations defined to sift out individuals who could not contribute effectively to the United States. They were confident that Congress and the American public would support them in the case of Jewish immigrants. These two sides largely talked past each other.

Geist liked aiding children but saw that many German Jews would make good US citizens. But to criticize the visa system directly would have undermined his career. This did not stop him from subtly trying to change the process. He took one initiative in September 1934, cloaked in a proposal to simplify administration at the consulates, to bring about greater use of the immigration quota. In a despatch to the Visa Division, Geist reviewed the history of the informal waiting list. He noted that the Berlin Consulate General now had a waiting list of seventeen thousand, and the waiting lists at all the US consulates in Germany totaled eighty-two thousand. The demand for immigration visas was heavy. Geist proposed to terminate these lists, forcing the applicants either to apply formally for visas or to withdraw. With the US economy improving, the consuls probably would be able to approve more. A Visa Division official recognized that terminating the waiting lists likely would "excite" the registrants (encourage them to apply) and predictably result in an increase in unemployment in the United States. He said it would be worth considering if Congress were to fail to reduce immigration quotas in the next session. Assistant

Secretary Carr agreed to keep Geist's idea in mind, but he declined to change the existing practice of keeping inactive waiting lists at the consulates.[18]

In late 1934, Geist spent a few days with his ex-colleague Messersmith in his new post in Vienna. Messersmith told Geist that Geist was ready to lead a major consulate general. This would have been a big step in Geist's career. The major stumbling block was that Nazi Germany was so complex and Geist had such good contacts that Messersmith wanted him to stay longer in Berlin. Geist said he was willing to stay on. Messersmith then prodded State Department officials to promote Geist two steps on the Foreign Service scale, but he received only one.[19]

The State Department's Pierrepont Moffat noted that Geist had served as acting consul general from late 1933, with a brief interruption, until October 1934. He termed Geist's reporting and protection work superlative, noted his energy, judgment, and discretion, and called his presence in Berlin a real comfort. He urged a commendation, and Secretary of State Hull quickly sent one.[20]

Geist needed some support from Washington because his relations with his new superior, Jenkins, were difficult. The new consul general seemed to take pleasure in notifying Washington when Geist's solution for the AP's Jewish photographers came unglued. Geist's suggestion that "non-Aryan" photographers apply for permission through the Reich Press Chamber failed when the Propaganda Ministry finally completely barred all Jews from the Reich Press Chamber. There was one exception: the son of a soldier had who died in the Great War. All others, including the *New York Times* photographic subsidiary, were excluded.[21]

Jenkins used the inside information from Geist's contacts, but in presenting it to Washington, he neglected to mention Geist's role in the intelligence, citing only an unnamed official of the Consulate General.[22] A year later, when the State Department proposed that Geist receive a part-time appointment in the Embassy, Jenkins responded that he could not spare Geist even part time. When the State Department nonetheless approved Geist's temporary deployment to the Embassy, Jenkins protested strongly.[23]

Their animosity dissipated after a long and difficult struggle involving a naturalized US citizen. A Cleveland resident named Richard Roiderer had gotten into trouble for criticizing Nazi officials in a notebook that had ended up in the hands of authorities, allegedly due to a vengeful love triangle. Claiming that the notebook contained military secrets, the police arrested him, and charged him with high treason. In other words, despite his naturalization as an American citizen, they considered him German. He was to be tried before a notorious and normally secret People's Court in Berlin. Geist found him a good lawyer, one Dr. Mogens von Harbou. Roiderer did not have his day in court for eleven months and spent them incommunicado in Berlin's Moabit Prison.

On the day of the trial, Geist and some US newspaper correspondents arrived early at the courtroom of the Berlin People's Court. Geist told the guard outside that the president of the tribunal had agreed to let him attend the trial because it involved a US citizen. In fact, the Ministry of Justice had denied Geist permission. The guard stressed that the proceedings were secret, but he let Geist pass, and the correspondents followed him into the room. In the trial that followed, the prosecution demanded five years in prison from a visibly weakened Roiderer. The judges ended up acquitting Roiderer, despite what they called strong suspicion against him, on the grounds that the prosecutor failed to prove that the defendant planned to publish his notes. Roiderer broke down and wept when the verdict was announced.[24] An innocent American triumphed over powerful Nazi forces: the story of his acquittal made the front page of the *New York Times*.[25] It seemed too good to be true, and it was.

It turned out Roiderer had been in Germany living off his deceased father's pension since mid-1932. Despite his status as a naturalized US citizen, he had stated to an American official that he hoped to remain in Germany indefinitely because he had been unable to support himself in the United States.[26] He seemed to forget that, as a US citizen, he should not get involved in German politics.

During his time in Germany, he compiled information about armaments under the control of the SA. The police arrested him trying to cross the border into Switzerland with his notebook. In prison, he confessed to all of the charges. His intention was to leave Germany for long enough to publish a story about these Nazi armaments.[27] It was reckless, almost suicidal, behavior.

Afterward, Geist and Jenkins took Roiderer to task. Jenkins thought Roiderer guilty under German law,[28] and he made this clear to him. He chastised him and ordered him to "make up your mind once and for all if you want to become a German or stay an American. . . . You had no business mingling in German politics. . . . We had an awful lot of trouble with you. You could never pay for all the work we have done in your case." According to Roiderer, Geist also told him he had no business getting excited about German barbarism as an American living in Germany.[29] Roiderer later commented: "Mr. Geist and Mr. Jenkins seem to have forgotten that the American taxpayer is paying them their salaries and that it is their business to protect this American citizen's interest—regardless of 'troubles.'" Roiderer felt not the slightest bit guilty and resented Geist's statement.

Geist did not disagree with Roiderer on the characterization of the regime: he himself charged that the regime was suffused with "gangster brutality." But Roiderer's recklessness had mired the consulate in a complex struggle to protect an American citizen for almost a year. In the end, Jenkins gave Geist credit for unusual tact and discretion in his handling of the case, saying he was largely responsible for the success.[30]

Geist saw that the Nazi regime's brutality was only increasing. He observed how Goebbels and the publisher of the hate-filled, semi-pornographic newspaper *Der Stürmer*, Julius Streicher, were gaining influence. The consul posited that anti-Semitism was partly a mechanism to distract the German public's attention from economic problems, but he only anticipated it to get worse. Geist expected new legislation to separate German Jews from other Germans and punish them in new ways, but in August 1935, it was not yet clear in what form.[31]

The following month, things would become known. Hitler took the occasion of the Nazi Party's 1935 Nuremberg rally to have the government bureaucracy promulgate laws with two complementary objectives: establishing racial criteria for citizenship and banning intermarriage and even sexual relations between German Jews and Aryan Germans. They barred Jews from employing female Germans under age forty-five. They relegated Jews, Sinti, Roma, and blacks (all non-Aryans) to the status of subjects.[32]

Neither Geist nor Jenkins sent the State Department a detailed analysis of the now infamous Nuremberg Laws, leaving this high-profile issue to the Embassy. But Geist followed up on the Nuremberg Laws with a long report on the political situation. He wrote that anti-Semitism was the common bond uniting diverse groups and factions within the Nazi Party, offering relief for the explosive forces in the movement. The conservative forces in the army, the nobility, and the upper ranks of the government bureaucracy found pervasive anti-Semitism discomfiting, and some men in these groups had Jewish wives. Nazi anti-Semitism divided the former Social Democratic workers, who disliked it, from the pro-Nazi workers, who sympathized with it. The Nuremberg Laws, Geist wrote, as well as indications of future expropriation of Jewish property, stimulated panic among Jews, with more and more of them seeking all possible ways to leave the country. Yet finding havens was still hard.[33]

In late 1935, the Consulate General and the State Department carried out an investigation of a trust fund designed to promote immigration to the United States. Emile Berliner, a German Jew, had immigrated to the United States in 1870, becoming a US citizen in 1880. He invented the microphone and a disc phonograph record, which made him a wealthy man. After his death in 1929, his widow, Cora Adler, also Jewish, inherited an estate of more than $1 million, the equivalent of about $15 million today. She established a trust fund of $50,000 to extend assistance to her husband's relatives in Germany. All of this took on new importance after 1933.

Jenkins was suspicious of affidavits of support signed by the trustee of the Cora Berliner Fund to help Berliner family members immigrate to the United States. A State Department investigator, however, found that trustee Joseph Sanders was well acquainted with the situation of the Berliners for whom he signed, and that they had resources to pay for their own transportation. The Berliner Fund was basically a second line of defense against the immigrants' poverty in the United States. Sanders's affidavits did not run afoul of even the State Department's strict interpretation of immigration laws and regulations.[34]

Geist knew someone nearby with substantial family resources—Dodd's least favorite embassy employee, Julia Lewin. Because of her brothers in the United States, the Swope-Lewin family had options to deploy funds on both sides of the Atlantic. We know very little of what they worked out to facilitate Jewish emigration or when and how they worked it out. But when Geist returned to the United States in October 1939, Lewin, who had preceded him, was anxious to contact him to learn the condition of "our endowment."[35] It looks as though Geist either authorized expenditures from this endowment fund or selected visa applicants to benefit from it.

In December 1935, one of the most powerful and most restrictionist State Department officials, Undersecretary William Phillips, visited Berlin, in part to get a firsthand look at the Embassy. By this time, the State Department's patience with Dodd had worn thin.[36] Geist, too, had new concerns and frustrations. The ambassador had never signed the advantageous lease that Geist had worked out for his living quarters, and there had been new disputes with Panofsky, his landlord. In turn, Panofsky's lawyer had turned to the Nazi government to help him collect what he was due from Dodd. While negotiating out of this mess with German authorities, Geist tried to put the blame on Panofsky, but privately Geist made it plain that Dodd was at fault. After relating this struggle and a series of Dodd's continuing complaints about his staff, Geist understated the situation when he described Dodd as not a very cheerful person.[37]

During Phillips's visit, Geist was ill and out of his office, but he came to see Phillips at his hotel. Geist made it clear to Phillips that he could secure favors from Himmler, probably the most powerful Nazi official after Hitler. Phillips was impressed, noting in his diary: "Geist has had the intelligence to get rather close to this man." He ended up leaving Berlin convinced that Germany was preparing to enlarge her frontiers to the east, perhaps in about two years, or as soon as she was in position to do so.[38]

Geist's forecast of German expansion followed a series of previous comments on Nazi foreign policy. In January 1935, a treaty-mandated plebiscite in the Saar region gave a contested territory a choice of what nation they would join. Selecting between Germany, France, and the status-quo French administration, 90.8 percent of Saar voters chose to rejoin a Germany under Hitler. Nazi leaders were almost drunk with their political success. One of Geist's American friends happened to be spending a couple of days with Hitler and Göring at Hitler's mountain retreat at Obersalzberg shortly after they heard the results. The Nazi leaders talked openly to Geist's friend about publicly announcing German rearmament in violation of the Treaty of Versailles. Geist reported this to Moffat, further bolstering his well-established view that Hitler would reign for a long time and that internal opposition was minimal.[39]

In March 1935, when Messersmith visited Berlin, Geist told him that the army now seemed to support the Nazi program. Messersmith was finally convinced that the longer Hitler remained in power, the greater a danger he became for Europe and the United States.[40]

In January 1936, Geist suffered from a hemorrhage caused by a growth in his bladder. The leading bladder surgeon at a Berlin hospital, Dr. Ringleb, initially thought removal of the growth would not be difficult, but he had to go in three times to get all the pieces, some of which he had to burn off. After eight days in the hospital, Geist was confined to his house afterward. To make matters worse, during this time Anna Geist suffered from an enlarged thyroid, which added to her serious diabetes and left her fighting for her life. She required daily injections and X-ray treatments.[41]

Sometimes serious illness followed by recovery concentrates the mind on essentials. In February 1936, Geist began to issue a series of penetrating reports and analyses that compiled the experiences that had been rushing at him for the past several years. In a long letter to State Department political adviser James Dunn, Geist comprehensively analyzed German political forces. He divided them into three basic categories, with subdivisions in each according to personal and institutional rivalries. Hitler and his chancellery headed the radical

Nazi forces, which also included the regional Nazi Party leaders, called gauleiters, and Party Secretary Rudolf Hess; the Secret Police led by Himmler; the Ministry of Propaganda headed by Goebbels; and others. The more conservative Nazi or pro-Nazi forces, with less influence, included the Air Ministry headed by Göring, the War Ministry under General Werner von Blomberg, and the Justice Ministry. The conservative non-Nazi forces included officials in the Finance Ministry, Economic Ministry, and Ministry of Foreign Affairs, but they had very little influence.[42]

The chief achievement of the Nazi regime, Geist said, was the creation of a totalitarian system, with Hitler as its high priest. Geist thought Germany eventually would have to choose between Armageddon and surrender. He did not believe Hitler would ever surrender. Instead, Germany would attempt to break through the ring of enemies gradually forming around it. A change of regime would become feasible only when Hitler was no longer alive.[43]

It was as if Geist had fused a photograph with an X-ray, showing the bones beneath the surface features of Nazi Germany.[44] Messersmith called this letter splendid, pronouncing himself in agreement with virtually everything in it. He added, "I know what a difficult time you must be having in many ways, but it is very much worthwhile and you will never regret what you are doing these days. There are those who know what it means, and the final record will do you justice."[45]

The State Department, meanwhile, asked Geist about a small number of Germans who had emigrated in stages, misusing visitors' visas in the process. Those Germans had received visas in Germany to visit Bermuda, submitting evidence that their visits would be temporary. Once there, they applied for immigration visas to the United States (under the German quota). Geist responded that the Consulate General would continue to be vigilant on visitors' visas. He explained that there were several reasons why Germans might apply for visitors' visas. For example, Germans with relatives in the United States believed that their mail back and forth went through censorship, and believed it was safer for them to correspond with relatives from a site outside Germany, or even to meet with them in person in the United

States. Geist asserted that he did not think any consul had advised them to do this, and he implicitly opposed any effort to punish the visitor-immigrants.[46]

Another opportunity to fund Jewish emigrants emerged in May 1936, and Geist figured out how to exploit it. David Glick, a well-connected lawyer from Pittsburgh, traveled to Berlin on behalf of the Warburg banking family and officials of the American Jewish Joint Distribution Committee. Glick explained to Geist that the Warburgs and the JDC wanted him to report on the results of the funds they had distributed in Germany. Geist decided to help Glick.[47]

On May 27, Glick and Geist drove to Gestapo headquarters at 8 Prinz-Albrecht-Strasse. A sign outside the building indicated that Jews were not permitted to enter; Geist snarled at it as they walked to the front door. Geist told Glick not to let the Nazis know that he spoke fluent German: Geist would serve as his intermediary and interpreter. Glick's impression of the Mephistophelian Himmler was someone who looked like a title searcher in the office of the recorder of deeds in a county government. He lacked pomp, he did not thump the table, and he did not particularly try to make an impression. But he had unusual, beady button eyes that radiated cruelty. Himmler summoned Heydrich, who struck Glick as a blond gorilla who would have made a good tackle on a professional football team.

Glick explained that he had come to Germany at the request of two men whom he did not name. He wanted to do his work quietly, and when he returned to the United States he would not seek publicity there or spread propaganda of any kind. He set out his purpose clearly: to assist the Jews of Germany to emigrate from Germany with as much money as German laws permitted. Glick said he understood that Germany wanted to facilitate the departure of Jews. Heydrich agreed that government policy was to facilitate the departure of Jews, and if Glick's mission was limited to that, he could count on the Gestapo's support and cooperation. Glick named the German Jewish organizations he sought to contact. Heydrich sent for the Gestapo's specialist on Jewish affairs, Dr. Karl Haselbacher, who joined them.[48] Heydrich explained the situation and instructed Haselbacher to work with Glick, putting all Gestapo facilities at his disposal. In his office Haselbacher showed off a file-card index containing the names, addresses, occupations, and activities of thousands of Jews throughout Germany. He handed Glick and Geist a list of leading Jews in various German cities and also his card with his private phone number: Glick could call him at any time in case of difficulty.[49]

Afterward, Jenkins noted the breakthrough of allowing "international Jewry," under the protection of the Gestapo, to contact German Jews. Geist's inside line in the Gestapo was paying off. Heydrich's cooperation indicated the possibility of a rational Nazi attitude toward Jewish emigration, Jenkins wrote, and Geist and Jenkins (Glick mistakenly remembered it as Geist and Messersmith) were amazed.

More than eighty years later, this meeting seems even more fantastic. The Warburg financial dynasty trailed only the Rothschild family as a Nazi symbol of "international Jewry." Born in Germany, Felix Warburg had emigrated to the United States, where he married the daughter of Jacob Schiff, a partner in the Kuhn Loeb investment banking firm. It later merged with Lehman Brothers. By 1935, Felix was chairman of the Joint Distribution Committee and mostly involved in philanthropy. Max Warburg was senior partner of M. M. Warburg Bankers of Hamburg. They were the two men behind David Glick's visit to Germany.

Geist almost certainly knew that Himmler and Heydrich had created a Reich Central Office for Combating Homosexuality and Abortion. An SS newspaper already had called for the death penalty for male homosexuals,[50] but Geist guided the representative of a wealthy Jewish clan into the hornet's nest of SS and Gestapo agents despite his own secret homosexual relationship with Erich Mainz. He arranged and got what he wanted out of the potentially perilous meeting with Heydrich. Operating on his own, Geist projected US interest in increased German Jewish immigration. His presence and his negotiating style built the bridge for Nazi negotiations with "international Jewry."

CHAPTER SEVEN

POST-OLYMPIC COMPETITION

In 1933, the Nazi government centralized all athletic organizations and stepped up the training of German athletes. Candidates for the German Olympic team trained under the personal supervision of Hitler's sports commissioner. Geist reported that Hitler himself visited athletes during a training course in 1933. With Germany scheduled to host both the Winter and Summer Olympics in 1936, Geist suggested that only the fear of losing the host's role might cause the German government to reverse its discrimination against Jewish athletes.[1]

The US Amateur Athletic Union voted not to participate in the 1936 games if the German Olympic Committee barred Jews from its team. Although the German Olympic Committee denied there was any discrimination, their assertion seemed doubtful to Geist. But it was the US Olympic Committee, not the government, that determined whether the United States would send teams to Germany. After an outbreak of anti-Jewish violence in Berlin and a rise in anti-Catholic actions in mid-1935, some leading American Jews, Catholics, and liberals stepped up an effort to pressure US sports organizations to boycott. In response, two leading figures on the US Olympic Committee, Charles Sherrill and Avery Brundage, went over to check if there were grounds to boycott the games. Sherrill, who previously had accepted Hitler's invitation to attend the 1935 Nuremberg Party rally, was not likely to be a harsh critic of Nazi Germany.[2]

Sure enough, the two emissaries reported back that Germany did not intend to exclude Jewish athletes from its team. Brundage and his publicity consultant issued a brochure entitled *Fair Play for American Athletes*, which blamed the American boycott movement on radicals, communists, and certain Jews. It advised the US government not to interfere, and it cited American involvement in the Great War as an example of unfortunate government meddling in European problems.[3]

Meanwhile, Dodd signed an embassy despatch describing the German Olympic Committee's maneuvers to bar German Jews from the German team.[4] (Only one half-Jewish athlete made it through the obstacles to play on the German hockey squad.) But the US Olympic Committee voted narrowly against further investigation of German conditions.[5]

Hosting the 1936 Olympics gave Hitler the chance to show off to millions that the country was partially recovered from the Depression. He did so via newsreels, radio, and the press. Conveying an image of strength and success was so important that in February 1936, after a Jewish medical student, David Frankfurter, assassinated the Nazi Party representative in Switzerland, Wilhelm Gustloff, the government prohibited party and public anti-Jewish violence in response to the killing. The reason: the Olympic Games.[6] It was unusual restraint for a regime accustomed to encouraging or tolerating anti-Semitic outbursts.

Mining heiress and socialite Evalyn Walsh McLean, owner of the Hope Diamond, was just the sort of American whom German officials hoped to impress at the Olympics. She lived and entertained on a large estate called Friendship nestled into the upper northwest corner of Washington, DC, where she once held a party for two thousand guests.[7] Senator Robert R. Reynolds of North Carolina, best known today for his June 1941 speech calling metaphorically for the construction of a wall around the United States to protect it from foreigners, courted but failed to win McLean.[8] (Instead, in 1939, at age fifty-seven, he married her nineteen-year-old daughter.[9]) A State Department official, pointing out McLean's political connections and influence, asked Geist as a personal favor to get her a room at the

Hotel Adlon, known for its exquisite service and its cathedral-domed hall. If anyone could get her a reservation there during the Olympics, Geist could.[10]

The famous aviator Charles Lindbergh also attended the summer games. Lindbergh considered Hitler a bit of a fanatic, but nonetheless a great man who could not have accomplished so much without some fanaticism. Eager to meet high Nazi officials, Lindbergh cultivated US military attaché Truman Smith. Most American spectators at the Olympics were wealthy sports fans who indulged themselves with a trip to Germany. Young American novelist Thomas Wolfe, who was neither wealthy nor particularly interested in sports, appreciated Hitler's Germany, but also captured something of the way in which it hijacked Olympic pageantry:

> The games . . . were no longer merely sporting competitions to which other nations had sent their chosen teams. They became, day after day, an orderly and overwhelming demonstration in which the whole of Germany had been schooled and disciplined. It was as if the games had been chosen as a symbol of the new collective might, a means of showing to the world in concrete terms what this new power had come to be.[11]

The Nazi regime took great pains to create the right setting, too. The sports grounds, arranged on an axis in Berlin-Charlottenburg, imitated designs from the Roman Empire. The Olympic Stadium itself was a double-ringed oval, with the lower ring below ground level and the upper ring towering over the grounds.

The Olympics were interludes in the process of expansion. In March 1936, after the Winter Olympics at Garmisch-Partenkirchen in Bavaria had ended, Hitler took a major gamble and moved German troops into the demilitarized Rhineland. Both the Treaty of Versailles and the 1925 Locarno Treaty had determined that German territory to the west of the Rhine River would be demilitarized, making any German invasion of France and Belgium more difficult. Now Hitler removed the buffer.

Britain and France protested weakly against the treaty violations, and the condemnation that followed from the League of Nations was also easily shrugged off by Hitler. With this one move, essential elements of the postwar peace settlement were in tatters: Hitler had massively shifted the balance of power in Europe without starting a war.[12] Geist recognized that Hitler had taken a decisive step that would encourage him to push against remaining treaty restrictions and other national boundaries. The outside powers failed to call Germany to account at a critical moment, Geist explained in a 1940 speech.[13]

Shortly after the Summer Olympics, Hitler decided to establish a special economic mobilization office headed by Hermann Göring. Spelling out his view of history as a struggle among nations, Hitler described the USSR and Bolshevism as an immediate threat to Germany. Bolshevism sought to eliminate those strata that had led mankind and to replace them with "world Jewry." Hitler wanted the German Army to become the best in the world in the shortest possible time, and he issued a law extending the draft, only recently introduced, to a two-year term of service. On December 2, Göring told his air force generals that Germany was already at war—only the shooting had not started.[14] Except, it had. The Spanish Civil War had begun and, like Italy, Germany already had sent planes to help the Nationalists under Generalissimo Francisco Franco.

Traditional authoritarians, fascists, communists, and liberal democrats all sought allies across the continent. On November 1, 1936, Mussolini declared that all European countries would revolve around an axis from Rome to Berlin. After its understanding with Mussolini's Italy, Germany concluded a pact with Japan. These moves were ostensibly directed against the Comintern and the possibility of Soviet expansion. The Anti-Comintern Pact eventually had fifteen signatories.

In January 1937, Geist wrote Messersmith that German radio was filled with bitter invectives against the "reds" everywhere, citing dangerous communist centers in Switzerland, Czechoslovakia, and France. According to the Nazis, the Jewish Bolshevik crowd invented and planted all anti-German stories, such as one about German infiltration into Morocco. Geist could not tell whether vehement denunciations of Bolshevism were mostly for German home consumption or to impress other countries to join Germany against the USSR. He compared Hitler to Don Quixote fighting against windmills but did not underestimate the danger of the German and Italian support of fascist movements elsewhere.[15]

Geist did not know which way the Roosevelt administration was leaning in its own foreign policy. In November 1936, FDR won a landslide victory over Republican candidate Alf Landon, gaining 60 percent of the popular vote and the electoral votes of all but Maine and New Hampshire. Virtually the entire country endorsed Roosevelt in what he then believed was his last run for the White House. Many New Deal programs proved to be popular and durable. But so far he had done little in foreign policy or with immigration.

In a speech in Buenos Aires on December 1, FDR signaled a more active foreign policy directed against Germany. In a time of isolationism represented by men such as Senator Reynolds of North Carolina, FDR spoke directly about the old hatreds and new fanaticism threatening conflict in the Old World. The New World, with common democratic bonds, could not simply ignore them, Roosevelt declared; it might be able to help avert catastrophe.[16] Even though the president did not hint at the need to rearm, the anti-Nazi thrust of his remarks was clear enough.

Two subsequent changes in the State Department gave Roosevelt's words added weight: he appointed Sumner Welles as undersecretary of state and Messersmith as assistant secretary of state. Their predecessors, William Phillips and Wilbur Carr, had shown little concern over Nazi domestic and foreign policies. Welles, whom FDR had known since childhood, became his man in the State Department. Roosevelt picked Messersmith in part because of his knowledge of Germany and his forthright opposition to the Nazis. If and when the second-term president decided to situate the United States against Nazi Germany's expansion, he had top State Department people to help him.[17] Both Welles and Messersmith paid attention to Geist's reporting and his warnings.

During his first term, President Roosevelt found immigration too sensitive politically, and Jewish immigration too combustible, for him to endorse publicly. German Jewish immigration increased gradually over time, but never approached the annual ten thousand target he had suggested in a private, fall 1933 conversation with American Jewish leaders.[18] Before and during his 1936 reelection campaign, Roosevelt avoided specific initiatives or proposals for Germany, but he did privately urge the British not to curtail Jewish immigration to Palestine.[19]

After Roosevelt's reelection, Messersmith wrote a long set of new guidelines on visa policy and practices, sending it to the State Department and recommending distribution to appropriate Foreign Service officers. The object of visa decisions, he stated, was not to maintain the United States as a place of refuge for all the dissatisfied and oppressed masses of other countries regardless of their ability to become good, productive citizens. But visa policies also were not designed to exclude classes of people based on race, religion, or political ideas, he argued.[20] One way or another, his message reached the White House.[21] Foreign Service inspector Jerome Klahr Huddle also noted that the character of German Jewish immigrants was unusual (in that it was so high) and that their American relatives sincerely desired to help them escape persecution.[22]

The push began to yield results. In early January 1937, the State Department formally told various consuls in Europe to judge whether applicants would "probably" become public charges, not whether they might "possibly" become public charges.[23] Judging if an applicant would "probably" become a public charge effectively made the process more lenient, since there had to be a high likelihood that the subject of inquiry would become a public charge. Determining that he or she might "possibly" become a public charge was the more stringent way of interpreting the law.

A. Dana Hodgdon, chief of the Visa Division in 1932–1933, had favored judging if applicants would possibly become public charges during his tenure as chief—and he had thrown up obstacles to Einstein's visa, too. In January 1937, he happened to be serving in the Berlin consulate with Geist. That same month, when asked to help interpret the new visa instruction, Hodgdon declared that the State Department now viewed German visa applicants more generously, accepting affidavits of support from distant relatives and friends in the United States. He noted that their sponsors were credible because they understood the unusual conditions in Germany.[24] It turned out that Geist's influence and the new visa instruction had unbent Hodgdon enough to recognize key elements of the situation in Germany.

This shift in the public charge clause aided German Jews seeking to reach the United States. In fiscal year 1936, nearly 7,000 Germans had received quota immigration visas, but for fiscal 1937 year (ending June 30) the total rose to more than 12,500. Some advocates for Jewish immigration pressed further. Representative Emanuel Celler of Brooklyn had introduced a bill to exempt refugees from the public charge disqualifier. But officials of the American Jewish Committee and Jewish immigration specialist Cecilia Razovsky joined Labor Department officials to oppose floor debate on Celler's bill. They believed that the immigration situation was as satisfactory as it could be after the new visa instruction, and they did not want to stir up illiberalism and hostility to aliens, in which case Congress might then reduce the quotas.[25] Geist agreed. He wrote about the visa situation in late 1937 in a letter that does not survive, but in response Messersmith expressed his pleasure at the visa results.[26]

Another indication of the change in both the interpretation of immigration law and the degree of political danger in Germany came in March 1937. Friedrich Brodnitz, Geist and Messersmith's "famous informant" from the Reichsvertretung who possibly had supplied Geist with the bound volume of all anti-Jewish laws, supplied the affidavits of support needed to complete his own visa application. Brodnitz, a thirty-eight-year-old physician, had a brother already living in New York, and that probably was enough under the new instruction.[27] It was good timing because Brodnitz soon ran into trouble with the Gestapo.

Geist acted quickly for his onetime informant. He personally introduced Brodnitz to the visa officer and got Brodnitz a US immigration visa almost immediately. Geist told him that the Consulate General would hold onto his passport until he was ready to depart; that seemed prudent in case the Gestapo decided to confiscate it. On

July 2, 1937, the two men held their final confidential conversation in Germany while walking in the woods of Berlin-Grunewald, where there could be no microphones. Geist wished him good luck in the United States, and Brodnitz departed the next day.[28]

In May 1937, State Department inspector Jerome Klahr Huddle came to Berlin for one of the periodic assessments of US operations. He confirmed that Geist basically had to train his superior, and Jenkins had not trusted the consul at first, but over time—due in part to Geist's diplomacy—they had managed to work things out. Huddle also candidly wrote that he previously had heard both good and bad assessments of Geist. Predisposed to doubt him and the quality of his work before Huddle's arrival in Berlin, the inspector found to his surprise that Geist had exemplary achievements in virtually all areas.[29]

Geist was firm, resourceful, tactful, effective in protecting American interests, and supportive of senior officers. He thoroughly grasped German domestic politics and foreign policy. He was a man of superior culture, able to give a popular lecture on literary topics, even on "an abstruse and baffling subject" such as the poet Robert Browning. American circles in Berlin were taken with his knowledge and his talent as a speaker. Only Geist's administrative work was less than top-notch, according to Huddle. But someone who took the time to appreciate Browning and Shakespeare was not going to ride herd on all his subordinates.

Huddle found that Geist adeptly handled people who visited the Consulate General; these included Jewish immigration and welfare workers from the United States. He was dignified and respected by his subordinates. He had far broader acquaintance with Germans than was customary in the Foreign Service, and he was able to deal effectively with minor German officials to resolve disputes favorably. Geist's contacts with Nazi officials were superior to those of any other embassy or consular official in Berlin. Huddle believed that no German official really respected any American, but insofar as it was possible, he wrote, they respected Geist.

Huddle reported that Geist's sister Anna lived with him in a comfortable, well-furnished apartment. She served admirably as his hostess, entertaining in a quiet, enjoyable manner. Only her precarious health endangered this slightly unusual household. Huddle did not even hint at Geist's sexual orientation, and probably got no sense of it from talking to others during his visit. Huddle wrote that Geist was eager to raise himself to a rank and post where he could do more political work, but if he were finally to leave Berlin, as before, it would be very hard to find someone to replace him.

From his new post in Washington, Messersmith found a creative solution. Having failed to persuade State Department personnel officials to promote Geist more than one step at a time, he arranged Jenkins's transfer to the post of consul general in London, simply leaving Geist as the senior consul in Berlin. At the end of October 1937, Geist became consul general in all but name. Geist also received an appointment as secretary in the Embassy, making him formally a diplomat as well as a consul. Before, he had to avoid stepping on the toes of embassy officials, but now he could write political reports whenever he got choice information. Messersmith expected that this arrangement would help the Embassy and the Consulate General coordinate their functions and reporting.[30]

With his new, more comfortable position, Geist dealt extensively with the recurring problems of German Jews. He specified that anti-Semitism at this point was less a matter of public sentiment and more a matter of laws, but that mattered little to those affected. So long as the Nazis held power, there would be no letup in the regime's severe anti-Semitic policies.[31] Geist recommended emigration to those who could qualify under recent looser American immigration standards. He continued to handle personally some visa decisions involving German Jewish Children's Aid.[32]

After his May 1936 interview in 8 Prinz-Albrecht-Strasse, David Glick had toured Germany and written up his observations in a sobering report about Nazi brutality and terror. The head of the Gestapo in one unnamed town told Glick that the treatment of the Jews was of no concern because they were only guests. Glick wrote, "He then went on to relate to me that in his particular section of Germany the Jews have been living for a period of two thousand years. My obvious reply to him was to ask how long should a Jew live in Germany in order to overcome the status of a guest? His reply was: 'Have you read the Fuehrer's *Mein Kampf*?'"[33]

In the spring of 1937, Glick returned for another effort, but the situation had worsened. On April 20, 1937, Nazi authorities dissolved B'nai B'rith, claiming activities hostile to the state.[34] The Gestapo seized B'nai B'rith's Berlin headquarters and eleven other properties across Germany, as well as liquid assets of the organization. Geist reported that the total value of property seized was about 400,000 marks, and B'nai B'rith was no longer able to pay pensions to its retired officials. Even its food bank reserves were confiscated. A week later, the total value of confiscations came to 2 million marks. The Gestapo arrested all the officials of B'nai B'rith in Germany and of the Reichsvertretung in Germany, too.[35]

After the Gestapo stopped Glick from proceeding with his work in Frankfurt am Main and Munich, Glick asked Geist for another meeting with Heydrich. This time Heydrich called upon his deputy, Werner Best, to join them. It may well have been the first time Geist met Best. In any case, they were fated to meet many more times before Geist left Berlin.

Glick pointed out that during his 1936 visit, he had kept his word about avoiding publicity. If the authorities wanted Jews to emigrate, they should help him now.[36] In the absence of a unified Nazi policy toward the Jews authorized by Hitler, putting something in writing constituted a risk for Gestapo officials.

Geist pressed forward on it. On the stationery of the Consulate General, Geist wrote out in German a brief understanding between Best and Glick. Addressed to American consular officials, it stated that some prominent Americans had donated to a fund to promote the emigration of German Jews. Glick represented them, and the Gestapo in the person of Best supported Glick's efforts. Geist signed as a witness to their discussion and the agreement. Best, however, did not sign it.[37] Geist wrote no official report about it either. This semiofficial document tried to bind Best as much as possible to something that he apparently felt he should not endorse in writing. But Glick could show it to local Nazi officials if he got into any trouble during his discussions with local Jewish organizations.

Werner Best had risen quickly to a position of influence in the Nazi regime through unorthodox means. Too young to have fought in the Great War, Best was part of the generation deeply stamped by the climate of wounded German nationalism in the postwar period. Twice arrested for stirring up trouble in the French-occupied Rhineland, he served about six months in prison. Afterward, he joined a circle of right-wing intellectuals around the writer Ernst Jünger. He studied law, became a judge, and also practiced politics. Working to coalesce diverse right-wing associations in the state of Hesse, he and his colleagues generally thought of a nationalist revolution from above. He initially took Hitler as plebian and dismissed the Nazis as a group without clear and serious goals. He doubted that they represented the political and intellectual elite needed to revitalize Germany.

After the September 1930 parliamentary election, Best realized that Hitler's ability to reach the masses was a powerful weapon for the right. He joined the Nazi Party on November 1, 1930, without ever having attended a party meeting. His first glimpse of Hitler in person came at Bad Harzburg in October 1931, where Best heard Hitler give a speech. Best later claimed that he was severely disappointed: there was no rhetorical magic, only banalities.[38] Whether or not this account is true, Best's first reaction to Hitler did not stand in the way of his growing attachment to the Nazi movement.

Soon after the Bad Harzburg rally, the German press published a story that leading Nazis in Hesse had several months earlier drawn up plans for a coup in which Best was implicated. American officials called the leaked documents "instructions for a Nazi dictatorship by terrorist methods" and "a political bombshell." The plans would have imposed the death penalty for failure to obey the orders of the Nazi storm troopers.[39] Best admitted that, after a mid-September 1931 meeting of Nazi deputies (and before the establishment of the Harzburg Front), he had drafted a set of contingency plans to respond to a Communist seizure of power. But American officials discounted this innocent interpretation: giving "subversive activity the character of measures of defense against Communists is in fact as old as the Nazi party itself." Best was arrested for treason, but the prosecutors could not eliminate the ambiguity in Best's work. And no one could demonstrate Hitler's involvement in a suspected coup because he was not involved. The Nazi press explained that these plans were the work of a private individual, not the party leadership. The charges against Best were eventually dropped, although he lost his job as a judge.[40]

Any conventional political leader might have fumed at Best for undermining the Nazi strategy of finding a legal political path to power. When Best was summoned to Munich for a personal meeting with Hitler, he might have expected as much. However, Best found that the Führer treated him like an old comrade, not a recent bandwagon climber. Hating and fearing the Communists, Hitler appreciated aggressiveness on the part of party members. The whole affair boosted Best's career and helped him reach Berlin.[41] Geist read about him in the German press long before they met in 1937.

Best was a resolute anti-Semite who considered Jews the committed enemy of the German people. He believed that the German people had to defend themselves, even if that meant the complete destruction of all Jews. He shunned an anti-Semitism of raw emotions, however, in favor of one grounded in what he saw as a rational assessment of national and ethnic interest.[42] But on a personal level, Best—at least compared to Himmler, Heydrich, Göring, and Goebbels—was cordial. His sincere intellectual interests dated back to his university days and his collaboration with Jünger. Beginning in 1937, he regularly published books, articles, and book reviews, as well as giving two or three lectures a month. He wrote on law, the judiciary, police and security, administration, and some political topics.[43] He believed that one could learn from history, and he had an interest in the United States as a successful imperial power.[44]

Such a person took some pleasure in the exchange of ideas. An avid reader himself, Geist knew that one way to develop ties with an author was to read his work and take his ideas seriously—or seem to. And Geist knew how to dissimulate. At a minimum, Geist considered Best a person worth cultivating for small favors, such as backing

Glick. At the maximum, he may have hoped to nudge Best away from the violent ends of his personal philosophy.

For the moment, however, matters seemed less promising. A few days after the meeting between Glick, Geist, Heydrich, and Best, a Gestapo official sent Glick a memo with the addresses of Gestapo offices in all the major German cities he intended to visit. He advised Glick to check in with the Jewish specialist in each city before contacting Jewish leaders. This is as far as Gestapo headquarters was prepared to go in writing.[45]

Geist threw himself into the work of defending Americans in Germany, where the stakes were higher than ever. Helmut Hirsch, a twenty-year-old Jew born to naturalized US citizens living in Germany, had lived in Stuttgart until 1935, and then in Prague. There he joined a group of anti-Nazi German émigrés known as the Black Front led by Otto Strasser, once a high Nazi official. Strasser, who had seen his brother Gregor executed in the Röhm purge, persuaded Hirsch to retaliate against Nazi persecution. Carrying a suitcase packed with enough explosives to blow up an entire building, Hirsch crossed into Germany but was arrested. The Nazi press accused him of a plot to assassinate the Führer, though Hirsch's actual target was the notorious regional party boss of Franconia, Julius Streicher, a champion of gutter-level anti-Semitic rhetoric and the publisher of the venomous newspaper *Der Stürmer*. A People's Court convicted Hirsch on March 8, 1937, and sentenced him to death. By that time, the State Department had concluded that he was in fact an American citizen because his father had registered his birth with the American consulate in Stuttgart.[46]

After visiting Hirsch in prison, Geist conferred with his attorney, who already had asked for clemency from Hitler. Geist wrote up his own arguments for the Ministry of Justice and spoke personally with Minister Franz Gürtner. On May 29, Ambassador Dodd received word that Hitler had rejected clemency for Hirsch. Embassy and consulate officials kept trying, and Hitler was again approached, but to no avail. Jenkins and Geist waited in vain to see Hirsch before he was executed on June 4. The prosecutor said he faced death calmly.

He was beheaded and then cremated. American officials were denied custody of his remains.[47]

The episode must have been a blow to Geist. He had failed to defend an American citizen from the depredations of a Nazi tribunal. And Geist knew that the episode would only feed into Hitler's belief that all Jews were conspiring against him.

In August 1937, Geist went home on leave to spend time with his family in Cleveland. Anna was too ill to travel with him, and he had to prepare his younger sister Jennie for the possibility that Anna might die soon.[48] By the time Geist returned to Berlin, Anna was in desperate condition. She was too weak to care for herself. Often in a stupor, she ceased to recognize anyone. He had come to terms with the prospect of her death, but this did not diminish the pain of seeing her suffer and lose her identity. He took her to a hospital and threw himself into his work. His letters to Messersmith show a man close to breaking down.

After a couple of weeks in the hospital, Anna began to improve. She was moved to a sanatorium, and surely through no coincidence, Erich Mainz took sick leave for more than a month in November and December. He probably helped with Anna's care as she convalesced in the sanatorium. Although she left the sanatorium by Christmas, Geist recognized that she could no longer manage in Berlin. When Anna was strong enough, in the spring of 1938, she went back to Cleveland to recuperate and to live with Jennie and other relatives.[49]

On October 5, 1937, Franklin Roosevelt stopped in Chicago on his way back from a train trip to the West Coast. The president had lunch with Cardinal George Mundelein, who had called Hitler "an Austrian paper-hanger, and not a very good one at that."[50] Hailed by crowds estimated at 750,000, FDR dedicated the Outer Drive Bridge over the Chicago River, which had cost the vast sum of $2 million. The *Cleveland Plain Dealer* called his speech at the dedication the most important foreign policy speech he had ever delivered.[51] He denounced unnamed countries that had violated treaties and international morality. The president warned Americans that geographical distance alone would not insulate them from dangers that threatened civilization. In a phrase that became famous, he called for a "quarantine of aggressors," and he also implied that the United States might need to step up defense spending to keep the peace. An aide said that a quarantine might mean at some future date cutting off certain countries from world commerce—what the twenty-first century calls economic sanctions.

The State Department cabled the text of the speech to all embassies and consulates abroad and offered to make it available to any foreign governments wishing to study it. A French government spokesman characterized the speech as marking the real entry of the great moral force of the United States into the world's troubled affairs. The *Plain Dealer* carried a huge headline on its front page: "Powers Stirred by Roosevelt Stand: Blast at Aggressors Hailed as Important Contribution to Peace."[52]

Roosevelt's quarantine speech challenged the climate of isolationism, particularly strong in the Midwest. After his address generated more criticism than support, Roosevelt mused about the man who tried to lead, then looked over his shoulder to see that no one was following him.[53] Geist understood this problem, having been there ahead of him.

Ambassador Dodd had taken leave during the summer of 1937 to recover from increasing stomach pains and severe headaches and to meet with the president. In his diary, Dodd expresses his inability to stand the pressure in Berlin much longer.[54] When, on August 11, Roosevelt favored him with an hour's talk and asked him to stay in Berlin a few months longer, Dodd took it as an endorsement.

The situation was complicated by the activities of his stand-in. That fall, the number two man at the Embassy, who was serving as chargé d'affaires during Dodd's absence, Prentiss Gilbert, had decided to attend that year's Nazi Party rally at Nuremberg on the advice of another embassy official. This broke with Dodd's precedent of refusing these annual invitations. Dodd wrote a letter of protest to Secretary Hull, which an unidentified high State Department official leaked to the press. This story created problems with the German government. The German ambassador to the United States told

Secretary Hull that, although Germany would not press for Dodd's immediate removal, the German government no longer welcomed him in Berlin.[55]

When Dodd met with FDR again on October 19, he asked to stay on in Berlin until March 1938. He had the impression that the president agreed and returned to Berlin unsuspecting. But just before Thanksgiving, Dodd learned that he had been dismissed. Geist and Mrs. Dodd ended up hosting the annual Thanksgiving Day dinner in Berlin. After what Louis Lochner called the most unceremonious departure of an ambassador he had ever seen, Dodd returned to the United States on December 29.[56]

Geist told Prentiss Gilbert that embassy officials should not reflexively do the opposite of whatever Dodd had done. Gilbert complained that he was in an impossible position: if he got too close to the Nazis, he would be criticized in the United States; if he was too unfriendly to the Nazis, they would freeze him out as they had Dodd. Geist told him not so: he should follow the precedent that he and Messersmith had established in Berlin of firmness in private negotiations. Gilbert welcomed Geist's help in the future.[57]

During Geist's stay in the United States, David Glick again had run into trouble. Two Gestapo officials had tried to get him expelled from the country. Glick already had filed a list of complaints at Gestapo headquarters about Gestapo mistreatment of Jews. He was waiting for Geist to return before seeing Best and the acting Gestapo specialist in Jewish affairs, twenty-eight-year-old Dr. Kurt Lischka. Glick expected all of them to have a heated conversation. But there was some good news. Glick had spent enough time in Berlin and Stuttgart to observe the US consuls and vice consuls: their attitudes and performance on visa decisions over the last six months (i.e., since the January 1937 visa instruction) were "as fine as one could ask for."[58]

Glick and Geist probably met with Best in late October 1937. On November 11, Geist wrote Messersmith a private letter about an unspecified conversation with Best. The report was "of the deepest interest" for Messersmith.[59] (Unfortunately, we have no other evidence of that meeting.) At that time, Glick was negotiating on behalf of approximately 120 Jewish prisoners in Dachau; they might be released if they could quickly leave for Palestine. This deal required not only Nazi approval but also visas for Palestine from British authorities in Germany, as well as financial support from the Joint Distribution Committee. Glick would have needed Best's support and probably also Heydrich's to get this done.[60]

If Nazi Germany simply wanted Jews to leave Germany, this kind of arranged exit would work. But if the Nazis intended not only to rob Jews but to persecute them, then the concentration camp was a more radical solution, and increased emigration alone might not satisfy the SS. With the American immigration quota more open than any time since the Depression, Geist wanted more information about the future. It was an important reason for him to cultivate Best.

The Gestapo's long campaign with the Jewish Telegraphic Agency in Berlin reached a conclusion. The Gestapo closed the JTA's Berlin office, charging it with endangering public safety and order. Geist asked Heydrich to explain, but he went out of town for a vacation. Geist then learned that the chief of the Gestapo's press department, a Dr. Klein, had charged the JTA with violating the 1933 agreement with the Gestapo (which Geist had negotiated). The Berlin JTA office was supposed to supply German Jewish newspapers with news from abroad. It was not allowed to send out reports about events in Germany. But special JTA correspondents from London, Prague, Vienna, and New York were writing about events in Germany after leaving the country to circumvent this rule.

Geist understood the fundamental problem: the Nazi authorities wanted to rid themselves of a hostile press influence and to shield their arbitrary anti-Jewish actions from outside eyes. But the JTA, Geist believed, made itself vulnerable by using a Berlin dateline for its stories: either the JTA officials had violated the 1933 agreement, or their datelines were false. On November 15, Geist turned over to Best evidence supplied by the JTA's London office that visiting correspondents had written each of the articles that the Gestapo found objectionable. All, however, carried "Berlin" in the dateline. After Geist summed up the evidence, Best still viewed it as inconclusive.[61]

Geist heard that American journalists working for the International News Service, AP, and United Press all felt that the JTA's use of the Berlin dateline reflected badly on American journalism. Perhaps more important, they feared that the JTA had magnified their own difficulties in Germany. Geist concluded that the Consulate General could not do anything more for the JTA. The German Foreign Office and Best himself reaffirmed the decision to close the JTA office at the end of December.[62] In his report to Washington, Geist noted without criticism that other American newspapermen did not consider the JTA a real news organization because it dealt only with Jewish-related stories.[63] Geist could have told the State Department, first, that Nazi policies toward the Jews were linked in subtle ways to other Nazi policies, and, second, that they were of great importance in and of themselves. All in all, this episode did not show Geist at his best.

In December 1937, Geist decided to attend one of Dr. Alfred Rosenberg's occasional evening gatherings for foreign diplomats and newspaper correspondents to mingle with high Nazi officials; the events were held at the Hotel Adlon. One of Hitler's oldest collaborators and an early editor of the main Nazi newspaper, the *Völkischer Beobachter*, Rosenberg had written "historical" polemics, such as *The Myth of the Twentieth Century*, filled with wild conspiracy theories about Jews and Bolshevism. Geist must have discounted Rosenberg, a Baltic German who had fashioned himself into an expert on Bolshevism and garnered an important Nazi Party foreign policy post, as a pseudo-intellectual. Nonetheless, Geist could at least pick up high-level gossip at the event.

Few diplomats and foreign correspondents showed up at the December 2 gathering. Nazi Party and Gestapo officials, and men from Rosenberg's own party foreign policy office predominated, among them Dr. Karl Bömer, who cordially introduced Geist to Rosenberg. A Nazi official gave a lecture so insignificant that Geist identified neither the speaker nor his topic. Then Geist circulated, speaking frankly, rather than diplomatically, to Nazi officials: "I told them why the United States condemned the Nazis on the Jewish question, on the church question, the matter of individual liberty, the freedom of the press and the general bellicose state of the world." He talked to Dr. Klein of the Gestapo and Bömer about the JTA controversy. Geist thought it extremely difficult to get concessions from them on any Jewish matters. But one Nazi Party official invited him to go to Munich for a meeting with Hitler's secretary Rudolf Hess, who might support more moderate policies. Concluding that it was worthwhile to keep in touch with such people, Geist made sure to affirm he thought it very harmful for US embassy or consular officials to give the Nazis the sense that the United States agreed with their policies. He singled out US military attaché Truman Smith as a stupid person who had tried to curry favor with Göring.[64]

Geist heard, rightly or wrongly, that Himmler was impatient with Hitler's "vacillation," pressing or hoping for more rapid pursuit of Nazi goals.[65] Geist did not know what this meant for German Jews. The possibilities ranged from easier emigration, forced emigration with all kinds of complications for Germany's neighbors, or worse. The foreign policy situation was clearer: although Hitler's November 1937 statements to top military leaders were secret and unknown to Geist,[66] Geist's many sources indicated that Hitler intended to expand to the east and west. Geist believed that the democracies were not going to get anywhere by bickering with dictators; they needed to organize themselves into a federation backed by sufficient military power. Otherwise, they would be subjected to "fire and steel" as soon as the dictators were ready for war.[67] It was a sobering and accurate forecast.

CHAPTER EIGHT

AUSTRIA AND FREUD

On February 20, 1938, Adolf Hitler ferociously attacked the foreign press for publishing "simply incomprehensible talk" about Germany.[1] Introducing Geist as the keynote speaker at the Washington's Birthday luncheon held by the American Chamber of Commerce of Berlin, the AP's Louis Lochner, who served as president of the organization, declared that American correspondents had adopted George Washington as their patron saint because he could not tell a lie. If he were alive in 1938, Lochner continued, he would have become a foreign correspondent because he would recognize that was the best place to show his love of truth. The crowd howled with approval.[2]

Lochner had worked in Germany since 1922. Born in Wisconsin and educated at the University of Wisconsin, Lochner had two children from his first marriage to an American who had died from the post–World War I flu epidemic, and one stepchild from his second marriage to Hilda Steinberger De Terra, a divorcée who was the daughter of a judge on the German Supreme Military Court. Lochner was fluent in German, steeped in German culture, and a serious Lutheran.[3] Fifty-one in 1938, he was two years younger than Geist. The two liked to work extremely hard and socialize with the rest of their hours, which brought them together. Lochner was very much the reporter and chronicler. He lacked Geist's power of analysis and his acting ability. But they both knew better than their professional counterparts how to operate in Nazi Germany.

Journalists and government officials of this time worked together more closely than they do today. Lochner once said that he would write "always the truth, but it is not always the whole truth." But privately he gave Geist material that was either too sensitive or too speculative to publish. Geist could not compromise his own confidential sources, but he likely gave Lochner occasional leads to stories in exchange. Their ties only increased after Lochner's stepdaughter volunteered to help on visa work at the Consulate General.[4] For obvious reasons, neither Geist nor Lochner recorded the details of their cooperation.[5]

As Geist's network of sources grew, he learned how to read into the information he received, as well as to delve deeper. Although other US diplomats and consuls in Germany reported on politics and foreign policy there, Geist surpassed them in his political insight and eloquence. The Department of State and the Foreign Service were the US civilian intelligence services of the day. The Office of Strategic Services, forerunner of the CIA, was not established until 1942. What US military attachés reported was often limited to the military capacity of the host country.

Geist's audience for his private political intelligence reports was small but select. One letter to Messersmith, for example, also went to Moffat, Undersecretary Welles, and Secretary of State Hull.[6] If Welles thought something important enough, he talked to FDR about it. In this way, a consul in a key post reached (and occasionally influenced) the highest levels of the Roosevelt administration. After many years of diligently establishing his sources, he was essentially America's best intelligence analyst in Berlin.

Nazi Germany worked hard to keep its plans secret. On November 5, 1937, Hitler met with a small group of high military and government officials. Fearing he might die early, Hitler wanted to give the equivalent of his last will and testament to those who would have to carry it out. War Minister Blomberg, Foreign Minister Neurath, and the heads of the three branches of the armed services joined Hitler at the Reich Chancellery. His military adjutant Friedrich Hossbach took notes and wrote a summary of the meeting days later. Hitler declared that Germany needed both land and raw materials to breathe, and this meant war. In the short run, Germany needed to absorb Austria and Czechoslovakia, which would help prepare for a broader war that he said might begin in the 1943–1945 period. For once, some subordinates pushed back. Blomberg, Neurath, and army commander in chief Werner von Fritsch warned that Britain and France would not stay out if Germany went to war in central Europe, and they argued that Germany was unprepared for an extended conflict. Chief of the Army General Staff Ludwig Beck, shown Hossbach's summary days later, even wrote a rebuttal.[7] This ambitious agenda was what Hitler was willing to reveal to a select few people in late 1937. It did not reflect the full extent of his hopes and his goals.

The criticism and rebuttal only led to other changes, set off by a personal scandal that touched the Nazi cabinet. Hitler and Göring had recently attended the wedding of War Minister Blomberg and a much younger woman, Margarethe Gruhn, whom Blomberg had met by chance. It emerged after the wedding that the bride had a police record for moral offenses—pornographic photos—and had been registered as a prostitute. After Blomberg refused to have the marriage annulled, Hitler forced Blomberg to resign.[8]

Army commander in chief Fritsch was far less pliant. His comments at the November 1937 meeting had been among the more confrontational, so Heydrich dredged up an old police file that dubiously claimed Fritsch was a homosexual. Himmler, convinced that the plague of homosexuality had infected the German Army, believed in Fritsch's guilt. Hitler, Göring, and Heydrich brought about a confrontation between Fritsch and the one unreliable witness against him. Insisting he had never laid eyes on the man before, Fritsch denied any homosexual acts. Werner Best interrogated Fritsch and other Gestapo officials delved into his past. Then the witness recanted, a case of mistaken identity, he said.[9]

Himmler and Heydrich emerged from the Fritsch trial temporarily tarnished and shaken, Heydrich even allegedly fearing a military coup and an army raid on Gestapo headquarters.[10] But Fritsch's acquittal did not save his job. Hitler decided to rid himself of a raft of underlings, and he went after not only Blomberg and Fritsch, but also Foreign Minister Neurath and other non-Nazi generals and diplomats. Throughout the weekend of February 4, 1938, there was a massive purge of dozens of officials who had shown even a shred of independence. In their place, Hitler appointed enthusiastic Nazis such as Joachim von Ribbentrop, the new foreign minister, and pliant tools such as General Walther von Brauchitsch, the new army commander in chief. Brauchitsch had his own marital and financial problems, which Hitler helped him resolve. Hitler dissolved the War Ministry, replacing it with a High Command of the Armed Services, headed by completely loyal general Wilhelm Keitel. Hitler made himself commander in chief of the armed services, disappointing Göring and perhaps also Himmler.

Geist wrote a commentary on the embassy despatch about these events. According to Geist's sources, Himmler himself had lusted for Blomberg's position and had much party support for it. Although Himmler had no substantive military qualifications, he was building up a military branch of the SS, later called the Waffen-SS. Geist's sources had Himmler withdrawing his candidacy, and the army officer corps taking the absence of a Nazi war minister as a victory.[11]

Geist added that the ouster of Blomberg and Fritsch largely resulted from earlier quarrels between Hitler and these two generals about Hitler's demand for additional living space and his determination to resolve this difficulty by force if necessary: he would not permit the German people to suffer deterioration of its agricultural capacity through overproduction and overfertilization. Here, with his discussion of the long-term Nazi goal of much more land, Geist had intuited the substance of Hitler's November 5, 1937, remarks, eliminating the noise of the personal scandals. According to Geist, the personnel changes amounted to a complete victory of the Nazi Party over the army. His interpretation has stood the test of time.[12] This quality of intelligence was rare in the 1930s. The world learned the details of Hitler's remarks in November 1937 only when prosecutors at the Nuremberg Trial turned up a summary of the meeting.

With the way cleared by the early February 1938 purge of potential dissidents, Hitler tried to bludgeon Austria into accepting a merger into Germany. Austrian chancellor Kurt von Schuschnigg responded first by accepting many of Hitler's specific demands, taking Austrian Nazi Arthur Seyss-Inquart into the government and agreeing to greater coordination with Germany. But when the Austrian chancellor began to sense an impending political disaster, he announced a plebiscite in which Austrians would vote on maintaining their independence.

Furious about the proposed Austrian plebiscite, Hitler prepared the army to act. Schuschnigg promptly resigned, and on March 12, German troops entered the country unopposed. An exultant Hitler came to Vienna and on the evening of March 13 announced the Anschluss, the incorporation of his homeland into Germany.[13] This step went beyond the Nazi coup that Geist had originally predicted, but he noted grimly that the army purge had led to the Nazi takeover in Austria, as he had reported.[14]

Less than a week after the Anschluss, President Roosevelt responded. Since Austria had become part of Germany, he suggested to his cabinet that the United States combine Germany's large and still unfilled immigration quota (25,957) with Austria's tiny one (1,413), giving Austrians a much better chance to immigrate to the United States. This step could bypass Congress. But when the president asked about increasing the German quota itself, cabinet members gave him a bleak assessment of likely congressional reaction, so he dropped that idea.[15]

The embassy staff in Berlin still were recovering from Dodd's mismanagement, and US tensions with Germany were high. Perhaps Roosevelt thought a Republican conservative, a career Foreign Service man, would ameliorate both difficulties. Yale-educated Hugh R. Wilson, who was Geist's age, had spent years in diplomatic posts in Switzerland and served a brief stint as assistant secretary of state. Once FDR appointed him, he was quickly briefed on the new developments in Germany by Messersmith, among others. Messersmith made it clear that although the United States wished British prime minister Neville Chamberlain well, Washington did not see how anything constructive could emerge from Chamberlain's "dangerous" policy of appeasing Germany.[16]

On March 13, 1938, Wilson approved Geist for the post of first secretary, the third-highest rank in the Embassy.[17] This appointment enabled Geist to contact the German Foreign Office when protection of US citizens required embassy involvement. Geist and the Wilsons had occasional meals together and talked freely. Geist's position in the Embassy came with perks, such as use of an embassy-owned car. Ease of transportation probably was a factor in another house move to the exclusive western neighborhood of Berlin-Grunewald, an area once promoted by Otto von Bismarck and famous for its extensive forest. Geist's next-door neighbor was former foreign minister Konstantin von Neurath.

Geist wrote Messersmith that Wilson treated him with "unusual friendliness," which he returned in kind.[18] He told Wilson stories of his early acting career and helped the Wilsons find a house in his scenic new neighborhood.[19] After six months in Berlin, Wilson evaluated Geist in glowing terms as "a man of unflagging energy, of high intelligence, good personality and humor. . . . I trust that Mr. Geist will be allowed to stay here . . . since his special knowledge would be hard to replace.[20] For Geist's part, he called his embassy appointment the highlight of his service.[21]

Geist did not probe the depth of their disagreement about the nature of the Nazi regime. Like many conservatives in Western democracies, Wilson thought that Nazi Germany's objectives were the correction of the "injustices" of the Treaty of Versailles. From this perspective, it was not worth a war to stop Germany from claiming or reclaiming German-speaking territories that had been stripped in a peace settlement that many considered unfair. Wilson also more or less blamed American Jews for creating an anti-German climate in the United States. He wished to avoid American involvement in a war in Europe at all costs.[22] Despite his new position in the Embassy, Geist wrote Messersmith that he had not changed his attitude toward the Nazi regime "one iota. . . . Respect, fear, and a sense of power are the only realities which these Germans understand."[23]

Yet Geist did not expect a war soon, if only because he thought the West was in denial. He hoped that by the time Western leaders came to their senses it would not be too late. The Nazi leaders, Geist predicted in March 1938, would coerce Czechoslovakia into ceding its border region, the Sudetenland, which had a largely German-speaking population. He believed that Germany would seize it without setting off a war and would disregard public opinion in the West. Germany would move to dominate rump Czechoslovakia, Poland, the Baltic states, Hungary, and probably Romania one way or another. Geist thought the other major powers were unprepared for a war to counter those moves. Germany would become so powerful that even a combination of European powers would not dare to move against it. Then Geist foresaw a German attack against the Soviet Union. It was not merely based on what Hitler had written long ago; officials in the Propaganda Ministry already were beginning to talk about preparations for it. Messersmith recognized that Geist was very well informed, telling him, "You are one of the very few people who has been able to foresee developments surely and clearly."[24]

By this time, Geist was as secure and as influential as anyone at the Embassy, and he controlled the Consulate General. He balanced his time between the two different roles, and no one challenged how he did it. On the other hand, the State Department remained sensitive about immigration quota issues and also involved itself in some individual cases. Geist's primary job as the senior consul, in which he encountered people facing personal and financial disaster, was more rewarding than playing Cassandra because he could actually solve problems and rescue individuals.

In March 1938, Franklin Roosevelt's speechwriter Samuel Rosenman received a letter from a friend in Germany about a Jewish dentist, Paul Laband, jailed for the crime of *Rassenschande*, or race "defilement." The Nuremberg Laws prohibited marriage or sexual relations between Aryan Germans and non-Aryans. Laband, reputedly one of the best dentists in Hamburg, was unable to apply for an American immigration visa because he had to appear in person at the Consulate General to do so. As he was still in jail, he could not. President Roosevelt suggested that Rosenman take this case up with Undersecretary Welles, who asked Messersmith to investigate why Laband had been disqualified for an American visa. Messersmith asked Geist to check and report back.[25]

Geist disentangled two related questions: (1) whether US consuls would disqualify a visa applicant with a police record of race defilement; (2) whether US consuls would accept a visa application from someone in prison or in a concentration camp because of race defilement. US immigration law barred anyone with a record of moral turpitude. But Geist determined the United States did not consider the Nazi-defined crime of race defilement to be moral turpitude, so a police record with this "crime" did not block a potential immigrant.

The US Consulate General in Hamburg *had* previously declined to accept a visa application from a prisoner, suggesting that he apply once released. But the Nazis sometimes took men released from prison and sent them directly to concentration camps, not technically part of the judicial system. Laband might never get the chance to apply for a visa in person. Geist knew that Nazi authorities often refrained from sending Jews to concentration camps if they possessed immigration visas to another country. He suggested a new State Department instruction authorizing consuls to accept visa applications from those in prison or in concentration camps for what the United States considered to be illegitimate reasons.[26]

The Anschluss of Austria brought in similar cases there. Raoul Auernheimer, an Austrian Jew who was a prominent theater critic, writer, and official of the international PEN writers' organization was sent to Dachau after the Anschluss. He had no chance to apply for an immigration visa, but he was desperate to get out. The German Swiss writer Emil Ludwig—born Emil Cohn—was a friend of Auernheimer and brought his case to Geist's attention. Senator Robert F. Wagner of New York also expressed an interest in Auernheimer. Geist spent months interceding with key Nazi officials, and Auernheimer eventually was released. He and his family emigrated to the United States before the end of 1938.[27]

The Austrian Nazi Party thirsted to settle scores with its political enemies, and anti-Semitic sentiments and violence spread to ordinary Austrians. Activists and imitators in the streets of Vienna surpassed

Germany's record of brutality over the preceding five years. German playwright Carl Zuckmayer, a liberal, happened to be in Vienna in March 1938. He recalled: "The underworld had opened its gates and let loose its lowest, most revolting, most impure spirits. The city was transformed into a nightmare painting by Hieronymus Bosch. . . . Unleashed here was the uprising of envy, of malevolence, of bitterness, of blind vicious lust for revenge."[28]

Anyone with a Nazi armband or with the gumption to pose as a Gestapo officer could make arrests or ask SA or SS officers to do so. Victims often could not tell whether they were dealing with government officials or with thieves and blackmailers. The most common public spectacle in Vienna was to force Jewish men and women into columns, allegedly to scrub the sidewalks of anti-Nazi political slogans from the ill-fated plebiscite. Mobs gathered around the slave laborers to gloat and sneer. Some "Aryans" were shamed, too, forced to wear signs proclaiming that they "piggishly" patronized Jewish merchants. Jewish store owners saw their businesses drop to virtually nothing but were forced to retain and pay their non-Jewish employees.[29]

Occasionally, brutality turned into murder. A well-known Jewish Social Democratic lawyer was stomped to death, as was the Austrian Jewish director of a chemical factory. Others were deported to concentration camps. Dozens of Austrian Jews committed suicide in the spring of 1938.[30] Press reports brought the eruption of hatred and violence in Austria to the attention of mainstream Americans.

Initially, the White House and State Department tried to work through John Wiley, the former diplomat in Germany who was now serving as American minister to Austria, to complain to Nazi officials or to save specific individuals. But Austria was now called a province of Germany (the Ostmark) that served as little more than a treasure chest of assets for greedy and ambitious Nazi officials. Wiley, whom Geist knew from his service in Berlin from 1930 to 1932, was downgraded to the position of consul general, and Nazi authorities delayed recognizing the formal authority of Wiley and other diplomats who had been assigned to Austria.[31] Meanwhile, Wiley's Austrian government contacts were either powerless or in a concentration camp themselves. On the night of March 12–13 alone, the Gestapo arrested about twenty-one thousand people thought to be a threat to Nazi rule.[32] Most were sent to Dachau.

Lochner went to Vienna in March and had lunch with Wiley to discuss their various difficulties. On the AP staff, Lochner had a Jewish photographer who was in protective custody in Vienna. He had gone to the Gestapo to obtain his release but was unsuccessful.[33] For Wiley's part, in two days 6,500 Jews had applied for visas to the United States, and others had sought to visit Belgium, the Netherlands, France, and Britain.

Wiley reported that eighty-one-year-old Sigmund Freud, despite his age and ill health, was in real danger. Founder and symbol of the hated ("Jewish") field of psychoanalysis, Freud had written of civilization as an imposed compromise with the individual's nonrational drives; a permanent peace between cultural constraints and passions or instincts was out of reach. He was not a particularly political man, but he firmly opposed the notion that humans could simply unchain their instincts. In this sense, the Nazis correctly viewed him as a philosophical opponent. In 1933, Nazi activists had included Freud's books in their book burnings. Freud commented then, "What progress we are making. In the Middle Ages they would have burnt me; nowadays they are content with burning my books."[34] It was not one of his better predictions.

Freud was a man of some resources. Nazi activists invaded his apartment and the office of his publishing firm. The Gestapo arrested and interrogated Freud's daughter Anna. Although Freud had no formal US connection, President Roosevelt asked Wiley to take up Freud's case with appropriate German officials. William Bullitt, the man who once had rejected Geist for employment due to some questions about his character, now was ambassador to France. He told FDR that Freud had well-placed friends in Paris, especially Princess Marie Bonaparte, willing and able to shelter him and his immediate family.[35] Bullitt also had written a psychoanalytic study of Woodrow Wilson with Freud, and he was anxious to extricate his coauthor. Bullitt warned the German ambassador to France that any mishandling of Freud would scandalize the world.[36]

Ernest Jones, the British founder of the London Institute of Psycho-Analysis, a member of Freud's inner circle, and a man with contacts in the British government, flew to Vienna to offer Freud a haven in London. Complaining that he was too old and too feeble to leave, Freud believed he could not get a permit to live anywhere else. He compared himself to the commander who wouldn't be leaving his ship. Jones quoted the second officer of the *Titanic*, who went down with the ship but was blown to the surface and saved when its boiler exploded. During interrogation later, the officer explained, "I never left the ship, Sir, she left me." Freud gave in but was determined to bring with him his entire family, including his in-laws, his physician, and his physician's family.[37]

Bullitt warned that he could not pledge more than $10,000 to support Freud's whole entourage, which numbered sixteen people, but as soon as Marie Bonaparte surfaced in Vienna, resources were no longer an issue. The problem was getting everyone out safely and legally. Nazi officials in Austria refused to give Freud a passport to enable him to emigrate, and everyone also needed exit visas.

This is when Geist entered the Freud conflict. Geist was aware of Roosevelt's interest in Freud and in Professor Otto Loewi of Graz, a pharmacologist who had won the Nobel Prize for Medicine in 1936, although neither of them had American connections.[38] If Geist negotiated on behalf of US citizens or American organizations, however, he might be able to squeeze in discussion of a few unrelated cases of prominent Austrians. It was all one could do in an age of national sovereignty, not universal human rights.

The State Department had asked him to try to obtain the release of nineteen men affiliated with B'nai B'rith in Vienna, most of whom had gone to concentration camps. With Himmler and Heydrich in Vienna overseeing the Anschluss, the arrest of political opponents, and the takeover of the Austrian police, Geist went to see Best at Gestapo headquarters in Berlin. The Gestapo did not control the concentration camps, so there would be no immediate solution to the issue of the B'nai B'rith affiliates. Geist also brought up several other cases involving Nazi mistreatment and beatings of American Jews in

Vienna. Geist had asked Wiley to gather as much information as possible, so that he could present the evidence to the Gestapo in Berlin and insist on punishment for the perpetrators. Nazi officials also had banned all foreigners from leaving Austria without an official certificate stating that they were not Jewish.

Geist's meeting with Best went very well. Geist went so far as to ask Best to prevent assaults on and humiliation of American citizens in Vienna, and Best said he would do everything in his power to do so. He arranged to have local SS and SA leaders forbid their men from mistreating Americans, and Nazi commissioner for Austria Josef Bürckel warned that he would punish further irresponsible behavior.[39] Geist also laid down an ultimatum about the ban on Jewish foreigners leaving Austria: cancel the order by 1 p.m., May 1, or he would have the State Department issue an advisory to American tourists to avoid Austria. At 12:15, Best told Geist that the Gestapo had withdrawn it.[40]

Geist then found the opportunity to travel to Vienna himself. Prentiss Gilbert, who was back to his position as number two man in the Embassy after the arrival of Wilson, recommended that Geist take a pouch of confidential mail to Wiley in Vienna by train. On May 5, Geist found Karl Haselbacher temporarily in charge of the Gestapo's Vienna office. Geist and Haselbacher had done business with Glick in Germany before, and their relationship was more than civil. Haselbacher confirmed the recent Nazi orders banning irresponsible action against US citizens. Then Geist took up with him "all the matters which we had pending in Austria . . . the case of Dr. Freud and others."[41] Later, Geist revealed that he had not wanted to step on Wiley's toes, but that the Freud case was the real reason he had gone to Vienna.[42]

Freud was fortunate that Geist had been so inclined. Haselbacher told Geist that the police had no further objections to Freud's departure and his papers were in order. The last obstacle was satisfaction of Freud's debt of 32,000 shillings (more than $8,000) to his publisher, but negotiations with Freud's creditors were underway to liquidate the debt. Freud convinced himself that emigration to Britain was worthwhile, not for his wife, sister-in-law, and himself—the old folks—but for his daughter Anna and the younger generation. His passport arrived on June 2, and he and the last part of his retinue left Vienna forever two days later.[43]

Another Geist intercession illustrates the problems of ordinary American Jews in Vienna. Max Heller had come to Vienna in 1937 after the death of his father. He remained there because his mother was ill, and he inherited the apartment building in which his mother lived. On April 25, SA men forced him at gunpoint to wear a sign urging Aryans not to buy from Jews even though he showed them his American passport.[44]

That evening, SA men invaded his home and carried him off, and the police said they were powerless to intervene. He was beaten and forced to sign a statement promising to pay 1,700 shillings (about $430), the amount one of his tenants had paid to his father several years ago as a premium to rent an apartment in the Hellers' building. The tenant told Heller, "You know how the times are now. You are a Jew, I am a Gentile, I have all the privileges and preference."

Geist and one of the Vienna-based consuls visited Haselbacher at the Gestapo's Vienna office on May 5. Geist demanded the arrest and punishment of Heller's assailants. Haselbacher told them that three of Heller's assailants had been imprisoned, the local SA group dissolved and, after one more interrogation by the Gestapo a few days later, Heller was able to leave the country.

Geist concluded that US officials in Vienna were making progress. Although difficulties would undoubtedly continue, American officials had perfected their technique and knew whom to go to to fix problems: "It was not until we were able to run down the responsible officials of the Secret Police in Vienna that the coordinated action with Berlin began to work effectively." He called the situation in Austria one of unbelievable misery and sorrow for innocent people: "But we who bear responsibility and must help where we can must keep going and do our best." It had been difficult for him to leave Berlin even for a one-day visit, but it had been worth it.[45]

Just before the Gestapo cleared Freud, its officials asked him to sign a statement that they had not mistreated him. Freud signed it, commenting, "I can most highly recommend the Gestapo to everyone."

Freud's excellent biographer Peter Gay called this a curious and risky act: Freud was lucky that these SS men did not notice his sarcasm.[46] Freud wrote sarcastically, but the comment was truer than he knew: Haselbacher was responsible for clearing up the remaining obstacles in the Freud case—and wanted some acknowledgment of it.

Another irony in the Freud case is visible only today. William Bullitt saw his eminent coauthor extricated from danger only with the help of Geist, whose career he had impeded during the Great War. But Bullitt never knew that.

Violence and intimidation in Austria and the increasing confiscation of Jewish property and assets in Germany generated a flood of visa applications and supporting documents from friends and relatives in the United States. Geist was responsible for seeing that the bureaucratic system worked as well as possible under difficult circumstances. The most consequential step he took was to rebalance quota allotments during this emergency. When Austria was independent, it had a tiny immigration quota of 1,413, but Geist now assigned 6,000 quota slots out of 27,370 (Germany plus Austria) to Vienna, where, by early July, there already was a waiting list of 20,000. Later, Geist raised Vienna's monthly allotment to 600 and the annual Austrian allotment to 7,200.[47] He could see that the monthly German quota was likely to be filled for the indefinite future.

In May, he asked for file cabinets to hold the applications and correspondence pouring in; when they did not arrive quickly, he asked for expedited shipment. In June, he asked for the appointment of another vice consul and several clerks for the Consulate General in Vienna. In July he requested five thousand quota immigration application forms and three thousand non-quota forms. In August he complained of an urgent need for several thousand quota forms.[48] In other times and places these would have been mundane problems and frustrations of office management, but here acknowledgments of applications and proper filing of affidavits of support could save people's lives.

Gestapo officials in Vienna issued individual expulsion orders specifying that if a Jew had not left the country by a given date, he or she would be sent to a concentration camp. Some Jews requested information about the status of their application, and when the Consulate General in Vienna sent out letters in response, they were treated as documents that offered some degree of protection against arrest. In a few cases, they secured the release of persons in concentration camps.[49] Wiley used his own salary to hire eleven additional staff and volunteers to handle visa correspondence, but even so, the staff could not cope with the visa work. He thought this was a matter of inadequate resources given the demand, but Geist believed Wiley also needed to organize visa work in the Consulate General better.[50]

The Anschluss and the abuses and atrocities in Vienna put new emphasis on America's role in Germany. Some insiders and outsiders may have thought the Embassy and Consulate General in Berlin undermanned. When the State Department raised the possibility of sending a new consul general to Berlin, which would have given Geist a new boss, however, Geist politely discouraged it—unless State wanted to transfer him. He liked his dual appointment and reinforced protection powers, and a new consul general would only get in the way. His duties were arduous and never-ending, but, as he told Messersmith in a letter: "I have acquired a technic [*sic*] during these many years, much of which you taught me, which makes it quite easy for me to tackle very serious cases with a pretty sure prospect of success. I . . . know where and when to strike, where and when to be aggressive and where and when to use more gentle methods. . . . But I should be very happy some day to go to Switzerland."[51] Geist once again stayed in Berlin. He never made it to his Swiss idyll.

Raymond Geist and his friend Julian Baker, around 1912. The Geists and Bakers both owned houses in the Villa Beach section of Cleveland. *Source: Raymond Geist Papers, Franklin D. Roosevelt Library (FDRL).*

Geist, probably dressed for "Julius Caesar" in New York City, around 1911. Geist worked for the Superintendent of Public Lectures then. *Source: Raymond Geist Papers, FDRL.*

Cartoon of Geist in Vienna, 1919, after he was appointed food commissioner for Vienna and lower Austria. *Source: Raymond Geist Papers, FDRL.*

Photo of Herbert Hoover, inscribed to Raymond Geist, probably 1919. Geist worked for Hoover's private relief organization in Vienna then. *Source: Courtesy of John Maller, Raymond Geist Papers, FDRL.*

Geist, probably around 1923 in one of his South American posts. Geist served there as vice consul. *Source: Raymond Geist Papers, FDRL.*

Geist in Berlin around 1930. Geist's command of German and his quick mastery of Germany's complex politics made him valuable to the ambassador and consul general. *Source: Raymond Geist Papers, FDRL.*

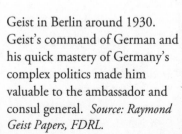

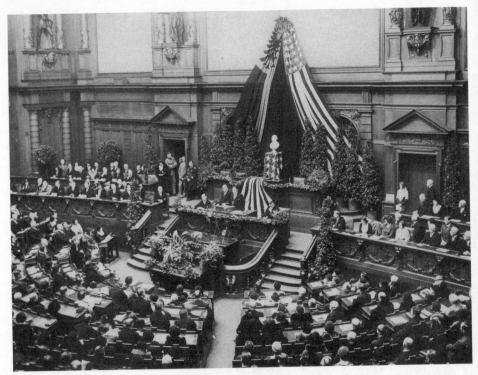

Geist's speech at the memorial service for German soldiers who died in the Great War, Berlin, September 1931. *Source: Raymond Geist Papers, FDRL.*

At a spa, September 1933. Erich Mainz, upper left; Raymond Geist, upper right; Anna Geist, lower left; unidentified woman, lower right. Mainz was Geist's lover. *Source: Courtesy of John Maller, Raymond Geist Papers, FDRL.*

Geist and Mainz mountain climbing in St. Moritz, Switzerland, September 1933. *Source: Courtesy of John Maller, Raymond Geist Papers, FDRL.*

Anna Geist ran her brother's household in Berlin as long as she was healthy. *Source: Raymond Geist Papers, FDRL.*

Hitler's invitation to Geist to a 1939 dinner for diplomats. Geist was then chargé d'affaires, the highest-ranking diplomat in the US Embassy. *Source: Raymond Geist Papers, FDRL.*

Geist after leaving the White House, December 1, 1939. Geist probably warned President Roosevelt just how dangerous Hitler and the Nazis were, but there is no direct record of their conversation. *Source: Library of Congress/Harris and Ewing.*

The Geist home in Bethesda, MD.
Raymond and Anna Geist lived
there, along with Erick Mainz, who
had Anglicized his first name.
Source: Raymond Geist Papers, FDRL.

Geist in the State Department, around 1940. He served as chief of the Division
of Commercial Affairs but also dealt with other matters related to Nazi Germany.
Source: Raymond Geist Papers, FDRL.

Geist's speech to Foreign Service trainees, around 1942 or 1943. The war opened more career opportunities for women in government. *Source: National Archives and Records Administration, photo 59-JB-167-1.*

Geist in Mexico City with Embassy staff at his retirement party in 1948. *Source: Raymond Geist Papers, FDRL.*

CHAPTER NINE

THE REFUGEE CRISIS

Geist rose to peak influence in Berlin just when the Roosevelt administration sought to accommodate more German and Austrian Jews in the United States and to resettle others elsewhere. Geist understood and helped navigate the difficulties of trying to accommodate refugees into immigration laws in the United States. He also foresaw that Germany's territorial expansion likely would complicate efforts for refugees, focusing international attention on basic questions of war and peace.

Hitler was far from satisfied with the absorption of Austria. Almost immediately afterward he met with Konrad Henlein, leader of the Sudeten German Party, which cast itself as the defender of the "persecuted" German minority population of Czechoslovakia. Hitler told Henlein not to compromise with the Czech government and to press for total freedom for the Sudeten Germans. Hitler and Henlein then launched an anti-Czech propaganda campaign. Hitler's secret goal was to destroy Czechoslovakia by the fall of 1938.[1] Nazi radicals believed, Geist told Messersmith, that they could once again bring about German expansion without war, partly because Britain and France were urging Czech premier Eduard Benes to make major concessions to Henlein.

Geist predicted that the democracies would not react strongly unless their own vital interests were threatened and that the United States would not align itself with the European democracies in the

absence of obvious threats to its own economy and national secu-
rity.² He believed that the Nazis themselves expected to go a long
way before anyone said "halt." The Western democracies, Geist wrote,
did themselves little good by proclaiming the message of peace and
goodwill: no peace could be established between the dictators and
the Western democracies. He regretted that so many Americans (he
could have included Ambassador Wilson among them) shared the
illusion that the United States could simply stay out of conflict: "We
cannot escape the evil fate which the rise of the dictators have thrown
upon us." The West had to envisage not only a defensive war, but a
war of tremendous offense as well. Messersmith sent Geist's letter to
Secretary Hull and Undersecretary Welles, in addition to officials of
the Division of Western European Affairs.³

By the late summer, Hitler was confident that the British and
French would not go to war on the side of Czechoslovakia, even
though France's alliance with the Czechs committed it to do so. Chief
of the Army General Staff Ludwig Beck, who disagreed with Hitler,
resigned on August 18, which opened the way for German aggression.
Nazi propaganda almost daily invented and denounced Czech atrocities against its German minority as a pretext for war.⁴

Messersmith tried to clarify the situation for the chairman of the
Senate Foreign Relations Committee: any guarantees that Hitler gave
about future German restraint would be worthless. Only the complete absorption of Czechoslovakia would satisfy the Nazi leaders, and
that would lead to further German moves in southeastern Europe in
preparation for a larger war. There could be no peace in Europe so
long as the Nazi regime remained in power, Messersmith concluded.⁵
This view was partly based on what Geist had written him.

Geist's optimism about the short-term prospect for peace rested
on a deeper pessimism. He believed that British and French leaders
would not stand up for Czechoslovakia, but if they were to do so, that
Germany would back off. He wrote afterward: "At the Embassy when
the clouds were the darkest they were questioning me as to the 'Geist
optimism'; and I still insisted that there would be no war."⁶

At the Nuremberg Party rally on September 12, Hitler declared
that Germany would go to war on behalf of the Sudeten Germans.

This brought British prime minister Neville Chamberlain to request what turned into two private meetings with Hitler in Berchtesgaden and Bad Godesberg. Then, on September 29, a summit conference of leaders took place in Munich. Hitler, Chamberlain, French premier Édouard Daladier, and Italian duce Benito Mussolini discussed the future of Czechoslovakia. The Czech government would be presented with a territorial settlement and offered the chance of taking it or going to war against Germany alone. Göring saw this as a means to secure territorial concessions already made in principle and to avoid a general war until Germany was better prepared. He drafted an agreement in advance, although the Italian ambassador presented it to Hitler as the work of Mussolini.[7] Geist did not have a source in Hitler's inner circle but probably did have one on Göring's staff. Geist wrote, "During those days I was in touch with people who knew and therefore held strong to my conviction to the end [that war would not break out]."[8] He was very much in the minority. Few people realized that Hitler really wanted war and backed off from it at Munich.

The Munich Agreement handed Germany Czechoslovakia's border regions, with three million Sudeten Germans, a major part of its border fortifications, and a significant fraction of its industry. Hitler guaranteed the sovereignty of what was left of Czechoslovakia, but the day after he signed the agreement, he said privately that he would annex the rest at the first opportunity.[9] The Munich summit later became, especially for Americans during the Cold War, a symbol of surrender to an aggressor who would only go on to demand more and take more. Yet even at the time, Messersmith told Secretary of State Hull that the settlement was unjust on both sides: What was the difference between Hitler taking something that never belonged to his country and Chamberlain and Daladier giving away something that never had been theirs? Despite his hatred of the Nazis and intense dislike of the settlement, Messersmith offered no practical alternative.[10]

The Czech crisis far overshadowed the Roosevelt administration's effort to resettle refugees. President Roosevelt had hoped to find up to ten places throughout the world that would take in substantial numbers of European Jewish refugees. For this reason, he invited thirty-two countries to discuss refugee problems in July 1938. FDR used the term political refugees—and avoided the term Jewish refugees—even when questioned about it: they were actual or potential refugees, he said, because of political conditions in their country. With anti-Semitism high in the United States and throughout much of Europe, he had nothing to gain politically either from increased Jewish immigration to the United States or from resettlement of Jews into other parts of the world. He went ahead nonetheless but adapted his rhetoric to the mood.[11] After Switzerland declined, France agreed to host the unusual refugee conference in the resort town of Évian, on the French shore of Lake Geneva. Undersecretary of State Welles suggested that resettlement of "surplus" populations from central Europe to other parts of the world would contribute to peace. In other words, liberal opponents of Nazi Germany and conservative isolationists both had reason to support Roosevelt's refugee effort.[12] But political spin was not enough to convince most isolationists.

FDR asked the prominent Republican attorney Henry Stimson to be the US representative at the Évian conference. Stimson declined because it was largely a Jewish issue, and he did not think the conference would succeed. Roosevelt then turned to another Republican, Myron Taylor, former chairman of US Steel, a Quaker, and a philanthropist. Taylor agreed. Inexperienced on refugee issues, he agreed to take along James G. McDonald, now chair of Roosevelt's Advisory Committee on Political Refugees, as a technical expert.[13] Roosevelt shunned bilateral negotiations with Germany, and he also did not want US involvement with the League of Nations, which had, amidst its other weaknesses, thoroughly demonstrated its inability and unwillingness to negotiate with Germany over the fate of German Jews. He hoped that the refugee conference would establish a new organization.

Geist helped prepare for the Évian Conference. He told Taylor that Nazi authorities were willing to allow German Jewish representatives to attend, but only as technical advisers, not as delegates. His (Gestapo?) source turned out to be well informed.[14] Nazi officials considered their treatment of Jews purely a domestic issue, and they resented foreign attempts to interfere.[15] Perhaps Geist was able to convince them that this issue and this initiative mattered to the president, and that Germany should consider its need for acceptable relations with the United States.

Before the conference, Foreign Minister Ribbentrop declared that Germany opposed removal of any German Jewish assets from the country. He also told British ambassador Neville Henderson that any anti-German "propaganda" at Évian would provoke punishment of German Jews. German Jewish representatives submitted a bland official memorandum to the Évian Conference, and, fearing reprisals, avoided any public speeches.[16]

Some two hundred delegates, diplomatic observers, reporters, and representatives of Jewish organizations gathered in the rococo-style Hôtel Royal d'Évian. During the discussions, representatives of Nicaragua, Honduras, Costa Rica, and Panama specified that they wanted no traders or intellectuals—then code words for Jews—and most other countries opposed further immigration generally. Only the Dominican Republic offered to take in a large number of refugees, and that offer turned out to be vastly exaggerated. The substance and the tone of the public proceedings crushed those who had hoped for immediate and substantial outside assistance. Out of the glare of publicity, however, committees carried out some work. The US delegation was able to secure its two main goals: to include Jews still in Germany under the term refugee, and to establish a small international organization called the Intergovernmental Committee on Refugees to negotiate directly with Nazi Germany over financial and emigration issues.[17] The United States would not bargain directly with the Nazi regime.

Ambassador Wilson then urged Taylor to confer with Geist because he was more familiar than anyone else with the process of negotiating to take Jewish assets out of the country. He suggested that Taylor invite Geist to London.[18] On August 3, Geist left, and the next evening he attended a large Intergovernmental Committee dinner at Claridge's. He stayed in London another four days.[19] Geist advised Taylor and the Intergovernmental Committee to take a low-key approach to contact with Nazi officials, delegating a deputy director to go to Berlin for preliminary negotiations.[20] Beyond that, Geist must have given the committee a primer on what might work and what would not work in Germany.

Geist surely would have said that Nazi radicals, including Hitler, regarded all Jewish assets as stolen property; they wanted both to punish and to exploit German Jews. They might allow some wealthy individuals to salvage a portion of their property if the greater part of it were confiscated. The Germans needed resources for economic mobilization. But they would not allow large numbers of emigrating Jews to take currency or property with them. Indeed, Ribbentrop already had declared as much. The Intergovernmental Committee would have to win the backing of someone powerful in Berlin to allow for an orderly exit of substantial numbers of Jews.

Officials in the German Economics Ministry and Hjalmar Schacht, still head of the Reichsbank since 1933, were simply too weak politically to bring about any real financial compromise with the West over Jewish emigration. In addition, the United States was not about to do anything that would result in an increase in German exports and the strengthening of Germany's economy. Most money for the support of immigrants to other countries or for financing Jewish resettlement projects would have to come from outside Germany, Geist would have told them.

Geist later briefly summarized his advice to Taylor in London. There was no way to convince or pressure Hitler and his immediate advisers to make any gesture whatsoever in favor of the Jews. But Jews who could leave the country might get something, provided that financial concessions were encapsulated in unpublicized private arrangements.[21]

In his report to Secretary of State Hull and Undersecretary Welles, Taylor praised Geist's valuable contribution to the refugee effort. For the time being, Geist, who had returned to Berlin, would work to prepare the atmosphere for a formal approach by the Intergovernmental Committee to the German government. He would not take any formal steps until he heard from the committee that it was ready. Taylor wanted to be able to show progress on finding sites for resettlement first.[22]

Washington lawyer George Rublee soon replaced Taylor as director of the Intergovernmental Committee based in London, while Taylor stayed on as vice chairman. The State Department delegated Robert Pell, uncle of later Rhode Island senator Claiborne Pell, to the committee, and he became deputy director. Taylor expressed confidence that emigration of Jews would appeal to the Nazi regime.[23]

German immigration to the United States stayed on pace to fill the annual German-Austrian quota of 27,370. Nonetheless, Nazi authorities frequently created difficulties. Police checked the tax records of Jews in Berlin painstakingly before they were issued travel documents. After the Consulate General issued some visas, German authorities seized the passports of the recipients, making the visas worthless: "It has not yet been ascertained whether there has been a valid reason for such cancellation or whether the cancellation is another and new form of Jew-baiting. The American Consul in Berlin [Geist] is looking into the matter," a Foreign Service inspector wrote at the end of July.[24] Walter Freudenthal of New Rochelle, New York, traveled to Berlin to discuss obstacles to the emigration and immigration of German Jews. He found it a pleasure to discuss his problems with Geist and his subordinate Halleck Rose. He congratulated the State Department afterward on having men of such caliber in Berlin.[25]

Geist improvised an arrangement for coping with the incoming affidavits of support signed by American relatives and friends of applicants: sending them out to the visa applicants. He thought would-be immigrants were better off holding their supporting documents, because they could show the police that they were making serious efforts to emigrate. When they reached their turn on the waiting list, they could bring them to the Consulate General. And the Consulate General could not file all these affidavits anyway; it was receiving hundreds of dossiers per week. But the State Department would not hear of this—their American sponsors were anxious, there was a need for confidentiality, and, perhaps most important, Geist's solution offered too much opportunity for fraud. The Consulate General was instructed to retain all visa materials in its files. It was a typical bureaucratic response to a creative suggestion.[26]

During September, Geist told a group of visiting Quakers heart-rending tales of woe—Jews thrown out of work, evicted from apartments, property confiscated, clients lost, and Jewish doctors banned from practice after October 1. Nazi authorities had just released specific new regulations banning Jewish lawyers from practicing their profession. Thousands of applicants per day besieged the Consulate General for much of the month, but the waiting list was now so large that they would have to wait three or four years for their turn to immigrate.[27]

On October 7, Nazi authorities invalidated the passports of all German Jews, including those who already had received immigration visas and visitors' visas to the United States but who had not yet left the country. Geist sought to get an explanation. He heard in advance that passports would be reissued under new regulations and with new stipulations. Two days later, he learned that the passports would contain a large, red letter J on the first page, and that all those who already had received visas to the United States would regain their passports.[28] It turned out that, at the request of Swiss police officials seeking to block the entry of unassimilable elements into their country, Werner Best had agreed to stamping Jewish passports with a J.[29]

Geist still sounded out the prospects for the Intergovernmental Committee negotiations. Perhaps this was one reason why he invited Best to his house for breakfast on Saturday, October 15.[30] Deputy director of the Gestapo, Best often had been helpful in the past. Geist must have wanted a private conversation with Best that morning, because he was planning to have a luncheon for various Nazi officials that day and he easily could have just included Best among them.[31] Perhaps he could convince Best that the current Nazi course of escalating persecution would alienate the United States. But there is no record of what they said.

Best had serious problems of his own. He was then engaged in a struggle with Walter Schellenberg and Reinhard Heydrich over the training of the Security Police, the term used for the Gestapo and the Criminal Police, and its relationship to the SS Security Service (SD). Best wanted a police elite that was university-trained in law and capable of making careful judgments about what was in the interests of the state. Schellenberg and Heydrich wanted a loyal and ruthless political elite. In oversimplified form, it was a question of whether the Security Police would be closer to a state police agency or to the SS, as well as who would control appointments to it. Best did not take the extraordinary step of publishing his dissident views until 1939, but it is conceivable that Geist learned of Best's conflict earlier. In any case, Geist could gain something from what Best was willing to say or from what he was not willing to say.[32] Best's acceptance of his invitation to breakfast is among the relatively few documents from his Berlin years that survived and made its way into the Raymond Geist Papers. More likely than not, this was a sign of some significance.[33]

Ambassador Wilson "helped out" with Geist's luncheon later that day, which likely meant that Wilson had the Embassy send invitations to German government officials and cover costs. The guests were men whom Geist called "my devils," key officials in the Gestapo, Berlin police chief Count Wolf Helldorff, and other officials in the Ministry of Justice and the Foreign Office. Helldorff had the final decision on whether to grant passports to rich or prominent Jews—there was supposed to be a blacklist of one thousand people forced to remain in Germany indefinitely, Geist reported. In fact, a few months earlier, Himmler had approved the strategy of keeping richer Jews in Germany as hostages, even though it seemed to contradict Nazi efforts to dump Jews across borders and to promote maximum emigration.[34]

Geist almost apologized to Messersmith for remaining on good relations with this crowd. His effort to entertain them was part of his strategy:

> Otherwise I could have little influence on the gates of the Concentration camps, which now and then I manage to pry open. I am now cultivating a new contact and that is the "secret" head of all the concentration camps in Germany, Gruppenführer Eicke, also head of the famous Deaths Head Brigade. I went to see him in Oranienburg Concentration Camp a few weeks ago. . . . You know I never give these things up and continue to follow the leads I get.[35]

Eicke had demonstrated his ruthlessness early as the first commandant of Dachau and as one of the murderers of Ernst Röhm. He had built and trained the Death's Head Brigade as a crack SS paramilitary force. The unit participated in the occupation of the Sudetenland. Eicke was the architect, builder, and director of the system of concentration camps in Germany. He was violently anti-Semitic and totally loyal to Himmler,[36] but he was willing to talk to Geist about individual cases.

Geist learned how to adapt to Nazi extortion and to stretch US visa policies in the process. He told Messersmith about the case of an unnamed man who could save $60,000 if he left Germany within thirty days, but whose turn for a US visa would not arrive for six months. Geist went to Frank Foley, passport officer within the British Embassy, and Foley arranged for a visitor's visa to Britain, so that the man could wait there until he received a US immigration visa.[37] Foley, as it happened, was a British Secret Service agent who was quite willing to spirit out substantial numbers of German Jews and did so in other ways, too. Geist and Foley began to cooperate in October and expanded the number of temporary visas in November. Any Jew waiting for a permanent home was safer outside Germany.[38]

Myron Taylor believed that the Munich Agreement improved the chance of a successful approach to the German government by the Intergovernmental Committee on Refugees. But Rublee wrote from London that British officials were not at all anxious for him to go to Berlin, because even preliminary and exploratory discussions might undercut other unspecified issues they considered more important.[39]

Geist recognized that Hitler was in a mood to defy those nations interested in doing something to help refugees, and no one should try to approach him for the time being. But if moderates in the German government could agree on a reasonable proposition, Rublee then would have at least some chance of success: "This is a very grave business and the success of the enterprise is a matter of life and death for thousands of worthy and innocent people. I shall certainly help Mr. Rublee in every way I can."[40]

A few days after his luncheon, Geist attended a big embassy dinner in honor of aviator Charles Lindbergh. The other guest of honor,

Hermann Göring, was the last one to arrive, holding a red box and some papers in his hand. On the cover of the box was a golden eagle holding a swastika, and inside was a decoration—a cross superimposed over a six-pointed star.[41] When Göring shook hands with Lindbergh, the field marshal awarded the American the Order of the German Eagle, which came "by order of the Führer." Lindbergh did not understand what Göring said but got the general message about his award. Later, Göring suggested a tête-à-tête with Lindbergh in the next room. Wilson jumped up to say that Geist could interpret better than he could. Göring questioned Lindbergh about his recent trip to Russia.[42] Geist found Lindbergh "was a little too stupid and dull for the conceited and verbose Göring," who decided to make a great speech. Geist encouraged Göring, who talked for half an hour straight, displeasing US military attaché Truman Smith, who considered Lindbergh his special property. Geist wrote to Messersmith afterward that Smith could have Lindbergh as far as he was concerned.[43]

Lindbergh told Ambassador Wilson that he was considering renting a house in Berlin for the winter, both because he was interested in Germany and because he thought it a safe spot to park his wife and children while he traveled around. If Americans criticized him for living in Germany, he would not return to the United States.[44] Nazi anti-Semitic measures and propaganda did not disturb him. This was the man who became the most prominent spokesman for the America First Committee in 1941. Isolationists in America First did their best to convince Americans that the United States had no interest in aiding Britain and France against Germany.[45]

After the Munich Conference, the Nazi regime intensified its anti-Semitic propaganda. Party activists damaged at least a dozen synagogues in Berlin with no resistance from local authorities. Meanwhile, the Polish government decided to invalidate the passports of many thousands of Polish Jews living abroad, most of them in Germany. Some of them never had lived in Poland. Nazi authorities wanted to hold onto rich Jews, but not poor-to-middle-class Polish Jews who might soon be ineligible to enter (or reenter) Poland. With their Polish passports expiring, Himmler ordered a mass deportation.[46]

On October 29, at 12:30 p.m., Geist met with Himmler at Gestapo headquarters, an appointment Himmler recorded in his schedule.[47] Himmler officially informed Geist of the ongoing deportations
of male Polish Jews, which he expected would be completed that evening. Women and children were not being deported, but Nazi authorities assumed they would follow their male relatives voluntarily.
Himmler said that they were not deporting any Polish Jews holding
American immigration visas. This was to say, in effect, that the rest
of these Polish Jews should be of no concern to the United States.
Ambassador Wilson immediately sent this information—attributed
vaguely to German authorities at police headquarters—to London for
Rublee, as well as to Washington and Warsaw.[48]

No one wanted the Jews with Polish citizenship. For three days, in
pouring rain, German and Polish authorities shuttled about sixteen
thousand people back and forth over the river marking the boundary
between the two countries near the Polish town of Zbaszyn. The de-
portees had no food or shelter. Eventually, Polish authorities set up
an internment camp to hold most of them; a small minority were allowed back into Germany. One of those was Berta Grynszpan, who on
November 3 wrote to her seventeen-year-old brother Herschel living
illegally in Paris. She and their parents were allowed with police escort
to return home to Hannover to get some essential items packed into
a valise. They had to leave everything else and all money behind and
return to Zbaszyn.[49] On the same day, Rublee requested a conference
with Geist if German authorities would allow him to visit Berlin.[50]

In September 1933, Geist and his sister had visited the Wartburg
Castle just south of the city of Eisenach.[51] The young Geist would
have loved it, and the mature man probably did too. Geist went back
to the Wartburg in November 1938.[52] Perhaps he found it a good site
for meditation.

The youth who yearned for major roles in the theater had come
a long way by age fifty-three. Many of his Foreign Service colleagues
recognized his unique contributions. He had helped to extricate Albert Einstein and Sigmund Freud from serious difficulties. Each day
the visa operations he supervised rescued people and probably saved

lives. His political reporting from Berlin focused on the greatest threat to Western civilization in history: he was trying to hold back the barbarians at the gates while he occasionally entertained them. His versatility was unmatched, and he exploited both his experience and his acting skills. He avoided the dangers of timidity and excessive reliance on bureaucratic procedure. "Nazi Germany is like no other country, and the methods of success here are peculiar to the soil and cultivation must be adapted accordingly," he wrote Messersmith.[53]

Messersmith again raised the possibility of getting Geist appointed consul general. Geist called the higher rank useful but in no way essential. Everyone already called him consul general, even Ambassador Wilson. If other US consuls in Germany had resisted his supervisory authority over them, it might have been different, but all of them supported him loyally. His appointment as first secretary in the Embassy and the widespread perception that the ambassador depended on him gave him de facto authority. The additional title of consul general would not make him any happier, he wrote.[54]

He was relieved that his sister Anna was recovering in the United States, and that he no longer had responsibility for her care. He hoped that she would regain enough strength for a needed thyroid operation.[55] Insofar as we can judge, his romantic relationship with Erich Mainz was a stable one. He attended church enough to follow the ins-and-outs at the American Church.

Geist's predictions had come true so often that he was now very confident, to the point of boastfulness, of his ability to sketch out the future in Germany. He kept up with internal Nazi politics and foreign policy day by day, hour by hour, which made it easy to project: "I shall soon write you another report which will give you the forecast for the next six months or year. There is nothing to be optimistic about. The dictators have won and . . . they are going a long way."[56] He was right about that, but he did not anticipate Kristallnacht.

CHAPTER TEN

KRISTALLNACHT

The Rehbock family, from the central German city of Gotha, was on the verge of emigrating. Earlier in the year, Ruth Rehbock had traveled on a visitor's visa to visit relatives in Chicago. They had pledged to support Ruth, her husband Hans, and their four-year-old son Rolf, and they filled out the necessary affidavit of support. Ruth returned to Germany with this crucial document, and the Rehbocks gathered the other papers and evidence they needed. They finally reached their turn on the US immigration waiting list. Receiving an appointment at the Consulate General in Berlin to obtain their immigration visas, they left Gotha several days early, taking a room at a hotel in the center of Berlin. From their hotel window, on the evening of November 9, 1938, the Rehbocks saw the modern synagogue on Prinzregentenstrasse go up in flames. They knew that something was seriously amiss elsewhere, too, because their house sitter in Gotha warned, in a prearranged coded message, that Hans should not return home.[1] The next morning, masses of frantic people blocked the entrance of the Consulate General, so that the staff had to enter and exit the building through the fire escape in the rear.[2]

Raymond Geist was not yet there. He had headed to the Wartburg Castle on the evening of November 9.[3] Walking through the streets of Eisenach the next morning, he saw burned synagogues and looted and smashed Jewish shops. Part of a pattern across the nation, the destruction was more or less arranged and cast as retaliation against the Jews.

An assassination triggered the violence. In response to the brutal deportation of his parents, sister, and thousands of other Polish Jews across the Polish border, on November 7, seventeen-year-old Herschel Grynszpan had shot a German diplomat in Paris. The diplomat, Ernst vom Rath, died on November 9, as senior Nazi officials assembled for the commemoration of Hitler's 1923 putsch in Munich. Propaganda Minister Goebbels suggested an organized pogrom employing the SA, and Hitler approved it verbally. SS and police authorities were instructed to control the violence across the country to ensure that it did not get out of hand, and then to follow it up with the arrest of twenty to thirty thousand Jewish men, focusing on the well-to-do. Goebbels, who wanted to make Berlin Jews suffer, personally ordered the destruction of the synagogue on Fasanenstrasse.[4] More than 1,400 synagogues across the country received the same treatment.

Youths and ordinary citizens joined the regime's forces in the destruction of Jewish owned or associated property in the capital. Thugs invaded Wertheim's, one of Berlin's largest department stores (in the process of being Aryanized), then rolled grand pianos through the gallery railings, and beamed as the pianos smashed to bits on the main floor six stories below.[5] The terrible events called Kristallnacht—night of broken glass—extended over days throughout the country. The SS and police carried out arrests and prepared to send tens of thousands to the concentration camps. Containing the violence was not easy; more than ninety German Jews were killed.[6]

Geist returned to his office on November 10, where he received one piece of good news. Nazi authorities in Vienna had previously told American Jewish medical students at the University of Vienna that they had to leave Austria without completing their studies. Geist had then given the Ministry of Education a list of affected students, at the ministry's request. On November 7, the ministry decided that it would allow the listed students to complete their degrees in Vienna. An Education Ministry official explained that this action came *not* out of any consideration for the students, some of whom had studied for years to become physicians, but as a friendly gesture to the United States. That gesture now sounded hollow. Geist nonetheless reported his success to Washington.[7]

The Rehbocks were unable to complete the process of getting their visas that long day. An official at the Consulate General told them to return the next day, but November 11 was Armistice Day (now called Veterans Day in the United States), and the Consulate General was closed for the American holiday. They told a Marine guard outside that they were in danger: they needed their visas as quickly as possible. Urging them to wait, he found Geist, who returned, opened the building, and gave the Rehbocks their visas. They quickly left Germany and settled in the Chicago area.[8]

Others, without visas, were not so lucky. Berlin police carried out the roundup of about twelve thousand male Jews, usually without obvious brutality, perhaps because of the presence of diplomats and foreign journalists, or perhaps because SS superiors preferred organized persecution to mob violence. Once these Jews were behind locked doors, SS brutality began, and it worsened when they reached the concentration camps at Sachsenhausen and Buchenwald.[9]

Kristallnacht was not only a humanitarian disaster. It punctured all Ambassador Wilson's hopes for better relations between Germany and the United States. At first, Wilson could not bring himself to record what had happened in Berlin. On November 10, he wrote in his diary, "Nothing to report." The next evening he and his wife dined with a Frau Friedheim, who was Jewish. Afterward, he went upstairs to read a book, while Friedheim told Mrs. Wilson "harrowing" stories about events of the preceding two days. Wilson wrote that he regretted that he could not block his wife from Jewish contacts, because there was nothing she could do for them except listen to their misery. Only on November 12 did he note in passing that some of the violence he had seen nauseated him.[10] Charles Thayer in the Consulate General sheltered Jewish families in his apartment until the storm subsided.[11] We do not know if Geist did the same.

On Monday, November 14, more than 1,500 people were lined up along the Bellevuestrasse outside the Consulate General and in its garden. Those applying for visas for the first time had little chance of getting them because the waiting list was more than 160,000. At best, they got documents demonstrating their intention to emigrate. Geist saw that those eligible for immigration visas received them and that they left the country, and he contacted police about arrested friends and acquaintances, telling Nazi officials that the United States had a specific interest in some of their prisoners.[12]

The next day Geist visited Best at Gestapo headquarters for what turned out to be a critical meeting. Best confided that Hitler himself had ordered this "terror," and Best could do nothing about it.[13] Geist's general strategy, honed from experience at these meetings, was to begin with individual cases in which the United States had a clear right to protest, then to probe and broaden the issues when it seemed possible. This time, it appears, Best went much further in laying out the future for German Jews, probably based on his conversation with Heydrich on November 14.[14] But it was a fate too terrible for Geist to process immediately. For the moment, he had to deal with one individual emergency after another. In any case, he would need additional evidence before he could even try to do something about what Best told him. On December 5, he returned to Best's revelation.

Some German Jews with US visas or US connections were beaten and abused in Sachsenhausen. Best helped Geist quickly to extricate about twenty people,[15] including the wealthy cigarette manufacturer and art collector Eugene Garbáty.[16] Until September 1938, Garbáty was largely insulated from Nazi persecution. In October, he and his brother Moritz were forced to sell their factory, worth nearly 10 million marks, for a small fraction of its value. Nazi officials confiscated their country estate near Dresden, worth more than 2 million marks, awarding it to the Hitler Youth organization. Released from Sachsenhausen through Geist's efforts, Garbáty bought his passport from the corrupt chief of police in Berlin, Count Wolf Helldorff, for 500,000 marks. He had to pay other fines, and the proceeds from the sale of his factory vanished. But he had managed earlier to pay off customs officials and get his valuable art collection out of the country. He soon became a US citizen and settled in southern Connecticut. Portions of the Eugene Garbáty collection rest today in the Museum of Fine Arts in Boston and the Metropolitan Museum of Art in New York.[17]

Fritz Warburg, formerly of M. M. Warburg, was another prominent German Jew sent to Sachsenhausen after Kristallnacht. Two of his brothers had emigrated decades before to the United States and had become American citizens. Paul M. Warburg is generally considered the architect of the Federal Reserve system, and Felix Warburg, senior partner in Kuhn Loeb, had been a major philanthropist and force behind the Joint Distribution Committee. Both had died, but they left families and a rich legacy. The Warburg connection with the United States gave Geist some leverage to intercede. It took a little time, but Geist got Fritz Warburg out safely, he reported to Messersmith. Warburg made his way to Sweden, becoming a Swedish citizen. He spent his last years in Israel, where he died in 1964.[18]

Geist and other US officials also complained to the Gestapo about other prisoners held since the Anschluss. Bruno Bettelheim, an aspiring Austrian Jewish psychoanalyst, had been interned in Dachau and then Buchenwald. Bettelheim had advocates in America. The well-to-do German American Agnes Piel, later Agnes Crane, whose daughter had lived with the Bettelheims in Vienna, had access to the American Psychoanalytic Association and the State Department, both of which inquired on Bettelheim's behalf. In late November, Geist asked Reinhard Heydrich personally to release Bettelheim, assuring him that the man would emigrate soon. But Geist warned Washington that Bettelheim's extended stay in the camps might make release difficult; Heydrich probably feared that Bettelheim would talk abroad about atrocities in the camps. Visa Division chief Avra Warren had to follow up in Vienna, where Bettelheim had applied for a visa. The prisoner emerged from Buchenwald in April and arrived in the United States in early May. In America, he had a long and controversial professional career, in which he applied his insights from the concentration camps.[19]

Herbert Schick, an American Jew living in Austria, was another prisoner, held in Dachau since June. Although Nazi officials considered Schick German, Geist reported on November 23 that he had obtained the Gestapo's written assurance that Schick would be released. Schick got a passport and sailed for New York on January 14, 1939.[20]

Meanwhile, Geist expanded the existing collaboration with British and French consular officials in Berlin, convincing them to accept persons "in desperate circumstances" whose turn for immigration to the United States would come within the next six to eight months. Some of those in concentration camps, once they had visitors' visas showing they would leave Germany shortly, were released and left Germany. Others in danger of arrest were not detained when they showed visitors' visas.[21]

On November 16, Geist asked the Dutch consul general to issue visitors' visas to people near the top of the US waiting list. The Dutch official asked for a summary of the proposal that he could give to his superiors in The Hague. Geist soon complained privately that the Dutch wanted some sort of American guarantee, which he could not give them. He didn't even have time to engage in "academic discussions" of a simple and practical matter: "By the time they [the Dutch] decide to help, the refugees will all be dead."[22] It was an indication of what he had learned from Best.

The AP's Louis Lochner wrote that all the foreign correspondents understated what they saw and heard during Kristallnacht, also avoiding statements that might endanger their sources. Nonetheless, the *New York Times* ran front-page articles for three successive days. One *Times* article compared the violence to the Thirty Years' War of the seventeenth century and the Bolshevik Revolution of 1917. The *Washington Post* used the analogy of the Catholic slaughter of French Huguenots in 1572. Nothing in recent western European history seemed appropriate. Newspapers across the country ran wire service stories prominently, and some published editorials. Press coverage across the United States was overwhelmingly critical of Nazi Germany, and that sentiment resonated with the American public—without, however, reducing Americans' resistance to increased immigration.[23]

On November 14, President Roosevelt met privately with Commissioner of Immigration and Naturalization James Houghteling, who probably argued that any weakening of immigration quota limits to benefit Jewish refugees would be politically and socially dangerous.[24] Secretary of the Interior Harold Ickes then told the president that the Columbia Broadcasting System had invited him to deliver a broadcast on Hitler's treatment of the Jews, and Roosevelt urged Ickes to accept. Both the White House and the State Department approved the advance text of Ickes's address, cutting specific references to Nazi leaders. Like the president, Ickes believed that Nazi Germany menaced Christians as well as Jews. Then he linked forced emigration and persecution with the danger of war: "There can be no peace if national policy adopts as a deliberate instrument the dispersion all over the world of millions of helpless and persecuted wanderers."[25] This connection between persecution and war stoked the fears of anti-Semites and isolationists.

Roosevelt maneuvered toward a midpoint between breaking relations with Germany and keeping silent about Nazi persecution. At his press conference the next day, FDR announced that the news from Germany was scarcely believable in a twentieth-century civilization; he was calling Ambassador Wilson home for consultation. Wilson never returned to Germany. Asked about the emigration of Jews from Germany, FDR endorsed the quota system and refused to commit himself publicly on where else Jews might settle—he said that plans were not yet ripe. At another press conference three days later, he added that ten to fifteen thousand German and Austrian Jews already in the United States on visitors' visas would not be sent back home. If Congress failed to act, they could remain, because "I cannot, in any decent humanity, throw them out." Siding with Secretary of Labor Frances Perkins on this action, the president overrode Messersmith and the State Department. But he faced political headwinds in Congress. Senator William Borah, a Republican isolationist, objected to any potential increase of immigration quotas and questioned the legality of extending visitors' visas.[26] Mild as Roosevelt's reactions might seem from the vantage point of twenty-first-century human rights, the United States was the only country to withdraw its ambassador as a reaction to Kristallnacht.

Just before he left, Ambassador Wilson met with Foreign Minister Ribbentrop. Wilson probably conveyed US "anxiety" about anti-Jewish violence witnessed personally by some US diplomats. FDR was taken aback when he heard Ribbentrop's response.[27] The president incredulously asked the State Department to confirm the claim that Ribbentrop had declared German Jews to be pickpockets, murderers, and thieves who had acquired all their property illegally. Ribbentrop said that the Nazi regime would take all their assets from them, then force them into urban districts frequented by criminals under close police supervision.[28] Nazi officials, such as Wolfgang Diewerge in the Propaganda Ministry, seriously believed that Grynszpan's shooting of the German diplomat in Paris was part of the longstanding international Jewish conspiracy against Germany.[29] Kristallnacht marked only the beginning of a sharp escalation of Nazi persecution.

Germany's economic czar Hermann Göring hosted about one hundred officials from various ministries and Nazi organizations at a lengthy meeting at the Air Ministry on November 12. The immediate outcome was a 1 billion mark fine on the Jewish community for the damages *they* had triggered during Kristallnacht, and an avenue for the complete expropriation of whatever resources would remain with the Jews after the fine. Heydrich wanted to organize emigration centrally, and Göring supported him. Heydrich opposed the establishment of closed Jewish ghettos in Germany because police surveillance would be difficult, but the term ghetto was in the air. During the last three weeks of November, Nazi officials debated how to regulate Jews who remained in the country. Werner Best drafted the legal basis for a central emigration authority and attended follow-up meetings.[30]

Counselor of Embassy Prentiss Gilbert reviewed the latest political trends for the State Department. Himmler and Goebbels led Nazi extremists, Gilbert said, even though Himmler often remained in the background and used *Das Schwarze Korps*, the SS newspaper, as the public voice of the SS. Separately, Gilbert reported that *Das Schwarze Korps* displayed pictures and caricatures of Roosevelt and Churchill side by side with photos and drawings of lynchings in the United States and Britain.[31] Himmler wanted to reconstruct Germany along almost fantastic medieval lines, according to his intimates. Göring was the single most powerful individual after Hitler, but he concentrated on military and industrial matters. Göring might disregard his own "moderate" inclinations to avoid criticism by Nazi radicals. Hitler reacted violently to foreign press criticism and intended to determine Germany's future course unilaterally, disregarding foreign opinion.[32]

On November 24, *Das Schwarze Korps* forecast the future of German Jewry. Segregated from the German population, Jews would be reduced to poverty and crime. They would undoubtedly thirst for revenge against Germany, and Nazi authorities could not permit them to create a breeding ground for Bolshevism. The government would exterminate the Jews as it exterminated other criminals—by "fire and sword." The result, said the newspaper, would be "absolute annihilation" of Jewry in Germany.[33] Geist read the Nazi press regularly and reported on occasional articles to Washington. In a propaganda state, the latest article was often a clue to the next policy. This story was Geist's second source about the future of German Jewry. Best had already alerted Geist to extreme peril for German Jews.

On Monday, December 5, Geist found time to deal with the general emergency. He dictated two private and confidential letters comprising nine single-spaced pages of emotion-laden, sometimes elegant prose. They revealed both his moral compass and his ability to adapt to his audience. The recipients were his superiors at opposite ends of the political spectrum.

Geist wrote Messersmith that the Intergovernmental Committee on Refugees might hope to accomplish something through a low-key visit by State Department official Robert Pell. Geist would eagerly assist Pell. Geist could not disapprove of US condemnations of Germany—"no condemnation is strong enough." But he feared that in reaction the Nazi regime would simply take out its wrath on German Jews. If the United States was going to uphold justice and principles of human dignity, it should "go all the way and prepare to attack the oppressor and bring about his destruction." Otherwise, the Roosevelt administration had to consider what would help or hurt the victims. Negotiations with German authorities to evacuate substantial numbers of Jews might make Nazi officials prefer emigration. Of course, the Nazis might well violate any formal emigration agreement, but it was worth a try.

Geist wrote, "They have embarked on a program of annihilation of the Jews and we shall be allowed to save the remnants if we choose." This was a struggle to save the lives of innocent people and spare them years of "indescribable torture and privations." He drew upon his grasp of history: this was cruelty unparalleled since the days of Nero. He drew upon his common experience with Messersmith: "Only we who sense the fanaticism and blindness rampant here know how dangerous it is to pursue a course of reproach when every sting will be promptly visited on the hostages." Geist essentially expressed the hope that Roosevelt would not further criticize Germany publicly.[34]

Geist conveyed a different message to Wilson, who disliked the administration's anti-Nazi course. Everything the Roosevelt administration was doing about Nazi persecution was either failing or unlikely to succeed, Geist wrote. Perhaps FDR thought that putting a new refugee organization together with US backing would give it enough prestige to impress the Nazis, but: (1) they were not impressed; and (2) they regarded it as a tool to place Germany in an unfavorable light. In fact, they considered it part of international Jewry's war against Germany.[35]

Unless the United States adopted a more conciliatory policy toward Germany, Geist wrote Wilson, the Nazis would simply block the work of the Intergovernmental Committee and go their own way. Here he revealed the most startling comments from his meeting with Best three weeks earlier.

> They are intending, as I hear from my friend, Dr. Best, to bring the Jewish situation to a close as rapidly as possible. They are intending to impose all the restrictions and hardships possible so that the Jews will be returned to the Ghetto and there encounter a form of existence through which they will inevitably perish; as I am sure the intentions are not to allow them to deteriorate to a certain low form of existence and then go on indefinitely, as one finds in the Ghettos of Poland. . . .
>
> The Germans are determined to solve the Jewish problem without the assistance of other countries, and that means eventual annihilation. They have already indicated that if the hair of a Nazi leader is touched there will not be a Jew left alive in Germany. This is a sombre and darkly portentious [sic] statement; but the warning must not go by entirely unheeded.

Again, Geist referred to the possibility of upholding the principles of humanity and justice, but that meant going to war and sacrificing the hostages. He knew very well how much Wilson hated the idea of war, so he tried to bring Wilson around to the notion of doing something positive for Jews still in the Reich. He hoped that Wilson would soon be able to return to his post in Berlin and occupy the new embassy building in the renovated Blücher Palace.[36]

Geist's letter to Messersmith is more eloquent, but his letter to Wilson is more specific. Geist wanted Wilson to take his language literally, and he offered up the name of one of his most credible and highest-level Nazi sources. Best offered insight into the purpose of ghettos that the SS was planning to establish somewhere, sometime. At some point, probably decades later when he organized his papers for posterity or his memoirs, Wilson wrote in pencil on Geist's letter, after Geist's words "sombre and portentious statement": "On this sombre note of real eventual genocide."

The term genocide was essentially unknown in 1938. Nor was the outlook in December 1938 what it became later—a continent-wide sweep and mass murder of Jews. Nazi officials sought to eliminate those German Jews who remained in the country. Plans for Jews across Europe and beyond would come later. But Best and Geist clearly recognized that once the SS set up ghettos for the Jews, they would die one way or another. Geist called upon his former superiors to help, or at least not to impede what he was doing to help. Best's comment, unknown until now, casts in a very new light Nazi Germany's plans to eliminate the Jews.

Geist apparently found a third source as well. In an affidavit written in August 1945 in preparation for war crimes trials, Geist wrote that Gestapo official Dr. Karl Haselbacher told him in 1938 that Germany was to be cleared of Jews, and that those Jews unable or unwilling to leave would be exterminated. Haselbacher soon left his position in Berlin to become head of the Gestapo in Düsseldorf. He died in a car accident during the war, so Geist had no reason in 1945 to withhold his identity as his source.[37]

Geist recognized that what he had done with Best's horrific comments—private letters to superiors—was a half measure. But he hesitated before sending such horrific predictions in official despatches to State Department officials unfamiliar with Nazi Germany. Would they think him an advocate of higher Jewish immigration to the United States, an alarmist who was exaggerating the danger? Yet he now reported officially, if only because, otherwise, Washington would not understand why he was so active in trying to get Jews out of Germany.

On December 12, Geist wrote to the Secretary of State,[38] officially but confidentially, that he believed the situation of German Jews would become desperate within the next two or three months:

> The pressure from relatives and other persons in the United States to assist [them] . . . will become very great, and every effort will be made to get them out of Germany, so that a large percentage . . . will be unable to wait for their visas and will attempt to flee into other countries. . . . Increasingly cruel pressure will be put on these people so that their situation in Germany will become intolerable, even entirely unbearable.
>
> With these kinds of pressures, other countries will not allow temporary admission of Jews unless they knew that the refugees would receive U.S. visas within a reasonable time.[39]

It was as far as Geist felt he could go. His sources indicated that action might come very soon, but Hitler had not yet determined the timing of his plans for war and his war against the Jews. The first ghettos were not established until after the German conquest of Poland. Ghettos in Poland posed fewer problems for the SS and police than ghettos in Germany would.

Geist struggled to fit Nazi barbarism into his view of history and of his ancestral homeland. He recalled his graduate studies in medieval life and literature at Harvard when he had "marveled that men could be so cruel, benighted, and murderous." But given their level of ignorance, superstition, and holy belief, the slaughter carried out by men of the Middle Ages now seemed almost natural to him. By contrast, he feared that future civilization would be nauseated with the name Germany for inflicting unspeakable horrors and cruelties on a fine and worthy people: "Even a thousand years of decent conduct would not wipe out this ineradicable stain." His mood in December 1938 fluctuated between gloom and satisfaction—gloom because of the tragedy he saw every day at the office, gloom at impending tragedy on a larger scale, but satisfaction that he still was able to save people.[40]

Trying to touch Messersmith's heart, Geist wrote about the fate of common friends and acquaintances, such as Clara Goldberger, who had had to leave her apartment and move to the slums of Alexanderplatz. Geist said he was looking after her like a child, and that she was getting a visa. The famous violinist Fritz Kreisler, already in the United States, was accused of making a false statement under oath that he was only half-Jewish; as a result, the Nazis were threatening to seize all his assets and property, and his wife Harriet in Berlin, an American citizen, was in personal danger. It took quite some time and effort, but Geist later arranged for Hitler to extend honorary "Aryanization" to Kreisler, who actually had four Jewish grandparents.[41]

Lilly Deutsch, the sister of the US banker and art patron Otto H. Kahn, asked Geist to get her out of danger after the Nazis seized all her jewelry and threatened her if she did not leave the country. (She was able to leave, but apparently died in Belgium in 1940.) Hans Bie, a former chief executive of the Allgemeine Kokswerke corporation, had been ruined and taken prisoner. He was losing his mind, but Geist was going to try to save him. Geist was surprised that the Nazi regime was cutting off people with means—"all have to sink into a horrible ghetto." Dr. Alfred Berliner, the Jewish founder of Siemens & Halske, predecessor of the modern Siemens firm, for fifty years one of the leading industrialists in the country and a former friend of Kaiser Wilhelm II, barely escaped death. Nazi officials threatened the seventy-seven-year-old Berliner with twenty years in a concentration camp because his nephew left an old army firearm in his castle. Geist successfully appealed to Göring through his adjutant General Karl Bodenschatz, and Berliner was spared. Berliner's wife, apparently a Christian, was Geist's landlady in Berlin-Grunewald.[42]

On December 8, before Messersmith had received any of Geist's personal or official warnings about Nazi plans, Messersmith gave his colleague and friend a response of sorts. The State Department's perspective was different from Geist's. The Munich Agreement giving Germany a portion of Czechoslovakia and then Kristallnacht had fundamentally transformed American views of Nazi Germany. The American public would have approved of breaking relations, Messersmith wrote. Bringing Ambassador Wilson back for consultation was the only possible action because mere words of disapproval would have seemed empty. The United States would make no moves toward appeasement of Germany and no moves toward improving commercial relations with Germany, despite the hopes of businessmen such as James Mooney of General Motors. The White House and the State Department would refrain from further public criticism of Germany—this was Messersmith's only point of agreement with Geist. But unless Germany changed its behavior substantially for the better, Wilson would not go back to Berlin. Expressing his own feelings, Messersmith said that according to many in the United States, Wilson had shown too much sympathetic understanding of the Nazi regime and had failed to present American views in Berlin forcefully enough. Now, Messersmith added, the recent barbaric actions of the Nazis against Jews and others had shaken Wilson.[43]

Messersmith praised Geist for doing a splendid job with visa operations. That said, Visa Division official Avra Warren was already on his way to Europe to inform consuls directly about what "we" (in the State Department) had to keep in mind. Secretary of Labor Frances Perkins was so sympathetic to the aliens in the United States and outside it that she had almost become an element of danger. Her extraordinary measures and backing of new legislation to stretch the quotas represented "hysterical action." Perhaps Messersmith thought her hysterical because she was a woman. The fact that Perkins had persuaded FDR to allow Jewish visitors to stay indefinitely still rankled Messersmith. But he did not regard it as a personal defeat alone. Messersmith declared that the United States was unable to serve as a haven for all the distressed people of the world; it had to preserve itself. If the United States increased the quotas, anti-Semitism would rise. That would make it hard to build opposition to Nazi Germany.[44]

The next day, Messersmith sent Geist a short note and a copy of his letter to Warren, bringing Warren up to date on problems with regard to temporary visas for refugees. He, Undersecretary of State Sumner Welles, and Visa Division chief Eliot Coulter had agreed on new limitations, which Messersmith noted to Geist, "may somewhat cramp your style in certain cases." US officials could not give formal written assurance to other countries that visa applicants near the top of the waiting list would be admitted to the United States within months. Other countries would regard this as a guarantee, and this would amount to mortgaging the quota. If something changed or went wrong, they would blame the United States. Messersmith declined to ban completely the practice of giving refugees US documents that helped them enter other countries but said that consuls would have to limit it to exceptional cases, as was originally done before Kristallnacht.[45] He rejected what Geist had done to get more Jews out of danger in Germany. Messersmith regarded the German immigration quota of 27,370 as the limit of American generosity; any attempt to create new loopholes or special admissions beyond that would stir up social problems and endanger the Roosevelt administration politically.

Warren, meanwhile, emphasized that any increase in the quota was extremely unlikely and that consuls should advise visa applicants accordingly. Messersmith wrote to Warren that, given the temper in the United States, any change in immigration law was likely to be a *decrease*. His assessment of public opinion and congressional sentiment was not far off the mark, even if it reflected his own preferences. In January 1939, the leader of anti-immigration extremists in the Senate, Robert Reynolds of North Carolina, asked Messersmith for a copy of the January 1937 visa instruction that "relates to the closing of the eyes of our consular agents abroad relative to the finances of applicants for visas to the U S of A."[46] It was a shot across the bow. Messersmith knew that Roosevelt would need Senate cooperation in 1939 to direct his foreign policy against Germany.

Messersmith admitted that there was a "racial background" to Kristallnacht but claimed that the main reason the Nazis went so far was an economic one. Germany's economic difficulties would lead the Nazis not only to confiscate the property of Jews, but also that of Catholics and eventually others. Messersmith saw the primary problem as the one he feared most—the Nazi regime was on course to seize property that it could use to prepare for war, including war against the United States. Despite his direct experience in Nazi Germany, Messersmith did not grasp the extent of Nazi leaders' hatred and resentment of "international Jewry," let alone factor into American policy the Nazis' threats to the existence of German Jews. Geist must have rued how his friend had reverted to his old economic determinism.

By contrast, Geist won an ally in Counselor of Embassy Prentiss Gilbert, temporarily also the top man at the Embassy (chargé d'affaires), who endorsed Geist's practice of handling Jewish matters in practical ways that would directly and immediately help German Jews. He called Geist exceedingly valuable in this regard. Gilbert wrote to Moffat that he had had long talks with Geist, who frequently said to him: "Don't make any formal protest in this matter high up until I see what I can do about it. . . . [When the individual concerned stands] directly before one's eyes, I must say I am greatly moved to accord with Geist's ideas."[47]

Amazingly, Geist's personal connections with Himmler and Heydrich still gained him access. Geist tried to get Heinrich Müller of the Gestapo to order German police to supply police records to German Jews now in other countries and who had applied to immigrate to the United States. To qualify for US visas they had to prove that they had not committed crimes. When Müller declined, Geist tried his luck with Himmler, who said he would take the matter under advisement. Müller came back to Geist with a nondecision: the Gestapo could not order such cooperation. There were no orders against it either, but the only way to ensure it would be for applicants to pay a $2 fee in advance in US dollars.[48] The SS and police had no interest in promoting German Jewish refugee emigration to the United States, but the regime needed foreign exchange.

Three visitors from the American Friends Service Committee— Rufus Jones, D. Robert Yarnall, and George Walton—asked Geist to get them an appointment with Heydrich to discuss how they could supply aid to and promote the emigration of German Jews and Christians whom the Nazis considered to be Jews. Geist told these Quakers that Nazi officials would want to see a specific plan. Nonetheless, he rushed off to Gestapo headquarters, leaving them in his office. After twenty-five minutes, they were called to join him, Heydrich, and two assistants. They raised the possibility of establishing a Quaker-run transit camp for emigrating Jews. Heydrich authorized them or their successors to travel across Germany to develop more specific plans. At their departure from Berlin shortly before Christmas, the Quakers thanked Gilbert and Geist for all their help, particularly noting Geist's success with the Gestapo.[49]

Geist must have wondered whether the Quakers had the connections, resources, and sense to establish transit camps away from German reach. If so, their plan would complement his own practice of giving out visitors' visas to prospective emigrants. If not, well, it was better not to think about that. In his meeting with the Quakers, Reichsbank president Hjalmar Schacht had told them, "Be quick, for nobody knows what happens in this country tomorrow."[50] But Geist thought he knew: war was coming, and the SS was translating its rhetoric into action. Two wars were approaching: a general war and a Nazi war against the Jews. Geist understood that they were connected, but he could not foresee their timing.

Hitler planned to give a speech to the Reichstag on January 30, 1939, to commemorate the sixth anniversary of his appointment as chancellor. Nazi "moderates" wanted Hitler to limit his attacks on the United States and on President Roosevelt in order to improve the climate for an increase in German exports. But Nazi radicals wanted a propaganda offensive to increase American anti-Semitism. If such an effort succeeded, it would transform American politics and bring Germany and the United States closer together.[51]

Through his Nazi sources Geist learned in advance that Hitler would attack Roosevelt directly, while positioning himself as the champion of the coalition of forces—particularly with Italy and Japan—against international Jewry, Bolshevism, and the democracies.

Before the speech, Geist told Nazi officials in plain terms that another Kristallnacht would terminate diplomatic relations and make the United States go on the offense against Germany. He also warned Hitler's adjutant Fritz Wiedemann that if Hitler attacked Roosevelt personally, it might have serious consequences.[52]

This was extraordinary behavior for a diplomat lacking specific instructions. Geist judged that Messersmith and others in Washington would let him gauge what might be accomplished through firmness. His warning got through and made an impact, if only a marginal one, on Hitler. Prentiss Gilbert reported after Hitler's speech that Göring had persuaded him to remove a section with personal polemics against Roosevelt, on the grounds that it would damage German commercial interests.[53]

Standing before the Reichstag on January 30, Hitler targeted Secretary of the Interior Ickes for stirring up anti-German sentiment in the United States. Hitler rebutted some of Roosevelt's prior claims, denying that Nazi Germany was hostile to religion, but the Führer attacked the Vatican and some Catholic priests in the process. He ridiculed the notion that Germany might attack the United States. He described the United States as having engaged in aggression against Germany during World War I and in the present. He claimed that Jews were responsible for stirring up anti-German sentiment in the United States, while the bulk of the American people rejected anti-German attitudes. But he did not mention Franklin Roosevelt.

Hitler mocked foreign critics of Germany's anti-Jewish measures. If the democracies were so concerned about these criminals, he argued, why could they not find any space in their territories or colonies to resettle them? He was obviously aware of the Intergovernmental Committee's difficulties in arranging resettlement, and he took pleasure in its lack of success. He also offered an alternative in the event of a war toward which he himself was inexorably moving:

> I was often a prophet in my life and was usually ridiculed for it. At the time of my struggle for power, it was chiefly the Jewish people who laughed at my prophecies that I would one day assume in Germany the leadership of the state and thus the entire *Volk*, and would then,

among other things, also bring the Jewish problem to a solution. I believe, however, that the Jews in Germany have already choked on the uproarious laughter of those days.

I wish to be a prophet again today: should international financial Jewry in and outside of Europe succeed in plunging the nations once again into a world war, the result will not be the Bolshevization of the world and thus the victory of Jewry, but the annihilation of the Jewish race in Europe.[54]

According to Hitler's biographer Ian Kershaw and other scholars, Hitler's association of war and genocide showed his genocidal intent, but not a specific plan.[55] It certainly was too soon for any serious consideration of gas chambers, and, as it turned out, deportations of German Jews to the east did not begin until the fall of 1941. But based on his conversations with high Nazi officials shortly after Kristallnacht, Geist saw the SS as already moving toward the killing of German Jews. Geist would not have registered such alarm about a slight possibility or a Nazi bluff.

Hitler's most infamous and most quoted speech acquires new importance in light of Geist's evidence. Hitler's rhetoric on January 30, 1939, capped a period of intense anti-Semitic efforts inside the Nazi regime, showing him that he would have the organizational support and manpower to carry out mass murder of Jews. This was now Hitler's preferred solution. It remained an open question when and how far he could carry it out. He could not resist signaling to the German public and the world what was crystalizing in his mind and in Berlin.[56]

Through his Nazi contacts and through his own firmness, Geist managed to delete one portion of this speech—the direct attack on FDR. Geist wanted to avoid a formal break in diplomatic relations largely for the sake of its potential effect on desperate German Jews. Fundamentally he was a hawk, but tactically he was a dove because the longer the United States maintained relations with Germany, the more people could emigrate to the United States.

CHAPTER ELEVEN

TESTING GÖRING

Geist could not have been surprised when, at first, Nazi officials did their best to ignore or slight the Intergovernmental Committee on Refugees.[1] A splashy presidential call to resettle refugees on a global scale and the Évian Conference shrank to a small refugee committee stuck in London. In December 1938, Reichsbank president Hjalmar Schacht went to London to discuss his own ideas for the emigration of a portion of German Jewry, along with Nazi confiscation of most German Jewish assets. Schacht sought to finance resettlement of Jews through a scheme involving an increase in German exports.[2] Rublee had long felt that if the committee did not at least try to negotiate with the Nazi regime, it would face strong criticism, and Schacht was the only government official even willing to talk.[3]

According to one of Geist's reliable sources, a few people in Göring's inner circle began to work on ideas for increasing Jewish emigration. They said they would try to persuade him to accept a reasonable plan.[4] That was enough to break the deadlock and to start negotiations. On January 10, 1939, Rublee, his wife, Deputy Director Robert Pell (a State Department official delegated to the committee), and a young assistant named Joseph Cotton Jr. arrived in Berlin, taking rooms at the Hotel Esplanade, near the US Consulate General. The American delegates were not optimistic about their reception.[5]

Geist was swamped with work already. Both the Consulate General and the Embassy were moving into the same newly renovated, long, three-story, neoclassical building known as Blücher Palace on the Pariser Platz, a stone's throw from the famous Brandenburg Gate. The chancery (embassy offices) and the main offices of the Consulate General were on the second floor, with the vacant ambassador's office facing the Pariser Platz. The ground floor contained the Visa Section, notaries, passport offices, citizenship offices, and welfare section. This consolidation would soon make Geist's daily routine slightly more manageable, but first, Geist had to organize and manage the move.[6]

To avoid even the appearance of government-to-government bargaining, American diplomats in Berlin kept out of the committee's negotiations with Schacht. At the first meeting on January 11, Schacht explained that he had to get instructions from Hitler prior to any substantive give-and-take. He laid out the situation much as he had done in London, dividing the Jews into the categories of wage earners, their dependents, and the elderly. Putting 45 percent of the Jews into the category of wage earners, he said that it might be possible for this group to leave over the next five years. (Schacht was dissembling or had no inkling of Hitler's plans for war.) He said he had categorical instructions (from Hitler) that emigrants could under no circumstances take any foreign exchange with them. Rublee cautioned that Western governments were "not disposed to consider" any increase in German exports as the price of removing Jews from Germany. They discussed possible use of the trust fund from confiscated Jewish property but came to no agreement. Schacht emphasized the need to move quickly because certain Nazi officials opposed these discussions. If negotiations lagged or broke down, the Jews might suffer.[7]

When Rublee's team showed up at the Reichsbank on Saturday morning, January 21, they were shocked to find that Schacht had been dismissed. No one else was willing to talk to them. Rublee telephoned Geist, saying in a jittery voice, "We understood if we were in trouble, you could help us."[8]

Geist already had invested much time and energy in trying to get refugee negotiations started. He knew that German Jews faced a dire future if these talks collapsed. A war would sooner or later bring an all-out Nazi assault against the Jews of Europe. He also knew that the "Jewish question" affected how Hitler viewed relations with the United States. Geist had to protect these negotiations because of the stakes.

Geist rushed to the office of Brigadier General Karl Bodenschatz, Göring's chief of staff, to stress that the Évian Conference and the Intergovernmental Committee on Refugees were FDR's ideas; if the Nazi regime snubbed Rublee's group, it might provoke the United States to break relations. Alarmed to hear that Rublee and the others planned to leave on an evening train to Paris, Bodenschatz promised Geist he would see Göring at 11 a.m. and get an answer by 11:30. Bodenschatz called Geist to say that the field marshal—Göring had been promoted to this rank—wanted negotiations to continue, and that he would appoint someone to replace Schacht. Moreover, he invited Rublee to his Berlin home to talk that afternoon. Geist went to the Esplanade to give the Americans the good news. Clapping Geist on the back, Rublee exclaimed, "Well, my boy, you certainly bring home the bacon." Geist laughed. It reminded him of what Messersmith used to say after he had pulled off successful maneuvers with Nazi officials in earlier years.

Geist accompanied Rublee to Göring's home, where the field marshal, Ministerial Director Helmut Wohlthat, Bodenschatz, and an interpreter awaited in a meeting room. Geist sat in the next room to maintain official distance. Bodenschatz brought him periodic updates on the discussion, which lasted almost an hour. Göring delegated Wohlthat to carry on negotiations with the committee. Geist thought that Wohlthat, another of his official "friends," was a good man for the job. Geist helped to draft the press release that the Germans wanted to issue right away: the thrust of it was that the negotiations begun with Schacht were continuing with Wohlthat.

Göring was anxious to find a solution of the "Jewish problem" and said that he was aware that this issue affected Germany's relations with other countries, particularly the United States. Wohlthat's conversations with Rublee would begin from the point where they had left off with Schacht. Göring emphasized the need to move rapidly—later, Myron Taylor would say that Göring warned he had at best six months. Göring claimed that only the Jewish question blocked good relations with the United States.[9] Geist wondered whether the continuing negotiations would yield practical results, but his intervention spared the committee an embarrassing, even humiliating, exit from Berlin. As Lochner put it, "At a dramatic moment Raymond jumped into the fray and two-fisted as he is fought his way right through to Göring himself. No other person in Berlin could have done what he did." Messersmith passed an excerpt of Lochner's letter on to Secretary Hull, Undersecretary Welles, and Moffat in European Affairs.[10]

Despite praising Geist, Messersmith had serious misgivings about the Intergovernmental Committee. He feared that Nazi officials would persuade Rublee to endorse an arrangement involving an increase in German exports to the United States. Messersmith complained that Rublee had selected his assistant, Cotton, possibly allied with "selfish financial interests," without consulting the State Department.[11] He feared that a negotiated refugee settlement might blindside the administration. High State Department officials believed that zealous advocates of Jewish refugees would unintentionally stir up broad hostility to Roosevelt's anti-Nazi foreign policy. The more liberal activists pushed humanitarian goals against prevailing public and congressional sentiment, the harder it would be for the president to persuade the public and Congress that US opposition to Nazi Germany was in the national interest.

In his 1939 State of the Union address, Roosevelt had drawn a sharp contrast between the democracies of the Western Hemisphere, supported by freedom of religion and good faith, and the dictatorships that threatened them. He condemned those who used propaganda and prejudice; they represented the first stage of aggression: "Long before any overt military act, aggression begins with preliminaries of propaganda, subsidized penetration, the loosening of ties of good will, the stirring of prejudice and the incitement to disunion." Most of all, he criticized neutrality legislation that might assist one side, rather than contribute to peace, and he noted that building up a strong US military force might deter war.[12]

The State Department wanted to avoid or remove practices such as abuses of visitors' visas or careless examination of affidavits of support, which might provoke the anti-immigration, anti-administration forces. There had been a nasty bribery scandal involving two clerks at the Consulate General in Stuttgart, and there were similar accusations about another US vice consul in Breslau giving out visitors' visas for payment.[13] Even where consuls and applicants acted in good faith, circumstances sometimes resulted in people being trapped in the United States. If those with visitors' visas remained beyond six months, they became illegal aliens. Roosevelt had personally ordered one mass exception, allowing visitors to stay after Kristallnacht, but the State Department did not want to repeat the practice of stretching visitors' visas.

Messersmith stubbornly defended the immigration status quo, partly because he thought it reasonable, partly because he wanted to create political space for the administration to oppose Germany's expansion. He disregarded anything that might interfere with that move, writing to Geist in mid-February, "I still believe that the only solution of this refugee problem is decent treatment of these people where they now are and we can't have that until there is a more reasonable Government in Berlin."[14] Geist saw and felt the human costs of Messersmith's view, but he did not have any leverage.

After Visa Division chief Avra Warren visited Berlin in January, Geist backed off, and even disclaimed, to some extent, his own arrangements with British and French officials regarding visitors' visas for those Jews slated to receive American immigration visas relatively soon.[15] When British passport officer Frank Foley met with Geist on January 12, Geist said he did not believe that many of the people who had gone to Britain temporarily soon would qualify for US immigration visas.[16]

On January 17, Geist told Lochner that US quota immigration rules were about to stiffen; only those well backed with assets would surmount the public charge barrier.[17] This apparently meant that the demand for visas was so high that consuls could be strict about the public charge provision and they still would be able to fill the quota. Geist could not have liked this change but bowed to superior authorities. He praised Warren for helping him think through other matters.[18]

Geist complained to SS officials that SS terror was impeding applicants for immigration visas. He threatened to stop giving out visas for the rest of the year if the SS and police made it impossible for his office to function smoothly. He told Himmler's press chief, another of Geist's "devils," that if they put another American Jew into a concentration camp, he would have the State Department invalidate all passports for travel to Germany: "They think I have the power to do these things and therefore it is safe to use them as threats. One has to be constantly at it day and night and never leave go. I feel that I have got some of these Nazis by the neck and that I cannot leave go of my hold." He expected to get visa work in Berlin on a solid and steady basis and reduce the crowds outside the Consulate General.[19]

On February 1, Wohlthat presented to Rublee's group a detailed German government proposal involving the emigration of 150,000 German Jews between the ages of fifteen and forty-five and who were capable of earning a living. Their dependents, estimated at 250,000, could follow only when the wage earners were well established abroad. That would, in effect, leave the young and old as hostages in Germany. The German government would take at least 25 percent of the remaining assets of German Jews to establish a fund that allegedly might go for resettlement or serve as collateral for a resettlement loan raised abroad. (No one outside Germany believed that this fund would actually be used to benefit emigrants.) Pell believed that Göring backed this program but needed additional ammunition to win Hitler over. As a result, Wohlthat insisted on visible progress with the establishment and funding of a resettlement foundation abroad before Berlin would carry out its commitment. Germany wanted assurance that the countries or places of resettlement would admit German Jews. The US negotiators "recognized" the German plan in principle, which is to say that they did not want to approve it but were willing to operate on the assumption that it might go through. The talks recessed while Nazi officials waited for a Western response. Rublee brought the German offer to the United States, and Pell returned to London.[20]

Geist saw that "monkey wrenches" kept recurring. He urged Lochner to ride the Nazi regime hard (with press criticism) if it failed to execute a refugee agreement. Nazi ideologue Alfred Rosenberg, meanwhile, warned the countries behind the Intergovernmental Committee that they must not create a Jewish state—that would give Jews too much power; he called for a Jewish reservation on the island of Madagascar, then part of France's empire.[21]

On February 10, Philip Bernstein, special correspondent for the Jewish Telegraphic Agency, came with his wife for tea with Geist before they left Germany. Geist thought Bernstein had done fine reporting in Berlin and Vienna over the preceding year without running afoul of the Gestapo. Geist used this social occasion to give Bernstein information he might use constructively in the United States.[22] Afterward, without naming Geist, Bernstein reported confidentially to the JTA that an American diplomat who was always sympathetic to the cause of German Jewry believed that: (1) the offer to Rublee was the best the Nazis would make; (2) the Nazis would live up to this offer; (3) American Jewry ought to cooperate with this plan, no matter how distasteful some of its terms were; and (4) American Jews should not oppose Ambassador Wilson's return to Berlin.[23]

Messersmith and others at State assumed that Bernstein had distorted Geist's views, especially in the claim about the Nazis living up to their offer. After Messersmith asked him to clarify, Geist offered a more nuanced summary, but he did not deny the thrust of Bernstein's report.[24] Geist *had* stated that Rublee got the most anyone could out of the Germans. The Gestapo did not favor the concessions Göring made, and Geist knew that the radical forces never would accept more. Geist wrote that the Nazi regime would carry out the general thrust of this plan, provided that the Intergovernmental Committee arranged destinations for substantial numbers of emigrants. With Göring and Hitler in favor, Geist did not believe that Himmler, Streicher, Goebbels, and other radicals would contest the general arrangement. They would chisel and victimize refugees, but they would carry out parts of the plan that worked in Germany's favor. Geist backed off from the quoted statement that American Jewry ought to cooperate fully, but he did not deny that the alternative to acceptance or continued negotiation was chaos (or worse). On the fourth point, Geist had long favored Wilson coming back to Berlin. Because Nazi officials themselves blamed American Jewry for Wilson's continued absence, Geist hoped to avoid any American Jewish protest against Wilson's return.[25] Geist believed that the Intergovernmental Committee's continued negotiations were critical because they likely would deter maximum persecution.[26] He was hoping to play for time, but the ground kept shifting.

On February 24, 1939, Counselor of Embassy Prentiss Gilbert suddenly died, apparently from a bad reaction to a medical injection.[27] His death must have shocked Geist, who was only two years younger. Not just Geist's boss at the Embassy, Gilbert had become his ally. Geist had lost both of his embassy superiors. As the senior officer present in Berlin, now he was formally in charge of the Embassy, with the additional title of chargé d'affaires.

On March 1, 1939, Geist got resolution of sorts on the case of a naturalized US citizen who'd been born in Germany but seized and imprisoned in a concentration camp after Kristallnacht. Werner Best wrote Geist that local authorities had considered Henry Weyl, born in Kippenheim, a German Jew. They learned otherwise, Best claimed, only when the US Consulate General protested. If they had known his citizenship, they would not have arrested him. Best said he had issued new instructions to prevent a repetition of this case. Geist told Washington that he would not fail to make use of Best's statement if cases like this arose in the future.[28] All the same, the case was not reassuring: local authorities certainly knew of Weyl's US citizenship, and Best's letter suggested that there might be future roundups.

On March 8, 1939, Geist obtained the text of an unpublished Nazi order directing authorities to arrange for the employment of Jewish workers in public and private enterprises as quickly as possible. The state had no interest in "letting Jewish labor resources remain unexploited." The only examples of employment given were factory work, construction, and land improvement—skilled labor or hard labor. Jewish workers were to be segregated from other laborers. This information coincided with earlier information gathered by Rublee suggesting a compulsory draft of Jewish labor. It was not a step toward emigration on a large scale, but Göring had approved it. Did this mean that Göring no longer supported mass emigration of Jews? It seemed ominous.[29]

Foreign policy events interfered with refugee negotiations as well. Hitler first worked to escalate tensions between Czechs and Slovaks and then exploited them. After the government in Prague deposed the Slovakian cabinet, Hitler decided to browbeat Slovak leader Father Jozef Tiso into declaring Slovakia's independence. Then Hitler summoned Czech leaders to Berlin, demanding that they accept a German occupation already in motion. Czech president Dr. Emil Hácha fainted during the negotiations after a German threat to bomb Prague, but an injection revived him. At 4 a.m. on March 15, he signed a declaration placing Czech territory in the hands of the Germans, and he telephoned orders to Czech troops not to fire on incoming Germans.[30] The destruction of Czechoslovakia surprised only those gullible enough to believe Hitler's promise at the Munich Conference that the Sudetenland was his final territorial demand.

Nazi persecution quickly reached the 118,000 Czech Jews and German Jewish refugees in Bohemia and Moravia, as Adolf Eichmann set up in Prague a Central Office for Jewish Emigration. Geist asked the German government not to impede the emigration of Jews there who had received visas to the United States or would soon receive them.[31]

German takeover of Czech territory and domination of the new Slovak Republic effectively ended British and French efforts to negotiate with Germany. In late March, Britain publicly volunteered to aid Poland in the event of a German attack, a move that enraged Hitler, who considered Polish territory as part of Germany's living space. Hitler began to prepare for war against Poland despite the new British policy. Initial Nazi propaganda directed against Poland concentrated on longstanding complaints about Danzig and the Polish corridor. Meanwhile, Nazi officials stated that they had virtually ceased relations with Britain, and they unleashed a cynical propaganda slogan that "God [should] punish England" for its wicked treatment of Germany. Perhaps that swayed gullible churchgoing nationalists. One of Göring's top officials in the Luftwaffe viewed US intervention in another European war as at most a remote possibility; the Americans would suffer 80 percent losses if the United States did.[32]

Geist decided to puncture this fantasy. At the home of a friend, he managed to have a "comprehensive conversation" with General Franz Halder, chief of the Army General Staff. Backed by his new title of chargé d'affaires and firm in his views, Geist got through to Halder: "He appeared to be very much disturbed over the possibility of America, in case of war, throwing the weight of her resources and support on the side of Germany's potential enemies." Halder had flirted at times with an anti-Nazi faction within the military, but he knew that a showdown in Europe was approaching. He did not want war, but he and the army pledged to do their duty and support Hitler no matter what his course:

> He [Halder] said Hitler had hoped that the western democracies would take a realistic view of Germany's fundamental position and not interfere in Germany's eastern aims but since England and France are now making diplomatic moves to block Germany's eastern expansion Hitler was looking again toward the west. . . . Unless fewer obstacles were placed in the way of Germany's eastern expansion it would be necessary for Hitler to end the opposition which might happen in the west.

Geist sensed that the top German military officers were apprehensive about a war with the West but concluded that the army was entirely subordinate to Hitler. He could now see that a German war against Poland might well expand into the West.[33]

German annexation of Czech territory made it harder for those seeking money and territory for German Jews. Myron Taylor and Undersecretary Welles agreed that the Intergovernmental Committee should carry on its efforts despite German-Czech events. Rublee resigned as director and was replaced by Sir Herbert Emerson. Myron Taylor took charge of the drive to establish a new foundation for resettlement of Jewish refugees. James G. McDonald, chair of the President's Advisory Committee on Political Refugees, agreed with Geist that Rublee had extracted the maximum from the Göring faction under prevailing conditions. Taking steps now might generate more favorable conditions later, whereas rejection or inaction would "bring lightning upon the Jews."[34]

In early April, Geist spelled out the likely alternative to the absence of progress on German Jewish resettlement. It would start with chaos and move toward mass murder. The Gestapo in Berlin was preparing 180 to 200 people per day for emigration, which involved giving them passports—the equivalent of a stern warning to leave the country in short order. Geist feared that pressure would be applied in such a way as to make orderly emigration impossible. Although Wohlthat was expecting to see Pell again, Pell had not yet delivered the progress abroad. Geist feared that Nazi officials would disregard the agreement with Rublee and handle the "Jewish problem" in their own way: "It will, of course, consist of placing all the able-bodied Jews in work camps, confiscating the wealth of the entire Jewish population, isolating them, and putting additional pressure on the whole community, and getting rid of as many as they can by force."[35] Geist had predicted the future: although he did not envisage extermination camps, this was in rough terms what the SS did during the Holocaust.

Another Quaker delegation visiting Berlin stumbled into an entirely untenable proposal originated by Max Warburg: the Quakers could set up and run transit camps for German Jews in the area of Hamburg. Geist believed that this would make the Quakers responsible for the placement of refugees from the transit camp. It might interfere with the Intergovernmental Committee's resettlement efforts and offer only the illusion of safety in the meantime. Jewish leaders in Berlin did not like the idea either, calling it a trap. Geist did not give the Quakers as much time as he had in December.[36]

On April 25, Wohlthat told Geist that he needed to see Pell urgently. Returning to Berlin, Pell met with Wohlthat to learn that he had worked out draft decrees establishing a central German Jewish organization and the trust for Jewish assets, and all the relevant ministries had approved them. They gave Jews a definite legal status in Germany, provided for education and religious practice, and offered training in fields that would facilitate success in emigration. Wohlthat said Göring would see that these provisions were enforced. Wohlthat said Hitler had invited him to dinner on April 28, expecting a report on the situation with the Intergovernmental Committee. He was "bitterly disappointed" to hear from Pell that the committee had not yet established a private fundraising and resettlement corporation. Göring found himself in a difficult position with Hitler, with "those who scoffed at Goering's plans for solving the Jewish problems beginning to say 'I told you so.'" Pell could not give Wohlthat anything concrete or definite, but they agreed on optimistic wording. Pell, convinced that Wohlthat was trying to deliver, also invited him to come to London for further discussions.[37]

Pell and Wohlthat had dinner at Geist's house on April 27. Geist was pleased, he later told Washington, that Wohlthat's draft decrees contained nothing particularly harsh, and seemed designed to facilitate Jewish emigration. He credited Wohlthat (acting on behalf of Göring) with keeping negotiations going and preventing recurrence of violence against the Jews.[38] But how sincere was Göring and how much leverage did he have as war approached? Wohlthat's dinner with Hitler, based on the account passed to German Jewish notable Wilfrid Israel, must have been hard to digest. Unimpressed with the inertia of the Intergovernmental Committee, Hitler refused to authorize Wohlthat to do anything further until the committee offered concrete plans. The alternative was brutal Gestapo attacks on the German Jewish community.[39]

On April 14, Roosevelt had tried an unusual maneuver to bind Hitler to previous statements that the German people did not want war. Posing as a friendly intermediary distant from European quarrels, the president sent Hitler a seven-page telegram asking him to declare that he would not invade or attack any countries on a list of thirty in Europe and the Middle East, starting with Finland and ending with Iran. Roosevelt asked for a ten-year German commitment to nonaggression. Such a commitment, Roosevelt said, would lower tensions, making it possible to reduce fears and regain security.[40] Hitler decided to answer with a speech to the Reichstag to assure himself of a worldwide audience. In the meantime, German diplomats asked the countries listed by Roosevelt whether they were consulted before FDR's appeal and whether they felt menaced. Fourteen of them criticized Roosevelt.[41] Geist reported that the Nazi press called Roosevelt's move something that only a "Jewish snob" could consider brilliant. Why would young leaders in Europe adopt the "war agitator" Franklin Roosevelt as their arbitrator and "father-confessor?"[42]

Hitler's speech to the Reichstag on April 28 was a major ceremonial event, open to diplomats and the press. Geist knew in advance that Hitler would attack the president sharply, but he thought it unwise to boycott the gathering in the former Kroll Opera House, across the way from Reichstag building gutted by arson in February 1933. His absence might be interpreted as not even taking the trouble to listen, he told the State Department. Chiefs of mission customarily attended such events, and he could withstand having his country and his president attacked. Half an hour after he left for the speech, a German courier delivered a translated copy of Hitler's text to the Embassy. It was the only written answer Roosevelt was going to get to his telegram.[43]

Geist climbed up to the special box for diplomats and honored guests in the balcony. He tried to make himself as visible as possible by sitting in the front row there, but the attendants insisted on having Nazi allies and supporters in those seats. He refused to go back farther than the third row, ending up behind Japanese ambassador Hiroshi Oshima. He had a good view of Hitler at the podium.[44]

Casting the whole speech as a response to Roosevelt, Hitler first offered a long-winded introduction about the ravages inflicted upon Germany by foreign powers and the Treaty of Versailles. He then seized upon a statement by Prime Minister Chamberlain that Britain could no longer trust Germany's assurances. Hitler thereby justified Germany's renunciation of the Anglo-German Naval Agreement of 1935, allegedly because that treaty rested on mutual good faith. He also renounced Germany's ten-year nonaggression treaty with Poland and laid claim to the international free city of Danzig as a German city. And he celebrated the victory of Generalissimo Francisco Franco's forces, supported by Germany and Italy, in the Spanish Civil War.

Eventually, Hitler got to FDR's telegram, which, he complained, reached the press before it reached him. Turning the charge of military expansion against the United States, he argued that the United States had intervened militarily six times since 1918 and that it had subjugated the North American continent not at the conference table, but by force. It respected international negotiations so little that it never joined the League of Nations. Hitler said that he had taken the trouble to contact the states listed by Roosevelt, and none of them said they felt menaced by Germany. He picked on minor inaccuracies and ridiculed Roosevelt's grasp of geopolitics. He cast himself as the ally of Arabs in the Middle East against Jewish interlopers in British-controlled Palestine. He called himself the savior who had conquered chaos and weakness in Germany, a country with one-third the population of the United States, but with less than one-fifteenth the territory. He suggested that the size of the United States led Roosevelt to think in terms of intervention anywhere, but he, Hitler, found his smaller nation precious and would stick to what mattered most. He finished, after two hours and twenty minutes of vigorous gestures and shouts, apparent earnestness and exaggerated sarcasm, bathed in sweat. American correspondent William L. Shirer thought his acting superb.[45] He was roughly in the position of a winner taking a geopolitical victory lap. The *Nation* commented that Hitler managed to come across as a "mélange of isolationist senators."[46]

Geist expressed the general diplomatic reaction that Hitler's real business was the dual attack against Britain and Poland, while his sarcastic treatment of Roosevelt was designed to generate laughter—and succeeded. But there was so much raillery that it undermined Hitler's sincerity, Geist thought, perhaps reflecting Nazi uncertainty about the policy to take toward the United States.[47] Despite being instant commentary, it was not an obvious take on the speech. Of course, Geist hoped that the White House would not overreact to Hitler's insults.

On May 4, Geist followed up with more analysis of the German public's favorable reaction to Hitler's effort. Even thoughtful Germans felt that Hitler had replied cleverly to Roosevelt without creating an unbridgeable gulf between the United States and Germany.

The average German felt it inconceivable that Britain and France would fight to assist Poland in keeping Danzig against the wishes of its German inhabitants—Danzig was actually self-governing under the supervision of the League of Nations. Many Germans felt that Hitler would manage to wrest Danzig and other territory from Poland without war, as he had done before with Czechoslovakia. In any case, they thought that fulfilling Germany's mission was worth some risk. Geist told Lochner that the Nazis might try to take over Danzig before May 12.[48] War might erupt soon.

On that same day, May 4, Myron Taylor brought a delegation of ten people to the White House to meet with the president, Undersecretary Welles, and Pierrepont Moffat of European Affairs about the proposed private foundation for Jewish resettlement. This meeting was necessary to overcome major American Jewish opposition to the Rublee-Wohlthat agreement. James G. McDonald and George Warren of the President's Advisory Committee on Political Refugees were allies, but several Jewish leaders, such as Joseph Proskauer, Lewis Strauss, and Henry Ittleson, were at best undecided. Taylor indicated that Göring had as much as said that he had six months to find a solution or else. Welles then read Geist's latest despatch, which started by describing his dinner with Wohlthat and Pell. It concluded: "The present negotiations can be continued between the Germans and the Intergovernmental Committee provided that . . . [it] can show reasonable prospects of providing opportunities for the migration of German Jews. Otherwise I believe that the Radicals here will demand a free hand to handle the Jewish problem in their own fashion."[49] Geist already had made clear what that meant. McDonald, who knew Geist, respected his views. Paul Baerwald, director of the Joint Distribution Committee and another of those in the delegation, was well aware that Geist had helped his brother get out of Germany.[50]

Judge Samuel Rosenman, Roosevelt's speechwriter and a prominent member of the American Jewish Committee, called for the establishment of an interdenominational foundation. Taylor accepted the principle, but said the Jews had to bear the greatest burden, because their coreligionists were the ones most threatened. It was the sort of debate that had delayed action before. Roosevelt intervened in this disagreement, stating that setting up a new organization was bound to take time. Was there not some existing organization that could be adapted? Some in the group objected, but the president stuck to his point. According to Moffat, FDR said, "We should tell the Germans in a fortnight,—not one day longer,—that an organization was in existence which could deal with the German Trust. It was not so much a question of the money as it was of actual lives, and the President was convinced that the warnings given by our Embassy in Berlin were sound and not exaggerated."[51] It is one of Franklin Roosevelt's least-known statements about what we call the Holocaust, and it referenced Geist's reporting.

During his dramatic first term, Roosevelt had tried to master and manage the multiple crises of the Great Depression by pushing through the programs of the New Deal and securing his control of government. He heard repeatedly about Nazi persecution of German Jews, but the level of anti-Semitism in the United States made him hesitate to take public steps to criticize Germany or to increase immigration substantially when the United States had so many other problems. Politically, his situation changed in November 1936, after he was reelected to what he believed would be his last term. Following the advice of more liberal supporters, Roosevelt and the State Department, through Messersmith and Geist, found ways to make greater use of the US immigration quota. After the Anschluss, FDR engaged directly with the fate of the Jews of Germany and Europe. But Germany moved toward war quicker than the negotiators could make progress on extricating and resettling Jewish refugees.

CHAPTER TWELVE

CHILDREN

In early 1939, Gilbert and Eleanor Kraus of Philadelphia took on a challenge to help German Jewish children immigrate to the United States. The national Jewish fraternal organization B'rith Sholom had a large new building outside Philadelphia on an eighty-five-acre property used as a summer camp. B'rith Sholom proposed to operate a group home for fifty children at least temporarily if the Krauses could bring these children from Germany to the United States. The fifty children selected by the Krauses showed how the US government worked (and still works), and George Messersmith and Raymond Geist made their rescue mission possible.[1] For once, the two colleagues and friends were on the same side of a sticky immigration problem.

In the background of the Kraus mission was a larger immigration story. In December 1938, Secretary of Labor Frances Perkins talked up a proposal to take in some thousands of refugee children in addition to the immigration quota for Germany. Advocates noted that Britain had accepted ten thousand German Jewish children after Kristallnacht as a response to the emergency; an American coalition ranging from liberal social worker Marion Kenworthy to the American Friends Service Committee was eager to follow the British example; and few believed that such children would take jobs away from Americans. But Perkins was an optimist. Many opponents of immigration objected to any increase, and the prospects for a bill in Congress looked highly questionable at best.[2]

At her husband's suggestion, Eleanor Roosevelt advised support-ers of a children's bill to recruit bipartisan sponsors in Congress, in-troduce the same bill in both houses, and muster all the Catholic support possible. FDR was very conscious of the influence of the ra-dio priest—that is, anti-Semitic radio broadcasts by Father Charles Coughlin. Eleanor attributed State Department opposition to fear of Congress, but it was more than that. A January 1939 public opinion poll indicated that a solid 66 percent of the public opposed the idea of admitting children outside the quota. Senator Robert F. Wagner of New York, a liberal Catholic Democrat, and Congresswoman Edith Nourse Rogers, Republican of Massachusetts, introduced identical bills on February 9 to allow ten thousand children into the country outside the quota for the next two years. Eleanor Roosevelt endorsed the bill a few days later. Franklin maintained a discreet silence.[3]

Gil Kraus met in January 1939 with Louis Levine, national chair-man of B'rith Sholom. A prominent and prosperous lawyer with a strong sense of right and wrong and an appetite for adventure, Kraus did not need much persuasion to consider bringing German Jewish children to safety.[4] One key contact was thirty-seven-year-old con-gressman Leon Sacks, a Philadelphia Democrat elected in the wake of Roosevelt's 1936 landslide. Born and raised in an immigrant neigh-borhood of Philadelphia, Sacks had a personal interest in Nazi perse-cution of German Jews. He and Kraus went to talk to Messersmith about the possibility of having children immigrate within existing laws and regulations.[5]

Six days before the Wagner-Rogers bills were introduced, Messer-smith professed sympathy for the principle of bringing child immi-grants to the United States but claimed that such bills had insuperable administrative difficulties. They would lead, he explained to Geist, to a deluge of applications. How could consuls ever determine which cases were the most meritorious? Whatever they did, they would face criticism. The political and humanitarian firefight would wreck their usefulness on immigration and severely weaken the Foreign Service. Messersmith had learned that Samuel Dickstein, chair of the House Immigration Committee, favored a children's bill, but that the vast majority of his committee opposed it. Others, such as Senator Robert Reynolds of North Carolina, were planning to introduce bills to cut the quotas. As a practical matter, Messersmith hoped for little committee discussion of immigration bills, and no discussion on the floor of the House and Senate.[6]

By contrast, Messersmith found Kraus and Sacks impressive and responsible. The B'rith Sholom group proposed to send the Krauses to Germany to "talk over certain matters with you and to go into certain aspects of the problems." Messersmith wondered whether they, both Jews, could do so without "serious inconvenience," meaning danger or threat. Could they even find a hotel room? He asked Geist to send him a very short cable: either voyage feasible, or voyage not feasible. A few weeks later, Geist wrote back, "Voyage entirely feasible." He must have checked with the Gestapo before answering so confidently.[7]

Finding fifty or so Americans with resources to fill out affidavits of support for children was a matter of networking and hard work, much of it done by Eleanor Kraus in Philadelphia.[8] A more difficult question was whether any quota numbers would be available for them. Berlin and Washington had to supply the answer.

Geist previously had served as the visa point man in Berlin for the Hilfsverein and German Jewish Children's Aid. Since 1934, with the assistance of the Department of Labor, they had brought about 350 German Jewish children to the United States.[9] Their program dwindled over time, partly because of resource issues in the United States. But after March 1938, an additional problem surfaced: the monthly quota allotments were almost always filled with adults and families. There were no slots waiting for additional children even if American families were willing to adopt or care for them. When German Jewish Children's Aid asked if the consuls in Germany could reserve a dozen quota numbers for children whose identities were yet to be determined under the existing arrangement, State's Visa Division said no.[10]

The Philadelphia couple thought they might convert quota numbers that went unclaimed near the end of the year—from people who had already emigrated elsewhere, died, or no longer could afford to emigrate.[11] But Messersmith, who had run the visa system when he was consul general in Berlin, knew it was not that simple. They would have to find children who had registered for visas earlier, placing them high enough on the quota list to inherit any vacant quota slots. In short, they would have to talk to Geist about who and where the right children were. He wrote Geist, "They [the Krauses] wish to get in touch with you and with the other visa-issuing offices in Germany to determine what families there are whose turns will be reached in the relatively near future. . . . They would then get in touch with the parents . . . and get proper affidavits from this country to cover the individual child."[12] They also had to drop their notion that B'rith Sholom pay for the passage of the children, because immigration regulations barred such assistance by an organization.[13]

Messersmith disclaimed State Department sponsorship of the Krauses and avoided any promise of favorable results were they to go to Germany.[14] All the same, Messersmith helped them work out a strategy through Geist, who was not exactly short of work in early 1939. Regardless, he painstakingly reviewed visa records of all the consulates in Germany to locate forty children formally refused visas and 526 children who would have qualified for visas but for insufficient affidavits of support.[15] Having already come up for their turn, they preceded all those still on the huge waiting list. If their families agreed to send them to the United States, they were prime candidates.

Advance publicity about the proposed rescue mission by the Krauses stirred up both opposition and confusion. How could the children enter the United States legally when the quota was filled each month? Some critics thought this mission was illegal because it must involve additions to the quota. The State Department stated repeatedly that this private effort was not outside the immigration quota. It did not publicly disclose the complicated effort to identify suitable child candidates, even to German Jewish Children's Aid. Another group of liberal opponents feared that this mission would complicate other rescue efforts—including the Wagner-Rogers bill. Rival Jewish organizations felt that they were better situated to find foster homes for children.[16]

Messersmith believed that, if the Kraus mission succeeded, the State Department could show that the immigration system ameliorated an immense problem. In Messersmith's eyes, the Kraus mission *would* in this sense undermine the chance of passing the Wagner-Rogers bill in Congress. The bill faced slim odds in any case.

On March 31, proponents of the Wagner-Rogers bill announced that, if their bill was passed, Quaker representatives would select Protestant, Catholic, and Jewish children. It was an effort to avoid the unpopular impression that this was a Jewish bill—even though the Nazis considered baptized children of Jewish descent to be Jews. A Gallup poll that month showed two-thirds of Americans opposed bringing in additional refugee children. Former undersecretary of state William R. Castle told Congresswoman Rogers that, if pressed, he would prefer to let in twenty thousand elderly Jews who would not multiply, rather than children. Claiming that refugees were building a Jewish empire in the United States, Senator Robert Reynolds founded a new organization dedicated to shutting out all immigrants.[17]

In this climate Gil and Eleanor Kraus visited Messersmith in his office in the sand-colored Victorian edifice today called the Eisenhower Executive Office Building, near the White House, a couple of weeks before they were scheduled to leave for Berlin. Eleanor remembered Messersmith being friendly, cordial, and noncommittal. After the Krauses obtained their passports at the State Department's Passport Office, one of Messersmith's assistants asked Eleanor if he could say something "off the record." Learning that they were parents, he urged her not to go because Germany was not safe for a woman. He said that war could break out at any time and, if it did, it might be difficult for Americans to get out of Europe. Eleanor was shaken. Gil agreed that she should not go. But Gil needed someone to help with all the work involved. They soon thought of the family pediatrician, Robert Schless, a widower who spoke fluent German. Schless agreed almost instantly to substitute for Eleanor.[18]

Messersmith wrote a cable to Geist introducing them and emphasizing their good qualities: "Both these men are very first class people and I am sure that you can depend on their reliability. I have told them to get in touch with you on their arrival and to consult with you continuously." Then Messersmith went through the motions of disclaiming any State Department sponsorship.[19] He knew that anti-immigration critics might later demand an investigation.

On April 7, the two Philadelphia men sailed on the *Queen Mary*, took a ferry across the English Channel, and went to Berlin by train via Amsterdam. Geist found them rooms at the Hotel Adlon, more convenient to the new Embassy-Consulate General complex than the Hotel Esplanade, where Ambassador Dodd had previously stayed. Work on the embassy compound in the Blücher Palace was not quite complete and not all US officials were moved in, but Geist, as acting chief of mission, was there.

Eleanor Kraus wrote in her memoir that Gil took an "immediate liking" to Geist, a man of imposing stature, a thick neck, and close-cropped hair. Geist offered them no assurances, but Kraus was relieved anyway; Geist seemed unflappable.[20] Then he made a surprising recommendation. There were children from Berlin and Stuttgart on his list, but the largest cluster by far was in Vienna. Why not go there?

The number of visa applications in Vienna had exploded in March–April 1938, following the Anschluss. The avalanche in the rest of Germany began in the summer of 1938, accelerating after Kristallnacht. More children in Vienna had reached the top of the quota list, and their parents were perhaps more desperate. Geist told Kraus and Schless that they would find it easier to work in one place, rather than try to pick children in different locations and herd them together.[21]

One disadvantage of Vienna was that Kraus and Schless would not work directly with Geist but with the officials of the Consulate General in that city. Nonetheless, they followed his advice and found rooms at the seven-story Hotel Bristol, located in the center of Vienna, with an art nouveau facade and an interior that blended Baroque and Biedermeier. Theodore Roosevelt and Marie Bonaparte had stayed there. The former owner, Samuel Schallinger, an Austrian Jew, had been forced to turn his property over to the government after the Anschluss.[22]

Selecting the children and completing necessary paperwork was overwhelming and exhausting. Kraus and Schless found the level of danger in Vienna manageable, perhaps because Geist had cleared the way for them. When they asked Eleanor to join them from the United

States, she rushed to do so. Gil met her in Paris, and they took the Orient Express back to Vienna.[23]

Geist had informed the Gestapo that the three Americans intended to screen the children at the Vienna premises of the Society of Friends (Quakers), where they would interview the families. Actually, they worked at the Jewish Community Building, known as the Kultus-gemeinde, where a young part-Jewish medical student named Hedy Neufeld helped them contact the families. When they finished their interviews and investigations, they made heart-wrenching selections based on which children could manage best without their families. Then they matched up documents for the children with American affidavits of support. Only then, in early May, did they proceed to the Consulate General for the visas they hoped to receive.[24]

Geist reported that, as of April 30, the consulates had 348 visas left over for the fiscal year ending June 30.[25] So there seemed to be enough visas for fifty children. But the Krauses and Schless ran into problems anyway. Their first problem was that Consul General Leland Morris was away on business, and his subordinates knew nothing about the rescue scheme. The second problem was that Vice Consul Parker Hart found the affidavits deficient because they lacked a seal from a certified public accountant. He said that the State Department had recently changed its rules to add this requirement. This was what Eleanor Kraus remembered in any case.[26] Hart was unsympathetic, or he looked hard for flaws in an unorthodox arrangement.

Geist's contemporary account was different, even if the result was the same. Once Kraus notified him that his group had selected the children, Geist transferred fifty unused quota slots to Vienna. But the Consulate General in Vienna had on file a significant number of applications from individuals with close relatives in the United States. Immigration regulations put these cases into a category called preference (first and second preference depending upon the closeness of the relation), ranking them above all non-preference cases. Geist quickly suggested to Washington that the preference system really was for the first ten months of the year, not for recycled visas during the last two months. He pointed out how much time and trouble the Krauses and

Schless had taken to get these children out. He recommended the fifty visas for the children in May, and visas for the Vienna preference cases at the beginning of July, when the new fiscal year would begin. But Visa Division officials in Washington would agree under no circumstances: preference cases would come first.[27]

When Leland Morris returned to Vienna, he discovered that visa issuance there was so backed up that the children could not undergo the required interviews and physical examinations before July. Morris told Gil Kraus that he might have better luck in Berlin with Geist. On May 6–7, with Schless remaining in Vienna, the Krauses, unhappy and unable to fall asleep, took the night train back to Berlin. Geist met them in his office on Monday morning, May 8. Eleanor wore a fancy new hat. Geist said he had been away from the United States for some time: he asked how much such a nice hat cost. Eleanor responded, "I would be ashamed to answer, particularly with my husband present." By then, Geist knew the visa complications better than the Krauses did, but he had not yet worked out the details of a solution. Geist let them explain the problem, and then he urged them to proceed as if the visas would materialize.[28]

Geist reclaimed the fifty quota slots from Vienna and delegated nine quota slots for preference cases in Vienna and an unstated number of preference cases in Berlin. No one could claim he had neglected the preference candidates.[29] Clearing the way for fifty non-preference visas, he introduced the Krauses to Vice Consul Cyrus Follmer, who scrutinized their affidavits and termed them "terrific," as complete as possible. Eleanor, Gil, and Dr. Schless still had to ferry the children to Berlin for their physical examinations on May 22, but they booked passage to the United States on the *President Harding*, set to sail from Hamburg on May 23.[30]

Geist wrote Messersmith that the Philadelphia trio would assemble the children in Berlin in a few days and, he believed, get the fifty visas: "Everything done has been within the framework of our immigration laws, and I am pleased to say that they have had my sympathetic consideration, and, I believe, to their entire satisfaction. Faithfully yours, Raymond."[31]

On June 3, the *Harding* docked in New York Harbor after gliding past the Statue of Liberty. Some of the older children understood that they were now beyond Nazi threats. The children waited on the ship until other passengers disembarked. Louis Levine, head of B'rith Sholom, and Congressman Sacks had by this time boarded to meet the children and to help with arrangements. Some children had relatives waiting to meet them. A group of reporters rushed to interview the children and their sponsors. Eleanor was as low-key as possible: this was a "quiet private project" involving some friends who wanted to bring children to this country. Calling for no publicity, Gil lost his temper. Even Congressman Sacks told the *New York Times*, "Oh, forget this. We don't want any publicity on it. The success of this is that we have not had any publicity on it all the way through." This statement spoke volumes about the political climate not only in Germany but in the United States as well. The *Times* published a short article the next day about the private rescue venture financed by fifty-seven Philadelphians.[32]

By this time, the Wagner-Rogers bill was on life support. A special joint House-Senate committee had issued a favorable report, but a majority of the Senate Immigration Committee seemed opposed, and its House counterpart was solidly against: only four of nineteen members clearly favored it, with eleven firmly opposed. When Representative Caroline O'Day wrote Roosevelt to ask for his support, he wrote, "File, No Action." During June, the Senate Immigration Committee amended the bill to give children preference but to count them under the quota. Senator Wagner disclaimed this mutilation, which would have displaced adults and families who had waited their turn. The Senate committee also favorably reported out bills to halt all immigration for five years and to fingerprint all aliens. None of these bills reached the floor of the House or the Senate.[33]

US laws and regulations were a sifting mechanism to determine which visa applicants would promote the national interest and prosperity of the United States. They would never work well for very large numbers of people fleeing for their lives. But Congress and the American public backed this system, and Congress had no intention of liberalizing it substantially. Under these circumstances, small victories were better than none.

On June 6, Gil Kraus wrote Messersmith that he wanted to come to Washington to offer his thanks, but, as the "father" of fifty additional children, he could not yet do so. He added, "I frankly wish to say that if it were not for the cooperation, within legal limits, of the Department of State and the Foreign Service, our accomplishment could never have been possible."[34] It was more than a pro forma thank-you note. Two bureaucrats who knew how the system worked and really wanted visas for these children resolved all the US visa problems faced by the courageous and dedicated Philadelphia trio.

On the same day, an unhappy conservative Republican senator, Rufus Holman of Oregon, having read of the children's arrival, wrote Secretary of State Hull: "I will be obliged if you will furnish me with a detailed statement of the manner in which these immigrants were admitted to the US under existing immigration law."[35] Only the Krauses, Schless, Messersmith, and Geist, putting their experiences together, could have answered the senator.

On June 20, Geist informed the State Department that the immigration quota for Germany for the fiscal year was completely filled.[36] Approximately 85 percent of the 27,370 immigrants were Jews, at least as defined by the Nazis.[37]

Three times Geist had gone out of his way to rescue children: with the Hoover organization's work in post–World War I Vienna; with the arrangement with German Jewish Children's Aid; and now with the Krauses. For the last two he had to overcome the opposition of both Nazi radicals and US restrictionists. These hard-fought victories vindicated his belief that the United States should maintain relations with Germany as long as possible.

CHAPTER THIRTEEN

TOWARD WAR

I n early May 1939, Alexander Kirk arrived to assume the position of chargé d'affaires in the Embassy in Berlin, relieving Geist of his job. The State Department told Geist that he should not feel slighted: the action was "based on considerations of rank. . . . From the Secretary down the excellence of your work has been recognized and commented on."[1] In the State Department efficiency report for the period ending July 31, 1939, Geist received a rare rating of excellent. After reviewing some of his negotiations with German government officials, Pierrepont Moffat concluded, "The work performed by Mr. Geist . . . all of which has a political connection, can only be described as colossal"—and he wrote in the German, *kolossal*, for emphasis.[2]

Kirk, three years younger than Geist, was a native of Wisconsin. His grandfather had founded what became the largest soap manufacturer in the country; Kirk received a private salary from the family firm. He had started in the foreign service almost a decade earlier than Geist, serving in Berlin during the Great War. He looked like the prototypical diplomat, lean, well dressed, and sporting a mustache.[3]

Kirk now had to analyze and report on Nazi capabilities and intentions.[4] He believed that Germany wanted all land previously taken from it in the peace settlement and great-power status as well. He knew little of the alarming intelligence that Geist and the AP's Louis Lochner had gathered over the preceding six years, and he apparently did not draw on their experience. As late as August 17, he said he could not believe that there was going to be a war.[5]

Lochner heard that Hitler had given an unusually forthright speech to leading German generals in January. The Führer had called the British decadent, predicting that Germany would dominate the world for five thousand years. He said that he probably would die young, so he had to accomplish the preconditions for German domination by 1940. Hitler's fantasy-like statements probably were derived from talk circulating among military men about two of Hitler's speeches: a speech of January 18, 1939, to cadets in the army; and a speech of January 25 to the senior army commanders. In the first, Hitler called the German people the strongest in the world and said he would build an equally powerful army for immediate deployment. In the second, he forecast that the Aryans would one day conquer the world.[6] In late May, when Lochner had dinner with Geist and Vienna consul general Leland Morris, they would have talked over such intelligence.[7] Geist had written in late January 1939 that if Germany were to obtain sufficient food and raw materials "the course of conquest would be straight ahead and to the limit unless they were stopped by a superior force."[8]

About the time Kirk arrived in Berlin, Lochner received a Pulitzer Prize for his reporting. His selection was unusual in that the AP rarely allowed reporters bylines in their stories. At a luncheon in Lochner's honor for all embassy and consulate general officials and their families, Geist delivered what Lochner called a "eulogy," embarrassing him so much that he wanted to hide in a corner.[9]

Geist received his own press tribute. Lithuanian-born Otto Tolischus, the lead *New York Times* reporter in Berlin since 1933, wrote a feature article on Geist for the *Times Magazine*. Nazi Germany was waging a totalitarian war, claiming absolute sovereignty for itself, while insisting that other powers observe "the laws of peace." All of this made Berlin the most difficult and the most important diplomatic post in the world. Personifying the "august" US government, Geist had become the best-known American official in Germany, Tolischus wrote. The article described Geist's protection work and visa supervision in glowing terms: he was *the* troubleshooter in Berlin. Reporter Howard K. Smith later described Tolischus as the ablest figure in the American press corps in Berlin.[10]

Geist continued his struggle to get endangered people out of Germany and neighboring countries. John Wiley, now US minister in Riga, wrote him about two of his friends, a Jewish composer and his fiancée, originally Austrian, now stuck in Antwerp. Although they had reached their turn for US immigration visas under the German quota, their applications in Belgium were judged incomplete because they did not show the absence of criminal records. US regulations, however, allowed for an exception when local police certification was not available. Geist told the US consul general in Antwerp that he had repeatedly discussed this point with the Gestapo, including with an unnamed high official (Himmler). In theory, such police certificates were available, but in practice they were not. Geist suggested that the consul general certify nonavailability and grant the visa.[11]

In the meantime, negotiations involving the Intergovernmental Committee on Refugees barely inched along. On May 20, Undersecretary of State Sumner Welles reported to President Roosevelt that Myron Taylor had succeeded in recruiting a list of twenty trustees, Jews and non-Jews, to a new Coordinating Foundation. Taylor offered to go back to London to link its activity with the Intergovernmental Committee, but an illness and an operation delayed his trip until July. Early Jewish fundraising for the Coordinating Foundation had modest success, and rival Jewish organizations fought over priorities.[12] It was not the united, urgent effort for which Geist and Göring's negotiator Wohlthat had hoped. Wohlthat felt himself in personal and political danger. When he decided to risk a trip to London to meet with Intergovernmental Committee officials, he sent word through Geist that he had to keep it all secret.[13]

Hitler and Himmler ignored what prospect remained for a negotiated emigration settlement as they looked toward a war that would only magnify the difficulties for Jews trying to leave Germany. War would also offer a lethal climate and a shield behind which the SS could operate.

US officials and businessmen visiting Berlin sought out Geist for assistance and for advice, and some observed him at work. An executive of the German subsidiary of General Motors tried to leave the country with plans for a new small, German-produced car in his pocket. After Nazi authorities arrested him, Geist rescued him and a couple of other American citizens working for GM. James Mooney, president of GM Overseas Corporation, called Messersmith to praise Geist as a "tower of strength" doing an outstanding job.[14] After a visit to Berlin, Frederick Davenport, chair of a unit within the Civil Service Commission, observed, "He just has it in him to be effective. He talks a language that German officials understand, and is, I think, regarded with great respect by them and by all who know him." Davenport said that when the time should come to appoint a full ambassador, Geist had the ability to do that job.[15]

In mid-August 1939, Geist escorted US postmaster general James Farley around Berlin, the most important stop on his European tour. Operating under the assumption that Roosevelt would not stand for reelection in 1940, Farley planned to be a candidate. He wanted to buttress his knowledge of international affairs and enhance his image.[16] Geist urged Farley not to accept an invitation from a Nazi Foreign Office official to arrange a meeting with Hitler, and Farley agreed.[17]

Farley was impressed by many new buildings in Berlin and by its general, sparkling-clean condition. He apparently visited the beach at Wannsee: "I remember one particularly fine bathing beach," he wrote after his trip. Everywhere, enthusiastic members of the Hitler Youth and other young people convinced him that Hitler had connected well with them. The few adult Berliners to whom Farley spoke did not want war but were grateful for everything Hitler had done for Germany. But soldiers marched everywhere in the city and on roads outside it. Farley thought they looked arrogant. Geist took Farley on a drive outside the city to see airfields and military compounds, protected by wire fences. Farley also asked if he could see a concentration camp, so Geist drove him north to nearby Sachsenhausen.[18]

The Inspectorate of Concentration Camps, the administrative center for all German concentration camps, was at Oranienburg; it was right next to Sachsenhausen. Geist had visited Gruppenführer

Theodor Eicke there before, and he knew the layout of Sachsenhausen, which was established in 1936.[19] A picket fence about five feet high stretched along the road, and outside it lay another one a couple of feet higher. Still, from the road, the two men could see those prisoners the SS guards were willing to display outside the camp. They wore prison trousers and white shirts, and Farley thought they looked healthy. Outside the camp perimeter they were building concrete and brick homes, quite substantial ones, for the officers. Farley refrained from taking photos but wrote that what he saw was similar to pictures of camp prisoners that had appeared in *Life* magazine.[20]

Most of the 6,500 Jews sent to Sachsenhausen after Kristallnacht were gone, either released or dead; only 247 prisoners in late August 1939 were Jews. Jews bore the yellow triangle and either a red triangle (for alleged political prisoners) or a green triangle (for alleged criminals); the two triangles, one pointed up and one down, were superimposed to form a star on the breast of their striped shirts. There may have been almost that number of homosexuals, who wore the pink triangle. All of the 6,500 prisoners, in various categories such as Sinti and Roma, habitual criminals, and others, had unique numbers stitched onto their shirts.[21]

On August 21, Geist gloomily concluded that war was about to break out, the first time he had said so.[22] But even worse, that evening Lochner received a bombshell—Stalin announced that the USSR would sign a secretly negotiated nonaggression treaty with Germany.[23] Formal signing of the Hitler-Stalin pact took place on August 23. The pact contained a secret protocol dividing eastern Europe into German and Soviet spheres of influence, clearing the way for a German attack against Poland without any threat from the east. The only advantage for the United States in this combination was psychological. Geist thought of totalitarian regimes as similar, if not similarly evil, and this pact put the two primary behemoths on the same side. Their alliance made it easier to arouse American dislike and distrust of Germany.

In the summer of 1939, the weakening or abolition of the Neutrality Acts was a political struggle still in progress in Washington. President Roosevelt also had had little success getting military expansion through Congress. Nonetheless, US military authorities had presented President Roosevelt with a strategic contingency plan to defeat Germany and her allies, it would require an American Army of ten million men. If the United States were to enter another world war, it would emphasize the war in Europe; American forces would hold Japan at bay as best they could in the Pacific until Germany could be defeated. The president now had at least some sense of where and how to navigate when political conditions would permit. The first stage would be economic and military assistance to Britain, not US entry into the war.[24] Geist, one of those who warned about the extreme peril Germany was posing to the West, likely agreed with this strategy, which put the onus of breaking relations upon Germany.

As the diplomatic situation worsened each day, Kirk complained to Lochner, "Hitler is a madman, so what can you do?"[25] Kirk told Farley that he thought the president had made a mistake in not sending an ambassador to the city, for a person with this rank might gain more respect from German officials. Foreign Minister Ribbentrop refused to meet with Kirk during the final crisis and for months after the war broke out.[26]

After a staged incident on the German side of the border at Gleiwitz, Germany "retaliated" by invading Poland on September 1. Britain and France declared war on Germany on September 3. Lochner, who had frantically covered the last diplomatic exchanges and the early fighting in Poland for the AP, accepted a German invitation to travel with German troops and witness some of the combat in the east.[27]

Another potential source of information for Geist was preoccupied, too. On August 18, Werner Best took part in a meeting with Himmler, Heydrich, and the commanders of five newly formed, battalion-sized SS and police units called Einsatzgruppen, mobile killing squads that were to follow the German Army into Poland. Hitler and Himmler probably had yet to issue basic instructions for the Einsatzgruppen.[28] On August 29, Best met with Heydrich and army quartermaster Colonel Eduard Wagner to secure army cooperation with the Einsatzgruppen tasks—such as arresting the tens of thousands of prominent Poles considered to be hostile. They were to be sent to concentration camps in Germany. This was to be merely the first step in eliminating Poland

and establishing permanent German domination and even partial annexation there. Wagner and other army leaders, not quite sure to what they were agreeing, raised no serious objections.[29]

On September 3, after a difficult battle with Polish forces in East Upper Silesia, Wagner said that draconian measures were needed. Himmler issued an order for insurgents to be "shot on the spot." Emanating from Hitler's special train in occupied Poland, this order was not given to the Army High Command, but to the SS and the Einsatzgruppen. As late as September 16, Best, who admitted that such an order was consistent with Hitler's prior statements, claimed not to know about it. But the order was confirmed in short order, and certain army officers who had earlier objected dropped the matter.[30]

It soon became clear that Hitler, Himmler, and Heydrich, all sending out instructions from conquered Polish territory, expected the Einsatzgruppen daily to carry out as many as two hundred executions of Polish nobles, intelligentsia, priests, and Jews. Hitler determined the broader goals: Germany was to annex parts of western Poland, rule over central Poland, and use the latter area as a dumping ground for those people displaced to make way for German settlers. He intended to neutralize the Polish elite and keep the mass of the Polish people at a low level of education.[31]

Best had lost his battle for a juridically trained police elite. His superiors Himmler and Heydrich subordinated professional training to loyalty and ideology. Nonetheless, Heydrich recognized Best's organizational and administrative skills. He was first given charge of Gestapo counterespionage and then, in late September, he became head of the administrative section (Section I) of the newly established umbrella police and intelligence organization called the Reich Security Main Office (RSHA).[32] Heydrich ran the whole RSHA.

While Best was preoccupied, Geist was incapacitated during the first half of September. He had driven himself too hard for too long, and he suffered serious, but only vaguely described, medical problems.[33] Psychological factors must have weighed heavily upon him. He could not do anything more to help his Jewish friends and acquaintances during the war, except for those who could quickly qualify for visas and get money from the outside to pay for passage to the United States. Most of the rest were doomed.

By the second half of September, Geist had recovered to the point where he could arrange the evacuation of wives and children of officials at the US Consulate General. He also persuaded at least some Nazi officials to accept an out-of-court settlement in the case of an American lawyer, Frederich Wirth Jr., arrested for currency smuggling. The case dragged on because officials insisted on a large fine that Wirth, although owed money by German clients, could not pay. Geist also met with Wohlthat, who claimed that the German government was still willing to cooperate with the Intergovernmental Committee on Jewish emigration. But because of the war situation, Wohlthat said, Jewish emigrants would not be able to take with them any articles in short supply in Germany; they could not spend (their own) money for personal transportation or shipment of their effects outside Germany; and the property they would leave behind would go to the successor organization of the Reichsvertretung to support indigent Jews.[34] To put it another way: if money were to come in from the outside to transport them, Germany would let them go without their possessions. This was little more than a fig leaf for complete expropriation, and it was unclear if Wohlthat could deliver even that.

Organized fighting in Poland ended in the first week of October. Germany and the Soviet Union together had captured a million Polish soldiers, about two hundred thousand fled across borders, and about one hundred thousand were killed or died. On October 3, Lochner heard either directly or indirectly from Geist that he (Lochner wrote "even Raymond Geist") did not favor US entry into the war at this time. Days later, the two totalitarian countries divided Poland between them.[35]

Geist seems to have tried to bolster his own position in Berlin. As the German siege of Warsaw neared its end in late September, Frederick Davenport, chair of the Council of Personnel Administration, wrote to the president to call for the appointment of a strong US representative with presidential authority in Berlin. To send a new ambassador to Berlin at that moment might signal acceptance of Nazi actions, Davenport observed, but someone with express presidential backing might meet with Foreign Minister Ribbentrop and others like him to convey the true meaning of the United States' nominal neutrality. The Roosevelt administration was then fighting hard in Congress for authority to sell arms on a cash-and-carry basis to belligerents, which would have benefited Britain and France, but not Germany, which lacked the requisite naval strength. (It passed Congress after fierce debate in November.) The perfect man for such a role under these circumstances was there already—and Davenport went on to list Geist's prior experience and achievements.[36] But it was too late.

On October 11, Lochner wrote, Geist surprisingly had left the country, having lost "a war of nerves" with the Embassy.[37] He apparently alluded to disagreements between Geist and Kirk, but it was not that simple. Geist's physician said he needed two months' rest.[38] Kirk thought him quite exhausted, as did those State Department officials who saw him in Washington more than six weeks later. Some of the documentation suggests that he suffered from serious dizziness; Geist himself wrote on November 9 that he remained too unsteady to meet with State Department officials.[39] Still, Lochner's diary suggests that Geist himself wanted to stay in Berlin with some kind of presidential authority and that he probably had asked Davenport for help. His body did not let him await the outcome.

Learning that Geist was about to depart, Hermann Göring asked to see him on Monday, October 9. Göring tried to persuade Geist to use his influence on President Roosevelt to make peace: that is, FDR should persuade the British and French to accept Germany's conquest and annexation in the east.[40] This was piling fantasy atop fantasy, but Geist made use of Göring's assumption that he could sway FDR. Geist said that if Germany were to bomb Paris or London, the United States would enter the war.[41] He didn't bother to mention that Congress had to approve a declaration of war, and he probably perceived that Nazi officials understood little of the US Constitution. Geist would not have taken seriously Göring's claim that Germany was satisfied with its gains, and historians have discounted it, too. It was part of an effort to sow confusion and division in the West. As early as October 14, Hitler talked privately about concentrating on the forthcoming war against Britain.[42]

On the evening of October 9, Geist left Berlin for Genoa, Erich Mainz serving as his valet and caretaker. On October 12, they sailed on the Italian ocean liner, the *Conte di Savoia*.[43] The seven-year-old ship had one unusual feature played up in its advertising—three huge gyroscopes installed in a forward hold to eliminate or reduce rolling on crossings of the Atlantic.[44] Geist, unsteady, probably needed the help. When the ship docked in New York Harbor on October 21, his sister Anna and a State Department special agent were waiting to help them with the formalities of entering the country and to ease his physical strain.

After Geist wrote a thank-you note to the State Department, they took a train to Cleveland, staying at the family house at Villa Beach. He told his State Department contact that he was feeling somewhat better, but still needed immediate rest.[45] Messersmith warded off people who wanted to see him; he needed time to recover.[46] Erich Mainz used his stay in Cleveland to file initial papers for naturalization; he had broken completely with Germany and wanted to become a US citizen.[47]

Geist did not go to Washington until late November. Most of his debriefing by State Department officials left only brief traces in the records. One anonymous official wrote, "He looks and acts a pretty tired sort of an individual." But the next day another official said that he gave an interesting picture of conditions in Germany and his view of the outcome of the war. A third official said he would not go back to Berlin and probably would receive an assignment in the State Department.[48]

Geist rose to the occasion for a meeting with Assistant Secretary of State Adolf Berle Jr. Geist said that the German public was unhappy about the continuing war with the West (although there was no fighting to speak of on land), but it would follow the government for a long, long time. The army would not jettison Hitler. Geist told Berle the story of his meeting with Göring on October 9. He thought that Germany was preparing for a long war, and he feared the eventual incursion of communism into central Europe. It was impossible, he said firmly, to make peace with the Nazis: "There cannot be, he thinks, any peace in the world so long as that machine is still extant." Geist expected the British and French to struggle militarily. The United States probably would have to enter the war to prevent them from being wiped out. The alternative was to convert the United States into a giant military organism analogous to the German version to guard against German-Russian expansion. The next day, Berle wrote that Geist had no illusions about the extent of German and Russian dreams; they contemplated air bases and outposts pretty much all over the world.[49]

President Roosevelt already had asked to see Geist,[50] and he received a fifteen-minute appointment in the Oval Office on December 1, with Undersecretary Welles also present.[51] The best source on the worst problem in the world, Geist would have repeated at least the thrust of what he told Berle. The three men may have discussed the situation at the US Embassy in Berlin as well. If asked, Geist would have said that to make a strong impression upon Nazi officials, FDR would need to send someone more forceful than Kirk and preferably someone of higher standing. (FDR did send Welles on a trip to Berlin in late February and early March for a brief set of meetings with high Nazi officials.) They also may have discussed Geist's future role in Washington. That is a plausible projection of a discussion that left no written traces. In any case, this meeting with the president capped Geist's long and extraordinary Berlin mission.

It seems that Geist impressed the president or at least reinforced FDR's own thinking. One sign came when GM executive James Mooney, eager to bring his own message from Göring about better relations, met Roosevelt a few days before Christmas. According to Mooney, FDR disclaimed any desire to tell the Germans what they should do about Hitler and reminisced about his early contacts with Germany and Germans, but warned, "I wish Germany would pipe down about dominating the world."[52]

When he began work in the State Department, Geist would have found it easier psychologically to focus on some other area of the world. He had not forgotten the desperation of those Jews seeking to leave Germany. But the choice was not up to him. He was out of Berlin but not finished with Berlin.

CHAPTER FOURTEEN

FROM AFAR

G eist rented a fifteen-year-old two-story house near the Naval Observatory in northwest Washington, DC, three miles from the State Department building and close to a major bus route. Its advantages also had a flip side: It was very close to Massachusetts Avenue, one of the city's major arteries, and the site of many foreign embassies. It was not very private. And with Geist lived Erich Mainz, who had Anglicized his first name to Erick, and who probably occupied something between an attic and a loft above the second floor. On his alien registration form, Mainz listed his occupation as landscape gardener, an occupation that did not require any kind of license.[1]

Geist decided to adapt his Berlin household arrangements in the Washington area. Once Anna joined them she could manage the household and serve as hostess as she had done in Berlin. Geist acquired the embassy car he had used in Berlin (it was shipped over from Copenhagen), and, after only months in the District, he moved to a nice Maryland suburban residential area within walking distance of a small swim and tennis club, and not much farther from a small commercial center in Bethesda.[2] He bought or leased a brick colonial that had plenty of room for Anna and Erick.[3]

Although Geist's comfortable house was typical of the neighborhood (called Edgemoor), he lived near a mansion built by Walter J. Tuckerman, a local aristocrat who stemmed from Puritan settlers in Boston and others who had participated in the Boston Tea Party.

Tuckerman was the main developer of the neighborhood and president of a major Bethesda bank as well. Local real estate experts today believe that at the time a restrictive covenant barred sales in Edgemoor to Jews and other minorities. The most detailed history of Bethesda does not confirm this but does note that the area was becoming "whiter." In any case, Geist would have learned one way or another that he had not escaped all anti-Semitism when he left Berlin. One wonders how much effort he had to put in to mask his homosexual relationship with Mainz from relatively conservative neighbors who favored Wendell Willkie over FDR in the 1940 presidential elections.[4]

Geist did not have to worry financially. On March 27, the State Department had nominated him for a promotion to Foreign Service Officer Class 3, with a salary of $7,000, the equivalent of at least $123,000 today.[5] He had come a long way since the day when he had to drop out of high school to support his family.

On February 26, 1940, the State Department abolished the Consular Commercial Office and replaced it with a new Division of Commercial Affairs.[6] With years of experience dealing with the problems of US corporations in Germany, Geist became its first chief. His appointment was announced on April 2.[7]

On April 9, 1940, Germany launched successful invasions of Denmark and Norway. A month and a day later, Germany attacked the Netherlands and Belgium, opening the long-planned offensive to conquer France, a thrust that had been postponed twenty-nine times. Belgium surrendered on May 18. On May 19, aviator Charles Lindbergh, Geist's least favorite visitor to Berlin, gave a speech in New York broadcast nationally by CBS radio. In an address entitled "Our National Safety" he nominally called upon Americans to build up US military strength. But Lindbergh directly attacked the foreign policy of the Roosevelt administration as likely to bring about an unnecessary involvement in the European war: "We are in danger of war today not because European people have attempted to interfere with the internal affairs of America, but because American people have attempted to interfere with the internal affairs of Europe." He offered a vague, conspiratorial explanation for US overreaching: "There are powerful elements in America who desire us to take part. They represent a small minority of the American people, but they control much of the machinery of influence and propaganda. They seize every opportunity to push us closer to the edge."[8] Many of his listeners understood that "they" meant the Jews. Lindbergh boasted in his diary that telegrams ran twenty to one in favor of his speech; letters about fifteen to one.[9]

Two days after Lindbergh's speech, President Roosevelt said to his New York state neighbor, Secretary of the Treasury Henry Morgenthau Jr., "I am absolutely convinced that Lindbergh is a Nazi. If I should die tomorrow, I want you to know this." The German military attaché in Washington called Lindbergh's speech courageous and "the highest and most effective form of propaganda."[10]

Assistant Secretary of State Breckinridge Long authorized Geist to give speeches in Chicago, Memphis, Atlanta, Birmingham, and Charleston to local chambers of commerce and similar organizations about his experiences in Berlin.[11] They followed Lindbergh's nationally broadcast speech. In the political climate of 1940, with sharp clashes between internationalists and isolationists and a presidential election coming in the fall, Geist's experience in Berlin became politically relevant. His speaking ability was well known, and he could reach the business community.

In his speeches, Geist stressed the combined danger from Nazi Germany and the Soviet Union. He appealed to his audiences with the title of his basic speech: "Seven Years of Socialism under Adolf Hitler." The Charleston Chamber of Commerce and other local organizations opened his May 24 lecture to the public.[12] Geist had plenty of stories to tell.

Geist described his one direct contact with Hitler, a March 1, 1939, diplomatic dinner during the period when Geist served as chargé d'affaires. The foreign guests and high Nazi officials were so conscious of Hitler that they stared at him constantly, as if he were from Mars. He acted like a monarch proud of his distinction and contemptuous of all other mortals. He did not converse but carried on a passionate monologue. When he stopped, conversation ceased. With visiting foreign statesmen, Geist had heard, Hitler likewise monopolized meetings with speeches or harangues. Hitler's real power lay in his ability to "perpetuate the myth of his infallibility."[13]

In his speeches, Geist did not mince words but was selective. He did not discuss Nazi persecution of the Jews, let alone Hitler's January 30, 1939, threat to destroy all the Jews of Europe. That might have given ammunition to Lindbergh and others like him. Geist, rather, concentrated on what a presumably conservative American audience would care about. What he had seen in Germany was "not merely of interest historically," not just of "academic interest." Hitler's methods were "schemes which any group of politicians might seize upon here or anywhere else." Geist expressed his fear "that we have those among us who would gladly sacrifice their liberties for the kind of precarious security which Hitler provided."

When Geist spoke in Charleston on May 24, the German offensive in northern France had cut off French and British troops; the evacuation at Dunkirk began several days afterward.[14] The rapid defeat of France, which many had seen as ready and well fortified, shocked the world. Even supposedly experienced observers concluded that France's debacle had nonmilitary causes; years of Nazi propaganda and espionage, eating away at France's will and ability to fight, lay behind its collapse.[15]

Books, newspapers, and films already had stirred up many Americans about the domestic activities of the Nazis and their would-be American collaborators. Sinclair Lewis's 1935 best-selling novel *It Can't Happen Here* focused on the danger of domestic fascism. But one of the hottest newspaper stories of 1938 was the FBI's arrest of a German spy ring that had infiltrated some parts of the American defense industry. The case prompted Warner Brothers to produce a thinly fictionalized version in 1939; it was titled *Confessions of a Nazi Spy*, starring Edward G. Robinson. This hit film stressed Germany's global objectives, identified the German American Bund as the prime agent of Germany in the United States, and warned the American public about the danger of Nazi espionage. Commercial success spurred repeated Hollywood imitations over the next several years.[16]

Fears of Nazi activity in the United States spread in 1940 even among knowledgeable State Department officials, some of whom also worried about the upcoming 1940 presidential election. Assistant Secretary of State Adolf Berle Jr., one of Geist's superiors, became convinced that some subversives were hiding among German refugees. Messersmith, only recently appointed ambassador to Cuba, allegedly found cases where Nazi officials tried to make use of German Jewish refugees in Havana through threats against their relatives in Germany. Undersecretary Welles asked Breckinridge Long (in charge of the Special War Problems Division), whose portfolio included the Visa Division, to tighten scrutiny of immigrants. With little restraint from above and with his own unhealthy paranoia about foreigners, Long set about the task of curtailing immigration from Germany. Long wrote in his diary about protecting national security by preventing the influx of aliens. He also wanted to put tighter checks on aliens in the United States and pushed for the transfer of Immigration and Naturalization from the Labor Department to the Justice Department.[17]

President Roosevelt still weighed whether to run for an unprecedented third term and needed to counter a plethora of isolationist opponents inside and outside the Republican Party. Critics such as Democratic New Dealer senator Burton Wheeler of Montana declared their opposition to being dragged into a war against fascism in Europe.[18] Roosevelt responded by trying to persuade Americans that Germany was a direct threat to the United States itself, warning that the Nazis were applying Trojan-horse tactics. Some senators and congressmen were even more alarmist, all of which explains why, in a June 1940 Roper poll, only 2.7 percent of Americans thought their government was properly handling the Nazi danger. In July 1940, another poll indicated that 70 percent of Americans believed that the Nazis already had begun to organize a fifth column in the United States.[19]

If asked, Geist would have been among the vast majority. He long had expressed concern about Nazi propaganda and espionage in the United States. In January 1934, he had written a lengthy despatch about nominally independent Germans, such as his former Harvard professor Friedrich Schönemann, who had returned to live in Germany, getting visas to visit the United States to spread pro-Nazi propaganda. He feared that such visitors, secretly financed by the Nazi government, would at a minimum cause tumult and disorder. He wondered if consuls could be instructed not to grant visas to pro-Nazi propagandists. But in his comment on Geist's memorandum, Ambassador Dodd thought the chance of any Nazi agents achieving results threatening civil liberties and the Constitution was very remote. In 1934, the State Department declined to use against Nazi-subsidized visitors a regulation that allowed consuls to bar visas to anyone who constituted a danger to public safety.[20]

In June 1940, however, Assistant Secretary Long told consuls to grant immigration visas to Germans only if those officials had no doubt whatsoever concerning applicants. He urged consuls to require more evidence to support visa applications, setting off a process that would, in Long's own words, postpone, postpone, postpone.[21] Consuls did not fully or immediately comply with guidance from Washington; they already had nearly filled the immigration quota for 1940. But they sharply reduced use of the German quota in much of 1941. This move kept some Nazis out of the United States but also prevented many legitimate refugees from coming.

Eventually, the State Department and Congress, which passed a bill to bar those who might threaten public safety, tried to preclude visa applicants with close relatives in Germany or the Soviet Union, even though the former were overwhelmingly opposed to Nazi Germany. Long and his Visa Division subordinates took a sledgehammer to the visa practices Geist had built up and overseen for the preceding five years.[22] Apart from the inhumanity of this cutback, Geist knew that this was not an effective way to combat espionage and propaganda.

Geist reported to both Berle and Long.[23] Long asked him to carry out a study of the food situation in Europe because Herbert Hoover, another isolationist, was criticizing both the Americans and the British for widespread civilian suffering. Geist, however, concluded that supplies of food in Europe were satisfactory.[24]

Berle oversaw a State Department unit called the Division of Foreign Activity Correlation, State's main intelligence organization during the war. In his August 28 diary entry, Berle complained about US companies in South America using Germans who engaged in anti-American propaganda. This followed an alleged secret order from

Hitler to Propaganda Ministry officials to prepare for war against the United States. Berle wrote that Geist would take charge of the effort to weed out such people and counter pro-Nazi activities.[25]

Geist increasingly spent time examining actual or potential Nazi agents and deciding which businessmen operating abroad could not be trusted. Geist understood the welter of Nazi organizations, and, beyond that, he was well connected with Germans who had come to the United States. He had multiple sources, and he was good at interviewing those under scrutiny. Some of what he did fit into his assigned mandate of commercial affairs, but, as in Berlin, he also engaged in intelligence and counterintelligence work. He became a senior adviser deployed when and where needed.

Geist judged people based on what he knew or could learn about them, not by stereotypes. Jakob Goldschmidt, a fifty-year-old German Jewish former banker, lived at the Savoy Plaza Hotel in New York. His lavish lifestyle and continuing connection with German industrialist Fritz Thyssen, who once had supported Hitler, raised suspicions. Thyssen claimed to have fled Germany for France to avoid a concentration camp. So, the real issue for the United States was its attitude toward Thyssen, who apparently wanted a visa to the United States. A State Department special agent reported that most German Jewish refugees in New York regarded Goldschmidt as a traitor to his people.[26] Geist withheld judgment about Goldschmidt but did not mark him as an agent of any kind. Thyssen, however, did not receive a visa.

Asked about Irving Sherman, an American Jewish banker who had worked in Berlin for years, Geist took a clear stand, writing that he had maintained contacts with high Reichsbank officials, but *not* with Nazi leaders. Geist said Sherman did not collaborate with the regime but merely represented his company well: "I always found him truthful and reliable and had a great deal of confidence in his general appraisal of the German situation. . . . I never had the slightest cause to doubt his patriotism. . . . He [Sherman] was not impressed by the temporary success of the Nazi program," showing extraordinary political acumen for a banker.[27] Not an endorsement of bankers, but certainly one of Sherman.

In mid-June 1940, Edmund Stinnes, a native German industrialist based in Switzerland, came to the United States nominally to expedite production of aircraft and other munitions for Britain. Stinnes claimed that he wanted to become a US citizen. But he intended to see the German consul general in New York and told the FBI that he would pass along anything useful. After that meeting, Stinnes called Geist to say that Nazi Germany was planning an air assault on Britain to last three or four days, or longer if necessary, to vanquish the British air force and gain mastery of the air. A land and sea offensive would follow. Stinnes said this campaign could begin at any moment. He believed that if the British could withstand the air assault for six or seven weeks, it would put Germany in an unfavorable position. Another participant at Stinnes's meeting with the German consul general, German commercial attaché Gerhard Westrick, claimed to be the personal representative of Foreign Minister Ribbentrop. After a German conquest of Britain, Westrick expected to direct German trade negotiations with the United States. This was very good intelligence. But at a time when many Americans found it impossible to distinguish between Nazis and Germans, could one trust Stinnes, whose wife and daughter were still in Switzerland? He was playing a difficult game by meeting almost simultaneously with Nazi officials and Americans.[28]

Geist had deep background. He knew that Stinnes, the son of Germany's most famous industrialist in the 1920s, was a Quaker, a former member of the Rotary Club of Berlin, and one of his and Messersmith's sources in the early years of the Nazi regime. Known as the black sheep in a conservative family, Stinnes had married the sister of Gero von Schulze-Gaevernitz, a naturalized US citizen.[29] But Stinnes had said that Germany would prefer to have Britain make peace on terms favorable to Germany, and Geist did not believe Hitler would stop short of total victory. Therefore, in reporting to the ever-suspicious Long, Geist was quite cautious, allowing that Stinnes could be serving German, rather than British, interests, but accepting his claim that a massive air assault on Britain was forthcoming. The Battle of Britain, as it became known, began on July 10.

Stinnes followed up, telling Geist about the propaganda activities of a nominally private New York–based office called the German

Library of Information, located in Battery Park. It published a magazine, *Facts in Review*, that was distributed for free to people all over the United States thought to be friendly to Germany. The June 24 issue of *Facts in Review* explained France's defeat and request for an armistice as the result of Germany's overwhelming military superiority and Britain's failure to supply France with enough military help. It twisted news events into sophisticated propaganda.[30]

Geist sent Stinnes's exposé to Berle's chief assistant, who asked the FBI to investigate the German Library. J. Edgar Hoover ordered surveillance of Dr. Matthias Schmitz, director of the library, and two of his assistants. This produced evidence of their subversive activities. Under legal pressure, Schmitz claimed that the library was a German government agency with diplomatic immunity. The State Department feared that it could not prohibit such official propaganda when pro-Allied institutions were engaged in similar efforts. Instead, it clamped down on the number of German employees at the library and limited their stay in the United States. In December 1941, the German declaration of war against the United States terminated the library and all other official German government posts in the United States.[31]

In September 1940, Geist reported that German naval attaché Helmut Rauber tracked the departures of ships taking munitions and war-related equipment from US ports to Britain; Rauber's data went to German U-boats in the Atlantic. Geist told Berle that Ulrich Freiherr von Gienanth, second secretary at the Embassy, and an employee named Fritz Wagner, met frequently at Wagner's home in Chevy Chase, Maryland; one or both had Gestapo connections, and they were up to no good. Berle asked the FBI to investigate both cases discreetly, without violating the Germans' diplomatic immunity.[32] The FBI found that von Gienanth had boasted to one of his girlfriends in Manhattan that he was the second-highest Gestapo official in the United States.[33]

Geist learned that the thirty-three-year-old von Gienanth formally worked for the Propaganda Ministry. His Gestapo claim was misleading, but he did work on intelligence and security issues as a junior SS officer, with a rank equivalent to that of a second lieutenant, and he held a position in the SD. Geist would, however, have been surprised to learn that in 1935 his friend/foe Werner Best had persuaded Himmler to bring von Gienanth, who had entered the Foreign Service, into the SS. In 1931–1932, von Gienanth had spent a year as an exchange student at Johns Hopkins University, and he knew the United States better than virtually anyone in the SS.[34]

Geist reported on the Nazis in Boston, too. Thirty-four-year-old Dr. Herbert Scholz, the consul general in Boston, was Himmler's close friend and an SS officer. (He allegedly was von Gienanth's superior in the Gestapo.) He had instructions to watch over German diplomats and consular officials in the United States to ensure their political reliability. Scholz reportedly was dissatisfied with the lukewarm attitude of the German chargé d'affaires, Hans Thomsen, and the anti-Nazi views of his wife. (Thomsen repeatedly cautioned Berlin against a vigorous program of clandestine warfare in the United States.) Berle sent blind copies of Geist's report to the War Department, the FBI, and the Office of Naval Intelligence. Technically, Scholz, an SS colonel, was in the SD, rather than the Gestapo, but by this time both of these two similar organizations were elements of the Reich Security Main Office. He flew a big flag with a swastika outside the four-story townhouse he occupied on Chestnut Street in Beacon Hill.[35]

In short, Geist tracked real Nazi agents, and his batting average was good. He generally did not disclose his sources, but one of his best was a former German consul general named Paul Schwarz, who was Jewish or of Jewish origin. In March 1933, when Schwarz was German consul general in New York, the German Foreign Office had suggested that he resign. He refused to return to Germany, went to Canada, and emigrated from there to the United States. He got a job as a stockbroker in New York although he had no experience. On the side, he helped to place German Jewish refugees.[36] By the late 1930s, Schwarz wrote a column for the anti-Nazi *New Yorker Staats-Zeitung*, edited by Bernard Ridder (later prominent in the Knight Ridder media firm). Schwarz became an American citizen in 1939. He was an extremely good source of intelligence because he maintained contact with German diplomats whom he had known for many years.[37]

Schwarz helped to supply evidence about the Transocean News Service, which spread Nazi propaganda in the United States and in

Latin America, coordinating its activities with the German Embassy and various consulates in the United States. The State Department's Division of European Affairs worried about its activities and influence in South America, calling it "a veritable plague of locusts." The Justice Department eventually prosecuted (and convicted) Transocean for failing to comply with the Foreign Agents Registration Act.[38]

Geist proposed to send Schwarz to South America to write newspaper articles, and, more important, to gather information about pro-Nazi activities there, in part from German diplomats. Moffat, who highly respected Geist, might have gone along with this proposal, but by this time he had become minister to Canada. The new chief of European Affairs, Ray Atherton, did not like this idea at all. When Berle asked Geist and Atherton to discuss the matter, Geist refused to back down. Atherton summarized their conversation politely but wrote a memo designed to sabotage State Department use of Schwarz. Berle then decided to leave such missions to the FBI.[39]

Atherton gave plausible reasons to object to the use of Schwarz, but, reading between the lines, one can see that Atherton was not convinced of the loyalty of a former German diplomat and German Jew. Geist's strong support of Schwarz did not endear him to Atherton. All in all, Geist learned that his unsurpassed expertise on Nazi Germany did not carry weight with entrenched bureaucrats with their own priorities and concerns. Perhaps it also mattered that Geist was not socially part of the club in the Division of European Affairs.

Geist had numerous discussions about the activities of General Motors in Latin America and in Europe.[40] One of his more interesting cases involved a report, passed along by a US consul in Europe, that James Mooney, formerly head of the GM Overseas Corporation, had had suspect negotiations in Paris with a German businessman named Eduard Winter. Geist dispelled the confusion. He did not believe that Winter was acting as a GM agent in Paris. He knew that Mooney did not trust Winter when he was in business in Berlin, and it was unlikely that Mooney had changed his mind about him. Besides, Mooney no longer ran GM Overseas Corporation, but was currently working on GM's defense production. Geist added that Messersmith viewed Mooney as dangerous, an appeaser of the first order. Geist thought him an unreliable meddler in things he did not really understand: "Mr. Mooney . . . [sees] no sense whatever in the present war . . . both parties should be compelled to make peace so that business could go on as usual."[41]

From Havana, Messersmith characterized the danger that Mooney posed, through his business connections in Germany and promotion of isolationism at home. He was "one of those Irishmen who is so against England that he would be prepared to see the whole world go down in order to satisfy his feelings with respect to England. In my opinion, he is as mad as any Nazi and is one of those who nourishes the hope that when the United States may turn Fascist he will be our Quisling or our Laval." Messersmith told Berle's assistant that Mooney had "several screws loose." Mooney had angered State Department officials by foolishly trying to serve as a peacemaker between Roosevelt and Hitler and interfering with Sumner Welles's visit to Berlin in March 1940, but Geist was closer to the mark in his assessment of Mooney than was Messersmith.[42]

After Germany declared war on the United States in December 1941, the American government shut all German diplomatic and consular facilities, interned German officials, and firmly cracked down on remaining German espionage activities. The FBI also ordered the Immigration and Naturalization Service to detain more than four thousand German and Italian aliens, as well as some American citizens sympathetic to Germany and identified as security threats.[43] The next year, the FBI captured a ring of Nazi saboteurs trying to damage US infrastructure; a military tribunal ordered the execution of six of them.[44]

Geist obtained information and located witnesses for the Justice Department's prosecution and conviction of American pro-Nazi propagandist George Sylvester Viereck.[45] Viereck, who had run a publishing firm based in New Jersey, was convicted of violating the Foreign Agents Registration Act in a case appealed all the way to the Supreme Court in 1943. He served three years in prison, but his sentence was overturned after the war.

Geist's domestic oversight activities diminished as time passed, but he still occasionally judged the attitudes of individuals, both inside and outside Germany, whose standing and attitudes toward the Nazi regime were uncertain. In December 1942, Leland Harrison, US minister in Switzerland, sought information about Carl Goerdeler, who recently had visited Switzerland and *might* be a key figure among military and industrial factions secretly planning to overthrow Hitler. Harrison asked what Messersmith and Geist knew about him. In spite of the fact that Goerdeler had held a government position (as price controller) until 1937, Geist endorsed him fully. Goerdeler was known as a moderate and a man of upright character. In discussions with Messersmith, he recognized the dangers and evils of the Nazi regime. Although his visits abroad were approved by the government, he was on the side of the opposition, Geist was convinced. Geist did not see Goerdeler as an active plotter in a coup but as a man who could prepare and organize respectable Germans to take power afterward. Again, Geist read what seemed to be conflicting evidence with sure eyes. Goerdeler was among the anti-Nazi resisters executed after the July 20, 1944, failed coup and assassination attempt on Hitler.[46]

In 1942, Geist stepped up his public and commercial appearances. At a speech to the National Foreign Trade Convention in Boston in October 1942, Geist defended the guiding principles of US foreign policy. Gone were the days when the United States could simply go its own way, disregarding the interests of other countries. With the fate of civilization hanging on the outcome of the war, the United States had forged a coalition of nations and peoples "committed to the survival of freedom and the advancement of civilization." The United States and the United Nations (the contemporary term for the Allies) had a big advantage over the Axis powers and collaborators: "The commitments of the latter are worthless; their diplomacy consists of deceitful manoeuvers; the assurances and pledges of their ambassadors and ministers are false and delusive."[47]

One of Geist's more important speeches was delivered at the May 1942 convention of the National Conference of Christians and Jews held at the Hotel Washington on 15th Street in the District of Columbia, a large beaux arts building within a short walk of his State Department office. By this time, Geist had learned to hew to wartime

policies, constraints, and areas of emphasis. Full of rhetorical flour-
ishes, his speech gave out few details of Nazi policies. The Department
of State, however, considered the speech important enough to issue to
the public as a press release.[48]

Geist offered his audience a loose version of what historians later
described as the theory of a "special German path" of development,
which allowed Hitler to gain widespread obedience among Germans.
Geist praised antecedents of rational and enlightened civilization
from ancient Athens to England's Magna Carta; Germany had ignored them. The Four Freedoms, which Roosevelt had proclaimed as
incontestable rights of mankind, were denied to the Germans.

Under more favorable circumstances, Geist explained, the Social
Democrats and the Catholic Center Party might have led Germans
during the Weimar Republic to realize political freedom like that
which Americans enjoyed, but nationalist, militarist, and aristocratic
forces kept hate and the desire for aggression alive, and Hitler drew
politically upon those sentiments. The Nazis concealed their pagan-
ism until it was too late for religious Germans—Protestants, Catholics, and Jews—to find common cause.

Geist had earlier written that Germans had flocked to support Hitler, at least until World War II began. But Geist now described millions of Germans aghast at early repressive measures against thousands
carried off to torture and death. The State Department and Office of
War Information (and the president) hoped to drive a wedge between
the German public and the Nazi regime, and Geist's speech fit into
that effort. Similarly, Geist described Nazi anti-Semitism without revealing its ideological depth or its level of support among Germans.
Conversely, he stressed that Hitler had merely delayed his sporadic war
against both Catholic and Protestant churches; they were doomed.

Geist denounced as unfounded Hitler's claims that German Jews
had offended the social order and German way of life. No other group
had contributed proportionately more to German renown, progress,
and greatness, Geist said. The abnormal brain of Hitler and his machine
had disenfranchised, humiliated, despoiled, tortured, murdered, and
finally deported Jews, despite the absence of popular anti-Semitism,

Geist declared. He called Hitler's anti-Semitism primarily political. Racial ideology, he stated (deviating from longstanding views), was a sop for Hitler's untutored followers, but also a cover for the Nazi purpose of seizing all Jewish wealth.

Many officials in the Roosevelt administration who spoke publicly about Nazi persecution during the war did so in general terms. They feared that Allied emphasis on Nazi persecution of the Jews might complicate Allied psychological warfare designed to weaken German loyalty to the regime, as well as to counter support for Germany in other parts of the world. Roosevelt waited until July 1942 to publicly condemn savage Nazi measures against Jews. Instead, administration officials looked for universal terms such as the Nazi assault on civilization.[49] It was not a coincidence that the title of Geist's talk was "Masters of Bigotry: Treason against the Human Race." Geist offered far less information about the Holocaust than he privately had forecast in December 1938 or in April 1939. He conformed to the administration's view of what should and should not be explained to the American public during an all-out war whose outcome still was in doubt.

In the fall of 1941, the Embassy in Berlin had sent to Washington a series of reports about new and sharper Nazi measures against German Jews. Forced to wear a yellow Jewish star with the word *Jude* in black letters, thousands of Jews were deported in contingents with a minimum of belongings either to the Lublin area or ghettos in Lodz and Warsaw.[50] A mid-November report suggested that many of those deported were dying—"being exterminated"—either from cold, starvation, disease, or outright massacre. It also summarized some of Goebbels's propaganda blaming the war on the Jews and threatening retribution. Goebbels alluded to Hitler's speech of January 30, 1939, in which he threatened the annihilation of the Jews of Europe, saying that Hitler's prophecy would be fulfilled.[51] Geist already knew that the Nazis would try to do so.

CHAPTER FIFTEEN

INDIRECT INFLUENCE

The first Nazi gassing program targeted Germans with serious mental and physical disabilities considered hereditary. Shortly after the war began, Hitler privately authorized their killing. He did not want to issue a law, fearing adverse public reaction, and a number of doctors wanted some form of authorization before they would dispose of patients, mostly in institutions.[1] They granted what they called "merciful deaths" to the "incurably ill," making it seem like euthanasia. Hitler's personal chancellery used codenames and euphemisms to veil this extensive process that murdered at least seventy-five thousand people through August 1941, but Geist found out about it anyway.

The Embassy in Berlin sent the State Department a series of reports about this Nazi "euthanasia" program. The author of the first embassy despatch, George F. Kennan (later, father of the Cold War containment policy), received at least some of his information from American journalists based in Berlin and in Switzerland, and from anti-Nazi resistance leader Helmuth James von Moltke.[2] Geist received copies of all the incoming euthanasia reports from the Embassy, not because they came within his sphere of responsibility for commercial affairs, but because officials in Germany and in Washington knew of his expertise and interest.[3]

One of Geist's friends, Sigrid Schultz of the *Chicago Tribune*, sent him occasional news from Berlin after he moved to Washington.[4] By the time Schultz returned to the United States in early 1941, she had gained a great deal of knowledge about the Nazi euthanasia program. She had located its administrative headquarters at Tiergartenstrasse 4. Schultz knew that Hitler's personal physician Karl Brandt and Philipp Bouhler of Hitler's private chancellery ran the program, and she mistakenly thought Heinrich Himmler was responsible as well. She did not want to publish this story under her name because she was going back to Germany.[5] But during her stay in Connecticut she likely would have given Geist this information one way or another.

Around the same time, the Embassy in Berlin sent to Washington a copy and translation of a letter written by Theophil Wurm, the Evangelical bishop of Württemberg, to the Reich minister of justice. It was a protest against the secret euthanasia killings. Consul General Samuel Honaker in Stuttgart, who had worked with Geist for many years, managed to acquire a copy of Wurm's letter, and Geist asked Assistant Secretary Long to read it.[6]

Such information about Nazi euthanasia (and exaggerated rumors about it) spread to higher levels in Washington and conditioned the US government's response to an unusual wartime request from the German military attaché in Washington. German doctors had diagnosed the son of General Friedrich von Boetticher as schizophrenic; in the mid-1930s, while living in Germany, the son also was indicted for treason. His father was able to quash these proceedings, but a separate German government decree ordered the son to report for compulsory sterilization. Since 1933, German law had authorized sterilization as treatment for persons with disabilities labeled genetic in origin. The younger Boetticher joined his father in the United States to avoid that procedure. When Germany declared war on the United States in December 1941, he was being treated in a psychiatric hospital in Towson, Maryland.[7]

During a meeting of the president's cabinet on December 19, Attorney General Francis Biddle mentioned that General Boetticher had requested "that his insane son be allowed to stay in a hospital in this country to prevent his being chloroformed if he were sent back to Germany." FDR then told the cabinet that the Nazi regime was doing away with wounded German soldiers on the battlefields and with the elderly generally. The president tended to absorb (imperfectly) what others passed on to him if it reinforced his view that the Nazis threatened all of humanity.[8]

Journalist William L. Shirer tried to bring the actual Nazi euthanasia killings to the attention of the American public in 1941, mentioning in his stories the possible use of poison gas. But Shirer failed to galvanize the media and the public. Even if the story were true, the victims seemed socially marginal. In a war for the survival of Western civilization, the fate of institutionalized German patients did not arouse strong emotions among most US readers.[9]

The Nazi euthanasia program served as a trial for methods of gassing later used against Jews, even if the first stage of what is now called the Holocaust involved mass shootings in the east. One way or another, Geist heard reports about multiple Nazi executions of Jews following the German invasion of the Soviet Union. He probably learned more than was published in US newspapers. But his sources in the Embassy and consulates then vanished. Germany's declaration of war after Pearl Harbor resulted in the automatic shutdown of the Embassy and US consulates in the country. Later reports about Nazi mass killings of Jews came from US outposts in nearby countries, particularly Switzerland. Geist was not in the regular State Department distribution chain for information about Nazi anti-Jewish policies.[10] Consequently, he was not informed when a report about the second Nazi gassing program arrived in Washington in August 1942.

The original telegram was stark.

Received alarming report stating that in Fuehrers headquarters a plan has been discussed and being under consideration according which total of Jews in countries occupied controlled by Germany numbering three and half to four millions should after deportation and concentrated be at one blow exterminated in order resolve once and for all Jewish question in Europe STOP Action is reported to be planned for autumn ways of execution still discussed STOP It has been spoken of prussic acid STOP In transmitting information with all necessary reservation as exactitude cannot be controlled by us beg to state that informer is reported to have close connections with highest German authorities and his reports to be generally reliable.

Gerhart Riegner, a Berlin lawyer who had settled in Switzerland after Nazi discrimination made it impossible for him to practice in Germany, drafted this telegram. As the representative of the World Jewish Congress in Switzerland, the Geneva-based Riegner sent regular reports to his superiors about Nazi killing of Jews.[11] This time, he wanted to reach Western governments and top World Jewish Congress officials as quickly and as safely as possible. He knew that the British and US consulates in Geneva could communicate securely with London and Washington through coded telegrams.

A British vice consul agreed to send one telegram to the Foreign Office for Sidney Silverman, chairman of the British section of the World Jewish Congress and a member of Parliament. The telegram to Silverman contained an instruction at the end: "Inform and consult New York." That reference to New York meant Rabbi Stephen Wise, head of the American Jewish Congress and the most prominent American Jewish leader. Riegner judged that the British Foreign Office would deliver a telegram to an MP, but he feared that the State Department might not send it to Wise. Having Silverman send the information to Wise was his backup plan.[12]

Riegner convinced US vice consul Howard Elting Jr. in Geneva to send his telegram to the US Legation in Bern, but Elting warned that higher-ups might discount the report and refuse to send it to Wise. The US Legation in Bern indeed was skeptical and said so in a cover despatch but telegraphed it to Washington anyway.[13]

Riegner's information did not resonate in the State Department. Paul Culbertson, assistant chief of the Division of European Affairs, drafted a letter to Wise discounting Riegner's telegram as one of many unreliable war rumors then circulating in Europe. Another official, Elbridge Durbrow, however, wrote "Do not send" (to Rabbi Wise). He thought that it would be unfair to the American public to spread stories of this kind unless officials had tried to obtain confirmation.

Furthermore, his draft response to the Legation directed it not to send future stories like this for dissemination to third parties (such as Wise). The sharp rebuke of the Legation was deleted from the final response but the short first paragraph remained: "In view of the apparently unsubstantiated nature of the information . . . and your skeptical comment[,] the Department has not conveyed the message suggested." Ray Atherton, chief of the Division of European Affairs, initialed the final version, and Undersecretary Welles initialed it on behalf of Secretary of State Hull.[14] Durbrow provided the dominant view in European Affairs: "It does not appear advisable in view of the Legation's comments, the fantastic nature of the allegation, and the impossibility of our being of any assistance if such [Nazi] action were taken, to transmit the information to Dr. Stephen Wise as suggested."[15]

On August 29, however, Silverman telegraphed Riegner's information to Wise. A condensed London-to-New-York version of Riegner's telegram conveyed the same horrific message. On September 2, Wise rushed to Washington and gave it to Undersecretary of State Welles. Welles, who had seen the longer version several weeks earlier, consulted the officials of European Affairs, who completely discounted the report of a Nazi plan for mass murder. They argued that the Nazis were putting Jews deported to the east to work. Welles accepted this plausible opinion: Why should they waste valuable labor? Wise asked Welles, "May we feel reassured?" Welles responded cautiously, "Who can tell, seeing that you are dealing with that madman [Hitler]?" He asked Wise not to publicize Riegner's cable until the State Department had thoroughly investigated the evidence of a Nazi program to kill millions.[16]

Welles must have seen the political risks. The high level of anti-Semitism in the United States and in other Western countries made it hard for many to feel sympathy for foreign Jews. Nazi propaganda constantly stressed that the Allies were fighting Germany only because of those people.[17] The US government and particularly the State Department were loath to emphasize Nazi crimes against the Jews. And the story was incredible in the sense of impossible to believe. Even if it should turn out to be true, it would have, they believed, nothing to do with winning the war. Were the story to gain publicity and credibility, Jewish groups would criticize the United States for doing nothing about it. These were among the reasons for the State Department to sit on the Riegner telegram.

As a matter of course, Riegner's telegram did not go to Geist in the Division of Commercial Affairs. Someone would have had to channel it to him because of his expertise—he was one of the greatest experts in the world on Nazi Germany. But he had no rank or title to confirm his hard-won experience. Geist's past efforts on behalf of German Jews made him suspect with some officials, and he was not on good terms with Atherton, chief of the Division of European Affairs.

To his credit, Undersecretary Welles asked US diplomats in Switzerland to gather as much information as they could. But that took months. During the interim, Welles could conceivably have spoken to Geist about the story, but there is no evidence that he did. In late November 1942, after other supporting evidence came to Washington, Welles told Wise that the available information "confirmed his deepest fears," and he encouraged Wise to publicize the story. But Welles was not willing to go public with his view, and he chose to bypass European Affairs, having taken in its negative stance.

Wise held a press conference about the Nazi "final solution of the Jewish question," announcing that the Nazis already had killed about two million Jews as part of their campaign to exterminate every Jew still alive in Europe. The *New York Herald Tribune* ran a front-page story, and the Associated Press gave it major coverage, too. The more cautious *New York Times* gave it modest space on page ten; the *Washington Post* put it on page six. News released by a private citizen did not carry official weight, even though Wise alluded to State Department confirmation of the information. State Department officials reacted badly to the stories, denying any confirmation and referring questioners to Wise.[18]

In retrospect, most major newspapers underplayed the story, but State Department officials still complained about a flood of mail to the president and to their own department. Petitioners wanted, among other things, a joint declaration denouncing Nazi barbarism, the opening of Palestine to a higher level of Jewish immigration, and the removal of barriers to the immigration of Jewish children to the United States.[19] Such wartime objectives were unpopular in the State Department.

In January 1943, Riegner tried again. He and his colleague Richard Lichtheim spoke with Consul Paul Squire at the US Consulate in Geneva, telling him about Nazi mass executions in occupied Poland. The daily rate was six thousand at one site, according to multiple sources. A certain number of Jews were spared and sent to labor camps. Deportations to the killing areas continued. By the end of March, one source claimed, no Jews would be left in Berlin or Prague. Riegner and Lichtheim hoped that the US government could use the information, but they at least wanted to get it to Rabbi Wise. This time, Minister Leland Harrison, having carried out one investigation for Welles already, considered the message of great interest, and he sent it on to Washington earmarked for Welles.[20]

Elbridge Durbrow claimed that Wise had misrepresented information he had received from the State Department earlier. Actually, he had received it separately through Silverman and Welles. Durbrow wanted Wise to know that the earlier case was a courtesy and an exception to normal practice. Atherton added that the Division of European Affairs was in a predicament because of the many requests for "official data." Durbrow drafted another telegram to Bern, discouraging the Legation from accepting reports for transmission to private parties. Allegedly, the Swiss might see this as a violation of their censorship. It was a thin excuse, but Welles signed off on this new instruction to the Legation in Bern.[21] European Affairs tried to shut down the flow of Holocaust-related information from Jewish sources in Switzerland. Again, as far as we can tell, no one consulted Geist about the accuracy or plausibility of the information.

By the spring of 1943, US proponents of some sort of government response to Nazi mass killings of Jews began to gain traction in the media and with segments of the public. In a May 4 speech, Assistant Secretary of State Berle—probably Geist's most important direct superior—expressed the canonical State Department view that only the invasion of Europe, the defeat of German arms, and the breaking of German power could stop the mass murder of civilians. But military victory would not come quickly, and that meant Nazi killings of Jews would continue unabated. The Allies still lacked the capacity to intervene militarily, but nonmilitary options ranging from information warfare to encouragement of neutral countries to take in refugees were within the realm of the possible. Media, administration, and congressional advocates of humanitarian action began to coalesce, reaching a critical mass in the fall. The Treasury Department, aided by one or more State Department insiders, began to build a case that the State Department and the British government were systematically obstructing rescue and relief measures on behalf of European Jews. As a result, on January 22, 1944, President Roosevelt established a new organization called the War Refugee Board to try to save the lives of those civilians persecuted and threatened by the Nazis and their allies.[22] It was a serious defeat for the State Department, all the more because Breckinridge Long lost control of the Special War Problems Division.

Long never recovered from his late-1943 testimony before Congress; he had claimed that the United States had admitted some 580,000 refugees, an exaggeration of at least 250 percent.[23] He had failed to consult Geist, who had intimate knowledge of visas and the process of immigration, nor, apparently, had he consulted State Department records. After Long's mistake was exposed, Congressman Emanuel Celler demanded his resignation. That took a while, but Long retired from the State Department in late 1944.

Out of the loop on refugee issues, Geist kept busy with uncontroversial State Department matters and bided his time. In mid-1943, Geist became chief of the State Department's Division of Communications and Records, which was in shambles. Within a short time he was able to lift morale and introduce new organizing principles for incoming documents. Whether he originated the new system or followed the suggestions of Miss Margaret K. Odell, on loan from the Remington Rand corporation, is unclear. Messersmith asked Berle to retain Geist in this job beyond his scheduled three-year stay in Washington, and Berle added his own praise.[24] But for someone who had dealt directly with Himmler, Heydrich, and Best, this lateral step must have seemed a disappointment.

Geist had not given up hope of dealing with Germany again,[25] but for the time being he had to exercise influence indirectly. The Office of Strategic Services, the forerunner of the CIA, used Geist as an occasional consultant. Someone with a sense of humor gave Geist the codename "Holy" since one meaning of *Geist* in German is spirit. He supplied information that seems to have helped Allen Dulles in Switzerland exploit one his best informants, Fritz Kolbe, an anti-Nazi German Foreign Office official who traveled frequently to Switzerland. Kolbe turned over copies of a massive number of German Foreign Office documents to Dulles. He supplied prime intelligence about Nazi policies outside Germany.[26]

In October 1943, Geist would have read, one way or another, of an astonishing story of Jews escaping from a roundup carried out by the Gestapo and Danish collaborators. Many Danes aimed to frustrate the seizure of their countrymen, and Danish fishermen helped ferry about 7,500 Jews to Sweden, which took them in. The central and mysterious figure in these events was Geist's old friend and foe Werner Best.

After repeated clashes with Heydrich, Best had departed from the Reich Security Main Office. In November 1942, Hitler appointed him Reich plenipotentiary in Denmark, formally the top post in the German occupation. Denmark received the lightest and most favorable treatment of all territories conquered and occupied by Germany, partly because of the Nazi appreciation of "Nordic" racial kinship, partly because of Germany's needs for agricultural imports and Denmark's willingness to do business. Best wanted to continue this cooperation, leaving the Danish government in place to conduct domestic policies.

Although the United States had done little up to October 1943 to try to bring about wartime rescue of Jews, on December 17, 1942, the Allied governments had issued a formal statement denouncing Hitler's policy of exterminating the Jews of Europe and threatening punishment of those who helped to carry it out. It reminded Nazi leaders of what they believed anyway—that Jews had powerful influence in the West, and that the fate of Europe's Jews mattered in Western capitals.[27] Best had multiple reasons for his less-than-stringent policies in Denmark, but he had to be aware that Germany's war situation was deteriorating.

When Danish resisters carried out acts of sabotage in the summer of 1943, German military commander General Hermann von Hanneken blamed Best for exercising too light a hand. Declaring a state of emergency on August 29, Hanneken disarmed the Danish armed forces and took the soldiers prisoner. The Danish government resigned. Hanneken, however, shunned direct German military rule, which was likely to irritate the Danish population further. Still an SS officer, Best complained to Himmler about Hanneken, trying to get the SS's backing against the military.[28]

Best knew that Hitler invariably blamed resistance and sabotage on Jews and their sympathizers, and the Jews of Denmark were still untouched. Best decided on disparate initiatives. He asked the permanent secretaries of the Danish ministries to operate as an informal council, more or less substituting for the Danish government. He asked Hitler, through the German Foreign Office, to let him "resolve" the Jewish question in Denmark. He asked Himmler to send him more police, which would let him operate with greater autonomy from the German military. Best's September 8 telegram to Hitler calling for a resolution of the Jewish question in Denmark was the expression of a delicate balancing act.[29]

Then, after Hitler approved the "final solution" of the Jewish question in Denmark, two of Best's key associates, Georg Duckwitz and Paul Kanstein, quickly backtracked. Duckwitz, German naval attaché in Copenhagen, had a long-established connection with Denmark and many ties with Danish politicians, particularly the Social Democrats. Although he was personally close to Best, he was horrified by this order. He notified two Danish Social Democrats and tried to smooth the way for Sweden to admit Danish Jews who could make it across the sound to Sweden. He started to warn Jewish acquaintances as early as September 17.[30]

Best's deputy Kanstein, who had links to the anti-Nazi resistance in Germany, also opposed this initiative to seize Jews as counterproductive in Denmark. Danish Social Democrats and radio broadcasts from Sweden, among others, began to warn the Copenhagen Jewish community of an impending Gestapo action.[31]

On the one hand, Best initiated an effort to seize Jews in Denmark partly to keep ahead of the action he knew would inevitably emanate from Hitler and other high officials in Berlin. On the other hand, he warned his superiors that Danish opposition combined with widespread anticipation of police action among Danish Jews made it unlikely that this action would be effective. On September 28, Best received from Berlin the order to launch the roundup of Jews, but he worked closely with Duckwitz, and he gave Duckwitz the actual date of the roundup. Best himself later claimed that "the Jews were warned with my knowledge and in accordance with my wishes." The police had orders to knock at the doors of Jewish houses and apartments but not to break in. The whole action was carried out as though its failure was to be expected. Yet Best could claim that the escape of most Danish Jews was not failure; Denmark would be free of Jewish influence. Perhaps their flight was the simplest way for him to resolve his multiple dilemmas.[32] So, the same man started and oversaw a roundup of Jews but also allowed about 7,900 people to escape to Sweden.[33] What happened in Denmark was the second occasion that Best leaked information about Nazi plans for the Jews, and the second time likely was easier than the first.

Geist frequently had told Nazi officials that the United States was an economic powerhouse and that Germany, out of self-interest, should stay on good terms with America. That guidance probably carried more weight with Best than with other Nazi officials, since he was both interested in the United States and intellectually capable of judging its strength. Geist also had mentioned that President Roosevelt was personally interested in the fate of German Jews. Whatever his motives, Best had warned Geist in mid-November 1938 about Nazi plans to kill German Jews. More than forty thousand German Jews then emigrated to the United States in the period after Kristallnacht and before the Holocaust began. Best must not have rued these secret conversations with Geist.

Very late in the war, Best tried to restore an American connection. Through an intermediary in Stockholm in February 1945, he offered to convey any US message to Himmler. Some high Nazi officials, probably including Himmler, hoped that they could use their hold on surviving Jews in the camps to extract better peace terms and/or personal benefits, such as immunity from prosecution. It did not work: guided by the Allied policy of unconditional surrender, the United States wanted no part of even indirect contact with Himmler. Himmler had to try his luck contacting instead the Swedish Red Cross and the Swedish representative of the World Jewish Congress.[34] But had Geist been in Europe, he might have wanted to see what he could do with Best one last time.

EPILOGUE

Geist fought against Nazi Germany indirectly through the Jewish children he helped to save. As they grew up, they contributed to the United States and to the war effort. Hans Arnold Wangersheim, born in Nuremberg in 1924, offers perhaps the most striking example. Raised in an Orthodox Jewish orphanage after the divorce of his parents,[1] he was among the 350 children selected by the Hilfsverein for sponsorship arranged by German Jewish Children's Aid through the Labor Department—the complex arrangement designed to protect against an immigrant child becoming a public charge. Geist engineered this method to give visas to Jewish children, protected it against Gestapo incursions, and oversaw it.[2]

Wangersheim received his US immigration visa in Stuttgart in January 1938.[3] He then was placed with a foster family in Janesville, Wisconsin, and he eventually attended the University of Wisconsin. Impressed by a Wisconsin football player named Howard Weiss, he changed his name to Arnold Weiss. During the war, while in the Army Air Force, he sustained leg injuries in a crash and could no longer fly. The Office of Strategic Services recruited him for intelligence work in Germany, making use of his native German. At the end of the war, Weiss, now twenty-one, moved to the Army Counter Intelligence Corps and was assigned to track down Hitler's last companions in his bunker in Berlin, partly in order to establish conclusive evidence of Hitler's death. (The Soviet Union had located Hitler's burned remains in Berlin but did not disclose this fact to the West for decades.) There were widespread rumors in the West shortly after the war in Europe ended that Hitler had escaped.[4]

In December 1945, Weiss tracked down Martin Bormann's aide Wilhelm Zander, who was hiding in a stone house in a small village near the Czech-German border. Weiss asked Zander, Why had he left the bunker before Hitler committed suicide? Zander said that Hitler had ordered him to make sure that important documents were preserved. Then he said, "I suppose you want the documents?" Weiss opened the envelope and saw *Mein privates Testament*, signed by Hitler on April 29, 1945, the day before he committed suicide.[5] Hitler's last will and testament gives as good a picture of his genocidal racism as any document we have. It was recovered through the indirect influence of Raymond Geist. Today, it lies in the US National Archives, along with many of the documents written by Geist and used in the preparation of this book.

At the end of the war, the Danes arrested and imprisoned Werner Best. Repeatedly interrogated in Denmark and elsewhere about his involvement in war crimes and crimes against humanity, he testified at the International Military Tribunal at Nuremberg in defense of the Gestapo-SD, which the Allies had indicted as a criminal organization. Many of his assertions were self-serving and mendacious. Best was fortunate in that he was tried in Denmark, not in France or in Poland, for his crimes were fewer and less serious in Denmark, and he plausibly could blame others for them. He continued to maintain that through Georg Duckwitz he had leaked information about the roundup of Jews in Denmark, and Duckwitz backed him up. Although the court initially sentenced him to death, an appeal reduced his sentence to five years, and he was released in 1951. He spent years lobbying in West Germany to commute the prison sentences of other Nazi war criminals. In July 1989, a West German state prosecutor indicted him for the murder of more than eight thousand people in France, but it was too late. He had died two weeks earlier.[6]

Anna Geist accompanied her brother to most of his foreign posts, making her own life in volunteer work, especially in religious activities and work with the underprivileged.[7] She ran his household and directed his entertaining during most of his time in Berlin and during his time in Washington and Bethesda. She was a major asset in his career, and she took pride in his success. After World War II, she lived with Raymond in Mexico, then went back their Bethesda house. Finally, she returned to her hometown of Cleveland, where she died on November 4, 1949, at age sixty-seven.

Erick Mainz became a US citizen on January 15, 1945, in Rockville, Maryland.[8] Six months later, he spent time with the Geists in Mexico City, Raymond's last post. While he was there and before flying back to the United States, he decided to make out a short will. In the event of his death, he bequeathed all his assets to "my life-long friend Raymond H. Geist, and I do hereby appoint him executor of my estate."[9] But Mainz long outlived his benefactor. He settled in Los Angeles, where he walked along the beach and enjoyed the ocean views. He became a licensed physical therapist. Eventually, he met Marie Smith Maller, and they married in 1963. He died in Santa Monica in 1994.[10]

In July 1945, Geist became counselor of embassy in Mexico, initially under his longtime friend and patron Ambassador George Messersmith. This step was part of their joint plan to return to Germany. President Roosevelt apparently once had offered Messersmith a future appointment to a high position in the occupation government of West Germany. Messersmith thought that in Mexico City he and Geist could exchange ideas, work out plans, and go to Germany together. Geist was exhilarated at this prospect.[11]

Geist prepared an affidavit for the International Military Tribunal at Nuremberg in support of the charge that Nazi leaders had planned and carried out a war of aggression in violation of treaties and international law. Geist's document supported the Nuremberg prosecution's case; it also recounted quite a few episodes from his years in Germany.[12] It got buried among the mountain of documents at the major Nuremberg trial, but it came in very handy for this book.

After President Roosevelt died on April 12, 1945, Messersmith's credentials were not strong enough to make him an obvious choice for a high US position in Germany.[13] By March 1946, Geist knew his prospects for a second mission in Germany had seriously diminished. In a letter to another Messersmith ally, he confirmed that "the late President Roosevelt had distinctly in mind that he [Messersmith] was the proper person to guide that country [Germany] into the ways of democracy and peace." Now it was hard to say what Geist's next assignment would be.[14]

After Messersmith was appointed ambassador to Argentina under the dictatorship of Juan Perón, Geist was not terribly eager to stay in Mexico City. Messersmith pushed him for the post of counselor of embassy in Bern, Switzerland, with Denmark, Norway, or Belgium as backups. Unexpectedly, however, the new ambassador to Mexico, Walter Thurston, pressed the State Department to keep Geist as his counselor of embassy, possibly until he reached the retirement age of sixty-three. Thurston judged Geist to be able, in good health, and well preserved at sixty-one.[15]

Geist was unhappy about this prospect. Returning to Washington for a physical exam, Geist told State Department officials that he had spent the prime years of his life in Germany, and he wanted to put his special talents to work there again. When this prospect fell through, he felt frustrated. He claimed that since he was seven years old he always had wanted to be an ambassador.[16] There was no trace of this goal in his diary.

Geist enthusiastically reviewed his work to help individual refugees leave Germany, his cooperation with the Intergovernmental Committee on Refugees, and, more recently, his effort to place 1,500 Polish displaced persons in Mexico at US government expense. He welcomed the prospect of going to Europe to work on refugee problems, perhaps with the International Refugee Organization.[17]

The State Department considered Geist for a different, related post—consul general in Jerusalem. But Loy Henderson, head of the Office of Near Eastern and African Affairs, changed his mind about sending Geist there, possibly because of Geist's background with Jewish refugees.[18] Henderson was no supporter of Jewish immigration to Palestine, let alone of a Jewish state in part of Palestine.[19] He proposed

Geist for Bombay (now Mumbai) instead. Geist then requested an appointment as chief of mission (ambassador or minister) somewhere, to achieve his childhood ambition.[20] But the State Department declined. So, he officially retired on August 31, 1948, at age sixty-three.[21]

In his letter of appreciation, Secretary of State George C. Marshall noted that in Geist's years in Berlin, "when political tension and, eventually, war made the carrying out of your heavy duties particularly difficult, you acquitted yourself in accordance with the highest traditions of the [Foreign] Service." Another letter of congratulations came from Dr. George Biggs, with whom Geist had lived in 1911. Biggs had helped Geist psychologically and financially at a critical time in his search for a career.[22]

In 1946 and 1947 Geist had repeated operations for the removal of tumors from his bladder.[23] After Anna's death, Raymond split his remaining years between Cleveland and Los Angeles. He too liked the beach, and he probably spent time with Erick. By 1954, probably knowing that he did not have many more months left, he allowed his name to be put forward for a West German decoration, the Commander's Cross of the Order of Merit. In a ceremony at the German Consulate General in Los Angeles on December 8, 1954, he received this honor for his tireless work to extract victims of Nazism from Germany. West German consul general Richard Hertz told him, "You not only served your nation well, but you rendered great service to humanity."[24]

A onetime German judge, Franz Bunzel, the son of a prominent democratic politician in the Weimar Republic, was one of those present. Like many German Jewish civil servants, Bunzel was forced to retire in 1933 under the Nazi Law for the Restoration of the German Civil Service.[25] He managed to stay afloat in Germany until Kristallnacht. Fearing that he was a Gestapo target, he went into hiding and then made his way to Amsterdam. It is likely that Geist helped him by telling the Dutch that he was due to get a US immigration visa under the German quota soon. With his fiancée Annaliese Münden, Bunzel emigrated to the United States in January 1939. They married and settled in Los Angeles.[26] Bunzel's presence at the ceremony symbolized Geist's rescue work in Berlin.

Raymond Geist died in Los Angeles on February 28, 1955. He was buried in Riverside Cemetery in Cleveland, with a simple headstone inscription: "Raymond H. Geist, 1885–1955." Geist left no spouse or children, and it would have been hard to compress his achievements into a few phrases on the headstone. His sister Jennie and her children survived him. One of Jennie's grandchildren, Susan Cooper, was of major assistance in the preparation of this book.

Geist was not a hero of the Holocaust in the mold of Raoul Wallenberg, the Swede who risked (and ultimately lost) his life in an effort to save tens of thousands of Jews in Hungary. Nor was he like Japanese vice consul Chiune Sugihara, who defied his government to give out thousands of visas to Jews in Lithuania before the Holocaust. Some might claim that, as a participant in a restrictive American immigration system, Geist was not a hero at all, but rather someone who did his job and who failed to back up his conscience with loud public protest. All the same, Geist's accomplishments show that refraining from public display of moral indignation sometimes could do genuine good.

Geist perceived a dire threat from Nazi Germany early, and consistently fought it until its collapse. He tried and occasionally succeeded in maneuvers unmatched by any other foreign diplomat. Had he been a consul with the worldview of Charles Lindbergh, far fewer German Jews would have found refuge in the United States.

Raymond Geist was proud to be the grandson of German immigrants to the United States. His West German honor cites this sentiment.[27] He took satisfaction in helping victims of Nazi persecution to immigrate to the United States, making it a stronger and better country.

Geist had read Hitler's book *Mein Kampf*, most likely well before Hitler came to power. Years later, Geist told his friend Louis Lochner that this book demonstrated a deductive mind: Hitler merely decided something was true, and afterward, everything else had to fit into his framework. It was the opposite of Anglo-Saxon empiricism.[28] Geist recognized the unique characteristics of this dictator and of the barbaric regime he built.

Geist would have thought it unlikely that any leader of a powerful developed nation would ever again depart so far from reality and from basic humanity, both in his vision of the world and in his own determination to destroy an imagined demonic enemy. All the same, Geist would have recognized that many national leaders and their supporters have seriously blurred vision brought about by extremist ideologies and prejudices. If they are stubborn, these leaders try to bend reality to their will, rather than adapt to it, using all the propaganda and tools of technology available to them. In this sense, the Nazi experience is still quite relevant.

Geist had the ability to cut to the essentials, so it is unfortunate that we have little of his political analysis of the rise of Nazism. But I will project what he would have passed on to us today. Men such as Brüning, Hugenberg, and Papen, who paralyzed German democracy for their own selfish political interests, only helped to bring about disaster and evil on a world-historical scale. To stop the Nazis short of taking power, all decent Germans would have had to overlook their many differences and stand together to defend democracy and human dignity. That guidance is timely and timeless.

APPENDIX

IN REPLY REFER TO

FILE NO. RHG:HP

THE FOREIGN SERVICE
OF THE
UNITED STATES OF AMERICA

DEPARTMENT OF STATE

Personal
& confidential

AMERICAN CONSULATE GENERAL

Berlin, Germany, December 5, 1938.

Dear Mr. Wilson:

Since your departure there has been no improvement in the general situation of the Jews and I am very
doubtful that the policy which our Government is following in this respect will yield any beneficial results.
You have no doubt seen Gilbert's telegrams regarding
his conversations with Dr. Woermann in the Foreign
Office and have carefully taken note of the observation
made regarding the possibility of the German Government
being willing to have conversations with Robert Pell in
some nearby country. You no doubt recall also in this
connection that substance of the advice which I gave to
Mr. Taylor last July when, on instructions from the
Department, I went over to London for a few days.
The advice which I gave to Mr. Taylor at that time was
based upon the convictions I had that under no circumstances could Hitler and his immediate advisers:
Göbbels, Himmler, Streicher, Rosenberg and others, be
persuaded to make any gesture whatever in favor of the
Jews. I do not believe, however, that this attitude,
adamant as it may be, precludes the possibility of
coming to some kind of financial agreement beneficial
to those Jews who might have the possibility of leaving
the country; provided always that the concessions
remain part and parcel of a private arrangement subject
to no publicity.

It may be that the President has conceived of the
International Committee which through his initiative
has been created as an organization with sufficient
prestige and importance to impress the Germans; but
this certainly is not the case. The are not only not

impressed

The Honorable
    Hugh R. Wilson,
        c/o Department of State,
            Washington, D.C.

-2-

impressed with the Intergovernmental Committee, but
regard it as an organization set up to place them
in an unfavorable light and to act as an instrument
of International Jewry. These prejudices can hardly
be counteracted and I am afraid now, unless we follow
a more conciliatory policy, they will do everything in
their power to render the work of the Committee abortive.
The action against the Jews is becoming more aggressive
from day to day, and hardly a week passes without the
promulgation of harsher measures. They are intending,
as I hear from my friend, Dr. Best, to bring the Jewish
situation to a close as rapidly as possible. They are
intending to impose all the restrictions and hardships
possible so that the Jews will be returned to the Ghetto
and there encounter a form of existence through which
they will inevitably perish; as I am sure the intentions
are not to allow them to deteriorate to a certain low
form of existence and then go on indefinitely, as one
finds in the Ghettos of Poland.

This is a very dark outlook from our point of view.
It means that the pressure on us for immigration visas
will continue with greater urgency than ever before.
With over 160,000 applicants now against the American
quota and the number increasing daily, there will be
no end to the agitation and political animosity.
I think we should take these facts into consideration
when determining our course of action.

I have written also in this pouch my views to
Mr. Messersmith and I shall gladly repeat them here for
what they are worth. I think we should follow up as
rapidly as possible any suggestion which the Foreign
Office here might give to discuss the question with
Robert Pell or anybody else who could talk unofficially
on behalf of the Committee. I think, too, that any
move which the Germans might make to meet our wishes
in the slightest should be the signal for your return
so that our relations do not further deteriorate. I
am convinced that nothing can be accomplished on behalf
of the victims by our maintaining a stiff attitude on
this question. My views are not based upon the precepts
of international diplomacy, with respect to which there
might be plenty of justification for our showing a
direct disapproval of the recent pogroms, but on a
realistic view of the Nazi psychology and the results

which

-3-

which our attitude will produce. Hitler will defy
any public rebuke, no matter from what quarter this
rebuke comes; and he will not hesitate to show this
resentment by going the whole way in asserting his
will. The result will only be a rapid deterioration
of the position of the Jews and possibly the confiscation
of all their wealth so that even a moderate scheme of
allowing them to take out a small amount in goods would
be impossible. The Germans are determined to solve the
Jewish problem without the assistance of other countries,
and that means eventual annihilation. They have already
indicated that if the hair of a Nazi leader is touched
there will not be a Jew left alive in Germany. This is
a sombre and darkly portentious statement; but the
warning must not go by entirely unheeded.

I believe the situation is a very grave one, and I
think everything should be done to bring about an
improvement in our relations as rapidly as possible.
No real good can be accomplished by our attitude,
unless we believe that in order to uphold the principles
of humanity and justice we are prepared to sacrifice
the hostages. But I take it that our Government is
desirous above all of bringing about an alleviation
of the position of the Jews still within the confines
of the German Reich. If so, we should not put ourselves
in a position where conversation and "persuasion" becomes
more difficult, if not impossible.

We cannot intimidate the Nazi Regime; therefore
I believe that when it is impossible to restrain them
by any show of moral disapproval, and being unwilling
to use force, we should not put ourselves in a position
where our influence is set at naught and where our
attitude might almost provoke the carrying out of a
policy which is our greatest anxiety to prevent.

We are trying to carry on here to the best of our
ability. I have been very successful in getting scores
of people out of the concentration camps and arranging
for their departure to another country. The French
and British have been willing to cooperate in this
scheme; but the Dutch who appeared to be at first
the most enthusiastic about helping found they could
do nothing. With regard to our immigration work, the
pressure from the United States is becoming much

heavier

-4-

heavier than from the Jews here. This indicates
the urgency of getting other countries to do something in a large way; otherwise the steady influx
of refugees into the United States over a protracted
period will create domestic problems for us which
might assume ugly aspects.

I need not tell you how much we miss you and
Mrs. Wilson, and how much more difficult our position
becomes without you. I find it much more to our
advantage when the work can be carried on in a spirit
of cordiality. These people seem so insensible regarding their official conduct; and I wonder whether or not
any good can be done by censuring them. They are so
convinced of the justice of their ways - the cult of
brute force - that it seems h opeless to appeal to
them on the basis of morality and fair play. I
emphatically believe that we have to be realists in
dealing with them, and take them as they are, always
being careful not to condone their actions and
standing strong on our own principles with the same
conviction and strength they maintain, but keeping
up relations so that we can do business and protect
our interests.

I hope it will not be long before you return to
your post. Good progress is being made with the
Bluecher Palais and I think you will be pleased when
we are nicely housed in the new quarters. The
requisition for the Embassy's new furniture is going
in with this pouch and it is very important that
shipment be made in time so as to have the building
entirely ready by the end of March.

With warmest regards, believe me

Faithfully yours,

Raymond Geist

ACKNOWLEDGMENTS

Each stage of this book had its own challenges. I was very fortunate to have the help of many people.

Melissa Jane Taylor generously shared a copy of Raymond Geist's State Department Official Personnel File. The size and quality of this file convinced me that it was possible to write a book on Geist. My agent Joe Spieler expressed enthusiasm about this topic from the beginning and helped guide me at various stages of the book. Clive Priddle, publisher of PublicAffairs and my editor, was willing to gamble on a book about a man whom history had largely ignored. His criticism and that of Athena Bryan at PublicAffairs helped me sharpen my focus on the continuities and key episodes in this book.

My former student Satu Haase-Webb helped me with some research at the Library of Congress; she also scoured social media and genealogy websites for traces of Geist relatives. Satu put me in touch with Susan Cooper, who had done a great deal of work on her Geist family history. My meeting with Susan and her sister Lisa Norden to talk about Geist and to view the small collection of family documents was one of the most exciting moments of my research. I built my knowledge of the Geist family upon the family history that Susan had already done. I am so pleased that the Raymond Geist Papers are now part of the Franklin D. Roosevelt Presidential Library, and I am grateful to its director, Paul Sparrow, for recognizing its value. Kirsten

Carter and Dava Baker helped to create the digitized Raymond Geist papers at the FDRL.

At the National Archives in College Park, Maryland, diplomatic records specialist David Langbart went way above and beyond the call of duty to guide me to all relevant indexes and inventories and to help me find records related to Geist. Eric van Slander and Paul Brown helped me find some material among military records at NARA. Caitlyn Crain Enriquez helped me locate a photo there.

I made a short but highly productive visit to the Herbert Hoover Presidential Library, thanks to the help of archivists Spencer Howard and Matthew Schaefer. Craig Wright arranged to photograph a key document there. Simone Munson at the Wisconsin Historical Society was of great assistance in Madison. Liz Schultz of the Oberlin Heritage Society filled me in on life in the town of Oberlin during the years that the Geist siblings lived and worked there. Melanie Hembera and Jürgen Matthäus each checked documents in the Bundesarchiv Koblenz related to Werner Best for me.

The archivists at the Harvard University Archives and at the Oberlin College Archives were kind enough to mail me material concerning Geist's studies in Cambridge and in Oberlin. Ralph Rehbock generously talked with me about his family's experience after Kristallnacht and sent me related documents. John Maller gave me basic information about Erick Mainz and sent me his photo collection. Patrick Kerwin helped me locate an important document in the William E. Dodd Papers at the Library of Congress. Alexia Haralambous looked up shipping information for me. Richard S. Levy and Eron Sodie answered specific questions.

David Langbart and Benton Arnovitz read every chapter carefully, correcting, polishing, and suggesting additions or changes, even on footnotes. They were way beyond helpful. Michael Dobbs, working on his own book, *The Unwanted: America, Auschwitz, and a Village Caught in Between*, traded some research information with me. I then benefited greatly from his careful scrutiny of, and suggestions for, my manuscript. He helped me to strive for a broader audience. David Engel, Lindsay MacNeill, Alexandra Lohse, and Katrin Paehler each went over key chapters for me and gave me their impressions. My longtime friend Marc Alexander gave me valuable comments on my first five chapters. My friend and colleague Norm Goda offered a careful reading of the near-final manuscript and helped me avoid numerous problems. Julian Bourg double-checked some endnotes for me at Harvard. I am grateful to all of them for taking time from their busy schedules.

My wife Carol read every page of this book in its earliest form—but not always right away. She criticized fuzziness and unnecessary complexity in my writing. She caught many errors. I did not show anything to others until she had commented on it first. She deserves credit for all that, and for putting up with my years-long fixation with Raymond Geist.

NOTES

Prologue

1. Adolf Hitler, "Reichstag Speech," January 30, 1939, www.ushmm.org /learn/timeline-of-events/1939-1941/hitler-speech-to-german-parliament. Translation of Hitler in Ian Kershaw, *Hitler: 1936–1945, Nemesis* (New York: W. W. Norton, 2000), 153.

2. Gilbert to Secretary of State, January 31, 1939, Record Group 59, 762.00/230, National Archives and Records Administration, College Park (hereafter NARA). Gilbert did not name the secretaries who attended, but there were only six men with this title. Geist was one of two first secretaries. Data on the number of secretaries courtesy of David Langbart, archivist at the US National Archives. As explained in chapter ten, Geist had a particular interest and stake in this speech.

Introduction

1. I have used selected Geist letters and despatches in several previous works. Also giving Geist substantial attention are Christoph Strupp, "Beobachtungen in der Diktatur: Amerikanische Konsulatsberichte aus dem 'Dritten Reich,'" in *Fremde Blicke auf das "Dritte Reich": Berichte ausländischer Diplomaten über Herrschaft und Gesellschaft in Deutschland 1933–1945*, eds. Frank Bajohr and Christoph Strupp (Göttingen, Germany: Wallstein Verlag, 2011), 70–137, and Michael Dobbs, *The Unwanted: America, Auschwitz, and a Village Caught in Between* (New York: Alfred A. Knopf, 2019), 30–40.

Chapter One: Visas

1. Herter to Carr, April 21, 1921, and Carr to Herter, April 21, 1921; Geist to Harding, January 14, 1921: all in Raymond Geist's Official Personnel

File, National Archives and Records Administration, St. Louis (hereafter OPF, NARA-SL). I am exceedingly grateful to Melissa Jane Taylor for giving me a copy of this file.

2. So Geist told Hugh R. Wilson, Wilson Diary, July 8, 1938, Hugh R. Wilson Papers, box 4, 1938 folder, Herbert Hoover Presidential Library (hereafter Hoover Library).

3. Martin Weil, *A Pretty Good Club: The Founding Fathers of the U.S. Foreign Service* (New York: W. W. Norton, 1978), 46–47.

4. Hugh R. Wilson Diary, July 8, 1938, Hugh R. Wilson Papers, box 4, 1938 folder, Hoover Library.

5. Weil, *A Pretty Good Club*, 46–47.

6. Carr to Herter, April 21, 1921, OPF, NARA-SL.

7. Carr's summary and memo for the files, July 21, 1921, and letters of recommendation, OPF, NARA-SL.

8. Richard Breitman and Allan J. Lichtman, *FDR and the Jews* (Cambridge: Belknap Press of Harvard University Press, 2013), 22.

9. Breitman and Lichtman, *FDR and the Jews*, 26.

10. Summary in Breitman and Lichtman, *FDR and the Jews*, 26. For purposes of the quota, nationality was determined by country of birth.

11. Copy of press release in RG 59, 150.626J-, NARA. Richard Breitman and Alan M. Kraut, *American Refugee Policy and European Jewry, 1933–1945* (Bloomington: Indiana University Press, 1987), 7–8.

12. Ravndal to Secretary of State, May 8, 1930, copy in RG 59, 123 G 271/115, NARA.

13. Jesse H. Stiller, *George S. Messersmith: Diplomat of Democracy* (Chapel Hill: University of North Carolina Press, 1987), 1–28.

14. Geist to Secretary of State, June 20, 1931, RG 59, 811.111 Quota 62/302; Messersmith to Secretary of State, January 5, 1931, and Visa Section to Messersmith, February 6, 1931, RG 59, 811.111 Quota 62/316, NARA.

15. Messersmith to Secretary of State, March 13, 1931, RG 59, 811.111 Quota 62/330; Geist to Secretary of State, September 10, 1934 (describing the situation in 1931–1932), RG 59, 811.111 Quota 62/465, NARA.

16. Geist to Secretary of State, April 13, 1932, RG 59, 811.111 Quota 62/381, NARA.

17. Walter Isaacson, *Einstein: His Life and Universe* (New York: Simon & Schuster, 2007), 394–399; Fred Jerome, *The Einstein File: J. Edgar Hoover's Secret War against the World's Most Famous Scientist* (New York: St. Martin's, 2002), 4.

18. Jerome, *The Einstein File*, 4; Isaacson, *Einstein*, 399.

19. Jerome, *The Einstein File*, 6–9.

20. Hodgdon to Phillips, September 21, 1933, RG 59, entry 707, 811.111, Einstein, Albert, Confidential File, NARA. Hodgdon defended

the position he had taken in 1932. Messersmith to Secretary of State, December 12, 1932, Messersmith Papers, box 1, folder 4, Delaware. On Carr, Breitman and Kraut, *American Refugee Policy*, 30–32; Ruth Shipley to Messersmith, December 10, 1932, Messersmith Papers, box 1, folder 2, Delaware.

21. Messersmith to Secretary of State, December 12, 1932, Messersmith Papers, box 1, folder 4, Delaware.

22. Lochner's letter of December 11, 1932, reprinted in Morrell Heald, ed., *Journalist at the Brink: Louis P. Lochner in Berlin, 1922–1942* (Xlibris, 2007), 100.

23. Messersmith to Secretary of State, December 12, 1932, Messersmith Papers, box 1, folder 4, Delaware.

24. This and what follows (except where noted) from Messersmith to Secretary of State, December 12, 1932, Messersmith Papers, box 1, folder 4, Delaware.

25. "Erklaerung Prof. Albert Einsteins an den Kongress," World Congress against the Imperialist War Collection, inventory number 3, International Institute of Social History, Amsterdam www.iisg.nl/collections/einstein/documents/worldcongress-3.pdf.

26. Geist's recollection quoted in Lochner's diary entry, May 6, 1939, Louis P. Lochner Papers, box 11, diaries folder, Wisconsin Historical Society.

27. *New York Times*, December 6, 1932, p. 1. Messersmith to Secretary of State, December 12, 1932, Messersmith Papers, box 1, folder 4, Delaware; Stiller, *George S. Messersmith*, 31.

28. Messersmith to Secretary of State, December 9, 1932, RG 59, entry 199, 811.111 Einstein, Albert, NARA. Shipley to Messersmith, December 10, 1932, Messersmith Papers, box 1, folder 2, Delaware. Stimson's press briefing, December 10, Messersmith Papers, box 1, folder 2, Delaware. http://udspace.udel.edu/bitstream/handle/19716/6001/mss0109_0028-00.pdf

29. "Americans Back U.S. Consulate in Einstein Quiz," *Chicago Daily Tribune*, December 11, 1932, p. 1.

30. Messersmith to Louis, December 12, 1932; Messersmith to Oswald Villard, December 15, 1932; Messersmith to Skinner, December 17, 1932; Messersmith to Shipley, December 30, 1932, all in Messersmith Papers, box 1, folders 3-6, Delaware. Messersmith to Feis, February 4, 1933, Hebert Feis Papers, box 123, Messersmith folder, Library of Congress.

31. Isaacson, *Einstein*, 401–405. Dodd to Secretary of State, November 22, 1933, RG 59, 862.4016/1326, NARA.

Chapter Two: The Rise of the Nazis

1. Mary J. Manning, "Being German, Being American," *Prologue* (Summer 2014): 17, www.archives.gov/files/publications/prologue/2014/summer

/germans.pdf. More generally, Michael Kazin, *War against War: The American Fight for Peace, 1914–1918* (New York: Simon & Schuster, 2017).

2. Undated [January 1918] letter in OPF, NARA-SL.

3. William Bullitt to Phillips, January 26, 1917 [1918], copy in OPF, NARA-SL.

4. Biographical statement, OPF, NARA-SL. *Oberlin Tribune*, February 19 and 21, 1919, Oberlin College Archives.

5. Biographical statement, OPF, NARA-SL. *Oberlin Review*, February 17, 1919. *Oberlin Tribune*, February 21, 1919, Oberlin College Archives.

6. His letter to his sisters, dated January 21, 1919, was published in the *Oberlin Tribune*, February 21, 1919.

7. Benson to USN Staff Representative, Paris, April 19, 1919, Raymond Geist Papers, Franklin D. Roosevelt Library.

8. Autobiographical statement, OPF, NARA-SL.

9. John Deak, "Ignaz Seipel," in *Austrian Lives*, eds. Günter Bischof, Eva Maltschnig, and Fritz Plasser (New Orleans: University of New Orleans Press, 2012).

10. Geist's description in *Oberlin News*, August 4, 1920, Oberlin College Archives.

11. "Austria-Hungary [*sic*] Wants for Food," *Oberlin News*, August 4, 1920, Oberlin College Archives.

12. On the Austrian telegram and on the feeding of children, Geist to Commander Baker, November 23, 1919, Belgian American Educational Foundation (hereafter BAEF), ARA Personnel, box 115, Geist folder, Hoover Library. By this time Geist claimed that 114,000 children in Vienna and another 36,000 in lower Austria were being fed.

13. "Radikale Aenderung der Versorgung," *Neues Wiener Journal*, October 24, 1919, http://anno.onb.ac.at/cgi-content/anno?aid=nwj&datum=19191024&seite=1&zoom=33.

14. Geist to King, October 25, 1919, Oberlin College Archives.

15. "The American Feeding Action," translated article in *Deutsches Volksblatt*, January 2, 1920, copy in BAEF, ARA Personnel, box 115, Hoover Library. See photo section.

16. Memorandum by E. G. Burland, January 2, 1920, BAEF, ARA Personnel, box 115, Geist folder, Hoover Library: "Dr. Geist contributed very valuable services in organizing the work with the E.C.F. [European Children's Feeding] in Vienna and Lower Austria. The only difficulty during these times was the fact that certain speeches and interviews of Dr. Geist were published, which caused some irritation to Capt. Gregory and Capt. Torrey."

17. Geist to Baker, November 23, 1919, BAEF, ARA Personnel, box 115, Geist folder, Hoover Library.

18. *Oberlin Review*, November 7, 1919.

19. Translated copy of comment, *Die Reichspost*, December 21, 1919, BAEF, ARA Personnel, box 115, Geist folder, Hoover Library.

20. Webb Waldron, "Doc Geist and Vienna," *Collier's*, February 14, 1920. Strictly Confidential, Chancellor's Office to the Editor of all Vienna Papers, January 2, 1920, copy in BAEF, ARA Personnel, box 115, Geist folder, Hoover Library.

21. These judgments are based on a close reading of Geist's Official Personnel File, NARA-SL.

22. Wilmersdorf location, Geist postcard collection, Raymond Geist Papers, Franklin D. Roosevelt Library.

23. Bernard V. Burke, *Ambassador Frederic Sackett and the Collapse of the Weimar Republic, 1930–1933* (New York: Cambridge University Press, 1994), 1–22.

24. Stiller, *George S. Messersmith*, 29.

25. Stiller, *George S. Messersmith*, 1–7, 27–29.

26. Messersmith to Secretary of State, January 12, 1932, RG 59, 362. 1115/6, NARA.

27. Brendan McNally, "Our Man in Berlin," *Rotarian*, October 2016, www.rotary.org/en/our-man-berlin.

28. Victoria de Grazia, *Irresistible Empire: America's Advance through Twentieth-Century Europe* (Cambridge: Belknap Press of Harvard University Press, 2005), 38–42.

29. Messersmith to Secretary of State, November 9, 1933, RG 59, 862.43 Rotary Club/7, NARA. Geist had joined Rotary in Montevideo in the mid-1920s, but Rotary has no record of his membership in Berlin. McNally, "Our Man in Berlin." The Nazi regime first interfered with Rotary chapters, and then, in 1937, shut them down.

30. Sackett to Secretary of State, January 7, 1933, RG 59, 862.00/2885, NARA. See also, Dodd to Secretary of State, October 26, 1933, RG 59, 862.00/3118, NARA.

31. 1931 performance evaluation, OPF, NARA-SL.

32. Burke, *Ambassador Frederic Sackett*, 43.

33. Burke, *Ambassador Frederic Sackett*, 50–53.

34. For a summary, Richard J. Evans, *The Coming of the Third Reich* (New York: Penguin, 2003), 93–94; the fundamental work, Hermann Weber, *Die Wandlung des deutschen Kommunismus: Die Stalinisierung der KPD in der Weimarer Republik* (Frankfurt am Main: Europäische Verlagsanstalt, 1969).

35. Larry Eugene Jones, *German Liberalism and the Dissolution of the Weimar Party System, 1918–1933* (Chapel Hill: University of North Carolina Press, 1988), 355–358.

36. Messersmith to Secretary of State, June 18, 1931, RG 59, 123 G 271/139, NARA.

37. Kennan Diary, June 1, 1931, George F. Kennan Papers, box 230, folder 21, Seeley G. Mudd Library, Princeton University.

38. Burke, *Ambassador Frederic Sackett*, 36–37, 53–55.

39. Geist to Mallory, September 25, 1931, and Geist to Secretary of State, September 25, 1931, RG 59, 811.43 Council on Foreign Relations/74, NARA.

40. Burke, *Ambassador Frederic Sackett*, 60–61.

41. Peter Hayes, *Why?: Explaining the Holocaust* (New York: W. W. Norton, 2017), 65–66.

42. Geist to Fletcher Warren, August 20, 1940, RG 59, 800.20211, Turner Ewart/3. On Turner generally, see Ewart E. Turner Papers, Temple University Libraries, Philadelphia, https://library.temple.edu/scrc/ewart-e-turner-papers.

43. Burke, *Ambassador Frederic Sackett*, 100–122.

44. Burke, *Ambassador Frederic Sackett*, 90, 95–108, 123–148.

45. Geist to Secretary of State, September 19, 1931, RG 59, 123 G 271/147, NARA.

46. Sackett to Secretary of State, November 16, 1931, RG 59, 862.00/2634, NARA. Ulrich Herbert, *Best: Biographische Studien über Radikalismus, Weltanschauung und Vernunft 1903–1989* (Bonn: J.H.W. Dietz, 2011), 110.

47. Herbert, *Best*, 109–111. Sackett to Secretary of State, November 16, 1931, RG 59, 862.00/2634, NARA.

48. Burke, *Ambassador Frederic Sackett*, 8. Sackett to Henry Stimson, personal, December 9, 1931, RG 59, 862.50/723, NARA.

49. Burke, *Ambassador Frederic Sackett*, 185–186.

50. Burke, *Ambassador Frederic Sackett*, 8. Sackett to Stimson, December 9, 1931, RG 59, 862.50/723, NARA.

51. Burke, *Ambassador Frederic Sackett*, 244.

52. Sackett to Secretary of State, September 2, 1932, copy in RG 59, 123 G 271/159, NARA.

53. Richard J. Evans, *The Coming of the Third Reich* (New York: Penguin, 2005), 281. Heinrich Hoffmann and Josef Berchtold, *Hitler über Deutschland* (Munich: Franz Eher Verlag, 1932). Wiley to Secretary of State, February 17, 1932, RG 59, 862.00/2703, NARA.

54. Goebbels's predictions in Wiley to Secretary of State, February 17, 1932, RG 59, 862.00/2703, NARA. Discussion of elections in Evans, *The Coming*, 281–282.

55. Wiley to Secretary of State, February 17, 1932, RG 59, 862.00/2703, NARA. See the discussion in Burke, *Ambassador Frederic Sackett*, 89.

56. Evans, *The Coming*, 282–283. Sackett to Secretary of State, May 28 and 30, 1932, RG 59, 862.00/2756 and 2757, NARA. Burke, *Ambassador Frederic Sackett*, 230–231.

57. Evans, *The Coming*, 283–285. Burke, *Ambassador Frederic Sackett*, 233.

58. Burke, *Ambassador Frederic Sackett*, 241–244.

59. Burke, *Ambassador Frederic Sackett*, 247.

60. Geist's Voluntary Report, September 22, 1932, RG 59, 862.50/742, NARA; Geist's Voluntary Report, the Economic Effects of the Papen Plan of September 4, 1932, May 4, 1933, RG 59, 862.50/756, NARA.

61. Feis to Western European Affairs, January 19, 1933, RG 59, 862.50/749, NARA.

62. Robinson Fire Apparatus Manufacturing to Geist, June 23, 1932, copy of letter (but not the report) in RG 59, 123 G 271/153, NARA.

63. Evans, *The Coming*, 298–302.

64. Burke, *Ambassador Frederic Sackett*, 268–269.

65. Ian Kershaw, *Hitler: 1889–1936, Hubris* (New York: W. W. Norton, 1999), 396–400.

66. Kershaw, *Hitler: 1889–1936*, 413–418.

67. Kershaw, *Hitler: 1889–1936*, 414.

68. On Geist's view, see his speech of May 21, 1942, RG 59, Press Releases, #239, May 21, 1942, NARA.

Chapter Three: Americans Encounter the Nazi Revolution

1. Messersmith to Secretary of State, January 12, 1933, RG 59, 862.504/322; Messersmith to Secretary of State, February 10, 1933, RG 59, 862.504/323; Messersmith to Secretary of State, February 20, 1933, RG 59, 862.504/324, NARA. Geist's reports on training apprentices, offering vocational guidance, and running public employment agencies are attached to each of these cover letters. The last report, on employers' associations, is in Messersmith to Secretary of State, March 23, 1933, RG 59, 862.504/325, NARA.

2. Klieforth to Secretary of State, January 31, 1933, RG 59, 862.00/2899, NARA. See also, Burke, *Ambassador Frederic Sackett*, 281.

3. Sackett to Secretary of State, February 6 and 7, 1933, RG 59, 862.00/2902 and 2903, NARA. Burke, *Ambassador Frederic Sackett*, 282–284.

4. Bella Fromm, *Blood and Banquets: A Berlin Social Diary* (New York: Birch Lane Press, 1990), 76.

5. Kershaw, *Hitler: 1889–1936*, 433; Evans, *The Coming*, 310.

6. Fromm, *Blood and Banquets*, 76.

7. I do not have an exact address. Mentioned in Geist's May 22, 1942, lecture, "Masters of Bigotry" (delivered before the National Conference of Christians and Jews, Washington, DC), www.ibiblio.org/pha/policy/1942/1942-05-22a.html.

8. Messersmith to Secretary of State, February 3, 1933, RG 59, 862.50/749, NARA.

9. Messersmith to Feis, February 4, 1933, personal, Herbert Feis Papers, box 123, Library of Congress.

10. Sackett to Secretary of State, February 6 and 7, 1933, RG 59, 862.00/2902 and 2903, NARA. Burke, *Ambassador Frederic Sackett*, 282–284.

11. Geist, "Masters of Bigotry."

12. See the summary of events in Evans, *The Coming*, 328–331. For detailed treatment, Benjamin Carter Hett, *Burning the Reichstag: An Investigation into the Third Reich's Enduring Mystery* (New York: Oxford University Press, 2014).

13. "Seven Years of Socialism under Adolf Hitler," 1940 address given by Geist to various Chambers of Commerce in the United States, Raymond Geist Papers, Franklin D. Roosevelt Library.

14. Evans, *The Coming*, 334–338.

15. "Seven Years of Socialism under Adolf Hitler," 1940 address given by Geist to various Chambers of Commerce in the United States, Raymond Geist Papers, Franklin D. Roosevelt Library.

16. Burke, *Ambassador Frederic Sackett*, 295–296.

17. Burke, *Ambassador Frederic Sackett*, 292–295.

18. The 1923 Treaty of Friendship, Commerce, and Consular Rights, www.loc.gov/law/help/us-treaties/bevans/b-de-ust000008-0153.pdf.

19. Stiller, *George S. Messersmith*, 36; Messersmith to Secretary of State, March 31, 1933, Messersmith Papers, box 1, folder 4, Delaware.

20. Stiller, *George S. Messersmith*, 36; Messersmith to Secretary of State, March 31, 1933, Messersmith Papers, box 1, folder 4, Delaware.

21. Geist Memorandum, August 16, 1933, copy in Messersmith Papers, box 2, folder 16, Delaware.

22. Messersmith to Secretary of State, April 6, 1933, copy in Messersmith Papers, box 1, folder 8, Delaware.

23. See George C. Browder, *The Foundations of the Nazi Police State: The Formation of Sipo and SD* (Lexington: University Press of Kentucky, 1990), 55–57.

24. Messersmith to Secretary of State, May 11, 1933, Messersmith Papers, box 2, folder 11, Delaware: also RG 59, 862.4016/1077, NARA.

25. The most vivid version is Messersmith's recollection in "Conversation with Goering on the break of relations," Messersmith Papers, box 18, folder 135, Delaware, but it is imprecise on some matters. Erik Larson, *In*

the Garden of Beasts: Love, Terror, and an American Family in Hitler's Berlin (New York: Crown Publishers, 2013), 3–4, discusses this case. The contemporary documents are in RG 59, 362.1121 Schachno, Joseph/1-8, NARA.

26. Messersmith to Secretary of State, August 19 and 21, 1933, and October 20, 1933, RG 59, 362.1113 Mulvihill/3, 11 and 16, NARA. On Geist's meeting with Interior State Secretary Grauert, Memorandum of August 18, Messersmith Papers, box 2, folder 18, Delaware.

27. Messersmith to Secretary of State, August 7, 1933, RG 59, 362.1121 Orloff, Walter/80, NARA.

28. Geist's Report of Interview with Orloff, August 2, 1933, attached to Messersmith to Secretary of State, August 7, 1933, RG 59, 362.1121 Orloff/80, NARA.

29. This is a concise summary of the multiple long documents in RG 59, 362.1121 Orloff, Walter, NARA. Particularly important is Geist's seven-page memorandum of August 2, 1933.

30. Phillips to Roosevelt, August 23, 1933, RG 59, 362.1113/4 ½, NARA. The listed cases were Leon Jaffe, Henry Sattler, Edwin Dakin, Nathaniel Wollf, Salomann Friedmann, Louis Berman, Hermann Roseman, Julian Fuhs, Edward Dahlberg, Joseph Schachno, Philip Zuckerman, and Daniel Mulvihill.

31. Robert Brooks to Hull, September 12, 1933, and Moffat to Brooks, October 3, 1933, RG 59, 362.1113/7, NARA.

32. Larson, *In the Garden*, 67–69, 103–105.

33. Moffat Memorandum, September 8, 1933, RG 59, 362.1113/9; Dodd to Secretary of State, September 8, 9, 15, 1933, RG 59, 362.1113/8 and 362/1113/28, NARA.

34. See RG 59, 362.1121 Johnson, Thorsten, and 362.1121 Diamant, Harry, NARA.

35. Messersmith to Secretary of State, November 15, 1933, RG 59, 362.1113/28, NARA.

36. For the ways in which Nazi officials presented themselves to Germans in the 1930s, see Claudia Koonz, *The Nazi Conscience* (Cambridge, MA: Belknap Press of Harvard University Press, 2005).

37. Raymond Geist, Establishment of a United German Protestant Church, August 31, 1933, copy in Messesmith Papers, box 3, folder 18, Delaware.

38. "German press, radio, film and theatre as a Political Instrument of the Hitler Government," September 11, 1933, Messersmith Papers, box 3, folder 18, Delaware.

39. Wikipedia, German edition, s.v. "Friedrich Schönemann," last modified November 24, 2018, 14:29, https://de.wikipedia.org/wiki/Friedrich_Sch%C3%B6nemann_(Amerikanist). Geist to Secretary of State, January 3,

1934, re Nazi Propaganda in the United States, RG 59, 811.00 Nazi/50, NARA. "October 25, 1933," in A Documentary Chronicle of Vassar College, https://chronology.vassar.edu/records/1933/1933-10-25-schoenemann-lecture.html. On the regulation of Nazi agents, see pp. 122, 338.

40. Cited by Abraham Ascher, *Was Hitler a Riddle?: Western Democracies and National Socialism* (Stanford, CA: Stanford University Press, 2012), 157.

41. Geist to Secretary of State, January 10, 1934, "The German Government's new educational methods and policies," RG 59, 862.42/77, NARA.

42. "German press, radio, film and theatre as a Political Instrument of the Hitler Government," September 11, 1933, Messersmith Papers, box 3, folder 18, Delaware.

43. Stiller, *George S. Messersmith*, 51.

Chapter Four: Very Private Lives

1. William Russell, *Berlin Embassy* (New York: Carroll & Graf, 2005, orig. 1940). Russell went on to write novels afterward.

2. Russell, *Berlin Embassy*, 12, 65.

3. Russell, *Berlin Embassy*, 12.

4. Information from Susan Cooper, Geist's great-niece, who got it from her grandmother. Interview of June 19, 2017, and subsequent email correspondence.

5. Postcard collection, Raymond Geist Papers, Franklin D. Roosevelt Library. Katrin Himmler, *The Himmler Brothers: A German Family History*, trans. Michael Mitchell (London: Pan Books, 2008), 166.

6. Stuart Emmrich, "36 Hours in Baden-Baden, Germany," *New York Times*, July 20, 2017, www.nytimes.com/interactive/2017/07/20/travel/what-to-do-36-hours-in-baden-baden-germany.html.

7. Information from Susan Cooper, Geist's great-niece, who got it from her grandmother.

8. Information from John Maller, whose mother later married Mainz. On Mainz's education, see Geist to McMillan, July 23, 1936, RG 59, 125.1953/691, NARA.

9. Telephone interview with John Maller, July 2018.

10. Mainz-Geist photos are in the Raymond Geist Papers at the Franklin D. Roosevelt Library.

11. Photo in the Raymond Geist Papers, Franklin D. Roosevelt Library.

12. Robert Beachy, *Gay Berlin: Birthplace of a Modern Identity* (New York: Vintage Books, 2014), 244.

13. Postcard collection, Raymond Geist Papers, Franklin D. Roosevelt Library. Information from Susan Cooper. Photos from the trip in Erich

Mainz's photo collection, thanks to John M. Maller, in the Raymond Geist Papers, Franklin D. Roosevelt Library.

14. Photos in my possession courtesy of John Maller.

15. Information from Susan Cooper. Documents in the Raymond Geist Papers, Franklin D. Roosevelt Library.

16. Information from Susan Cooper.

17. All this came from his autobiographical statement in his application to the Consular Service. OPF, NARA-SL.

18. Diary entry of January 15, 1908, Raymond Geist Papers, Franklin D. Roosevelt Library.

19. "History," About CSU, Cleveland State University, www.csuohio.edu /about-csu/history.

20. Geist's autobiographical statement, OPF, NARA-SL.

21. Geist's autobiographical statement, OPF, NARA-SL.

22. His letters to his mother have not survived, but she repeatedly commented on his letters and on the money. See Raymond Geist Papers, Franklin D. Roosevelt Library.

23. Anna Geist to Raymond Geist, October 9, 2005, Raymond Geist Papers, Franklin D. Roosevelt Library.

24. Diary entry of March 5, 1908, Raymond Geist Papers, Franklin D. Roosevelt Library.

25. Information from Susan Cooper. On the loan, also Wilbur J. Carr, Memorandum for the Files, July 21, 1921, OPF, NARA-SL. On tuition, diary entry of February 17, 1908, Raymond Geist Papers, Franklin D. Roosevelt Library.

26. Geoffrey Blodgett, *Oberlin Architecture, College and Town: A Guide to Its Social History* (Kent, OH: Kent State University Press, 1985), 20, 30.

27. Information from Liz Schultz, director of the Oberlin Heritage Society, and Susan Cooper.

28. Diary entries of 1908–1909, Raymond Geist Papers. Also, Ira C. Painter to President King, Oberlin College, December 13, 1907; King to Painter, December 21, 1907, Oberlin College Archives.

29. Oberlin College yearbook.

30. They also objected to his use of Oberlin College stationary. Information from Susan Cooper. Ira C. Painter to President, Oberlin College, December 13, 1907; King to Painter, December 21, 1913; Painter to King, December 23, 1907, Oberlin College Archives. Geist got high grades in oratory.

31. Diary entry of April 23, 1908, Raymond Geist Papers, Franklin D. Roosevelt Library.

32. Diary entry of February 22, 1908, Raymond Geist Papers, Franklin D. Roosevelt Library.

33. Diary entry of April 1, 1909, Raymond Geist Papers, Franklin D. Roosevelt Library.

34. Oberlin College transcript, copy in Harvard University Archive, UAV 161.201.10, box 38, Cambridge, MA.

35. Jones to Houghton, March 5, 1918, OPF, NARA-SL.

36. Interview with Susan Cooper, June 19, 2017.

37. See OPF, NARA-SL.

38. Harvard University Archives, UAV 161.201.10, box 38.

39. Information from Susan Cooper.

40. Flier and information from Susan Cooper and Liz Schultz, Oberlin Heritage Society.

41. Web Waldron, "Doc Geist and Vienna," *Collier's*, February 14, 1920. Also, information from Susan Cooper. See photo section.

42. Geist's diary, October–December 8, 1911. Raymond Geist Papers, Franklin D. Roosevelt Library.

43. Information about Norma Reinhart from Susan Cooper and from Geist's diary, December 8, 1911, Raymond Geist Papers, Franklin D. Roosevelt Library.

44. Extract of letter from Geist to Mrs. Biggs, diary entry of January 28, 1912, Raymond Geist Papers, Franklin D. Roosevelt Library.

45. Geist's diary, October–November 1912, Raymond Geist Papers, Franklin D. Roosevelt Library.

46. Postcard collection, Raymond Geist Papers, Franklin D. Roosevelt Library.

47. Autobiographical statement, OPF, NARA-SL. R. S. Shank to R. C. Bannerman, May 19, 1921, copy in OPF, NARA-SL: "Geist had great hopes of having all his expectations of the German people fulfilled, but . . . he was deeply disappointed at conditions which he found there, especially at the numerous 'Forbidden' signs which he saw everywhere and Mrs. Biggs remembers distinctly Geist denouncing the German governmental system."

48. Diary entry of April 6, 1914, Raymond Geist Papers, Franklin D. Roosevelt Library.

49. Autobiographical statement, OPF, NARA-SL.

50. Formal title: "The Vocabulary of Layamon, with Particular Reference to Semantics." Diary entry, May 27, 1916. See also, Webb Waldron, "Doc Geist and Vienna," *Collier's*, February 14, 1920.

51. Recommendation in Kittredge to Bullitt, January 22, 1918, copy in OPF, NARA-SL.

52. Greenbough to Dear Sir, January 22, 1918, OPF, NARA-SL.

53. Wikipedia, German edition, s.v. "Friedrich Schönemann," last modified November 24, 2018, 14:29, https://de.wikipedia.org/wiki/Friedrich_Sch%C3%B6nemann_(Amerikanist).

54. Information from Susan Cooper, interview of June 17, 2017.

55. Information from Susan Cooper.

56. Geist's diary, January 14, 1918, Raymond Geist Papers; Date of death in Geist's passport application, April 19, 1919, Raymond Geist Papers, Franklin D. Roosevelt Library.

57. Geist's diary entry following December 12, 1912, Raymond Geist Papers, Franklin D. Roosevelt Library.

58. Messersmith to Secretary of State, June 26, 1934, and undated Moffat note to Wilson, copies in OPF, NARA-SL.

Chapter Five: Probing the New State

1. Alon Confino, *A World without Jews: The Nazi Imagination from Persecution to Genocide* (New Haven: Yale University Press, 2014), 29.

2. Richard Breitman, Barbara McDonald Stewart, and Severin Hochberg, eds., *Advocate for the Doomed: The Diaries and Papers of James G. McDonald, 1932–1935* (Bloomington: Indiana University Press in association with the United States Holocaust Memorial Museum, 2007), 31.

3. Saul Friedländer, *Nazi Germany and the Jews: The Years of Persecution, 1933–1939* (New York: HarperPerennial, 1998), 1: 20.

4. Gordon to Secretary of State, April 10, 1933, RG 59, 862.4016/615. McDonald heard that the boycott was curtailed because of Hindenburg's concern. Breitman, Stewart, and Hochberg, *Advocate for the Doomed*, 43–45.

5. Messersmith to Secretary of State, April 19, 1933, and June 17, 1933, RG 59, 862.4016/714 and 1181, NARA. On the shift toward government measures, see Friedländer, *Nazi Germany and the Jews*, 1: 27–39.

6. Geist to Secretary of State, June 8, 1933, RG 59, 362.1154 Jewish Telegraphic Agency/9, NARA.

7. Messersmith to Secretary of State, July 26, 27, and 31, 1933, RG 59, 362.1154 Jewish Telegraphic Agency/17 and 24 and 25, NARA.

8. Edgar Ansel Mowrer, *Triumph and Turmoil: A Personal History of Our Times* (New York: Weybright and Talley, 1968), 217–219.

9. Breitman, Stewart, and Hochberg, *Advocate for the Doomed*, 45.

10. Stiller, *George S. Messersmith*, 42.

11. Larson, *In the Garden*, 75–76.

12. Lochner's letter of May 26, 1933, reprinted in Heald, *Journalist at the Brink*, 120. Letter of September 21, 1933, on page 138.

13. Geist to Secretary of State, February 27, 1934, RG 59, 362.1154/25, NARA.

14. Mentioned in Hodgdon to Carr, May 15, 1933, RG 59, 862.4016/5, NARA. On Switzerland's policies, Greg Burgess, *The League of Nations and*

the Refugees from Nazi Germany: James G. McDonald and Hitler's Victims (London: Bloomsbury, 2016), 20.

15. Abraham Ascher, *A Community under Siege: The Jews of Breslau under Nazism* (Stanford, CA: Stanford University Press, 2007), 110.

16. The Dodd family's account of FDR's advice appears in Dodd's post-humously published and edited diary. The original version did not survive, and the published version probably reflects changes by Dodd's children. William E. Dodd Jr. and Martha Dodd, eds., *Ambassador Dodd's Diary, 1933–1938* (London: Victor Gollancz, 1942), 22–23.

17. Larson, *In the Garden*, 43. Diary entry of April 6, 1933, in small note-book entitled Memoranda for 1929–1930, 1932, William E. Dodd Papers, box 59, Library of Congress.

18. Larson, *In the Garden*, 43. Robert Dallek, *Democrat and Diplomat: The Life of William E. Dodd*, 2nd ed. (New York: Oxford University Press, 2012), 196, has Dodd determined to be positive from almost the moment he set foot in the country.

19. Larson, *In the Garden*, 65.

20. Larson, *In the Garden*, 48. Stiller, *George S. Messersmith*, 41.

21. The literature on Dodd is extensive, and I have constructed a short composite from the following: Larson, *In the Garden*, and David Mayers, *FDR's Ambassadors and the Diplomacy of Crisis: From the Rise of Hitler to the End of World War II* (New York: Cambridge University Press, 2013), 36–52.

22. Larson, *In the Garden*, 85. Wilbur Carr, Strictly Confidential Memo, June 5, 1935, Wilbur J. Carr Papers, box 12, Library of Congress.

23. Born in St. Louis into a German Jewish immigrant family, she had married a German Jew, becoming a German citizen and living in Berlin. After her husband died in a swimming accident, she regained her US citizen-ship and returned to her job at the Embassy.

24. Thomas Irmer, Immigrant Entrepreneurship, s.v. "Gerard Swope," last updated March 4, 2013, www.immigrantentrepreneurship.org/entry.php ?rec=61.

25. Wilbur Carr, Strictly Confidential Memo, June 5, 1935, Wilbur J. Carr Papers, box 12, Library of Congress.

26. Larson, *In the Garden*, 62.

27. Breitman, Stewart, and Hochberg, *Advocate for the Doomed*, 293.

28. Geist to Dodd, June 24, 1935, William E. Dodd Papers, box 46, general correspondence G, Library of Congress.

29. Geist's comments to Wilbur Carr, Carr's Strictly Confidential Mem-orandum, June 5, 1935, Carr Papers, box 12, Library of Congress.

30. William Phillips Diary, December 20, 1933, William Phillips Papers, call numbers bMs Am 2232, Houghton Library, Harvard.

31. See Stiller, *George S. Messersmith*, 93.

32. Quoted by Larson, *In the Garden*, 166.

33. Mowrer, *Triumph and Turmoil*, 224–225.

34. Larson, *In the Garden*, 78–79.

35. Kirkpatrick to Secretary of State, April 26, 1934; Geist to Secretary of State, April 30, 1934, RG 59, 862.918/47-49, NARA.

36. See Gerhard L. Weinberg, *The Foreign Policy of Hitler's Germany: Diplomatic Revolution in Europe, 1933–1936* (Chicago: University of Chicago Press, 1970), 164–167; Kershaw, *Hitler: 1889–1936*, 492–495.

37. Geist to Secretary of State, December 15, 1933, RG 59, 862.4106/1336, NARA.

38. Kershaw, *Hitler: 1889–1936*, 495; Victor Klemperer, *I Will Bear Witness: A Diary of the Nazi Years, 1933–1941,* trans. Martin Chalmers (New York: Random House, 1998), 41–42.

39. Geist to Secretary of State, December 15, 1933, RG 59, 862.4016/1336, NARA. See also Koonz, *The Nazi Conscience*, 115. This division was a rival to the Nazi Party's own Office for Enlightenment on Population Policy and Racial Welfare.

40. Geist to Secretary of State, January 19 and 24, 1934, RG 59, 862.4016/1345 and 1347, NARA.

41. Richard Breitman, "American Diplomat Records Regarding German Public Opinion during the Nazi Regime," in *Probing the Depths of German Antisemitism: German Society and the Persecution of the Jews, 1933–1941*, ed. David Bankier (Jerusalem: Yad Vashem Books, 2000), 501–510.

42. Leonard Baker, *Days of Sorrow and Pain: Leo Baeck and the Berlin Jews* (New York: Oxford University Press, 1980), 161–167.

43. Friedrich Brodnitz, interview by Herbert Strauss and Joan Lessing, June 21, 1977, AR 25385, Center for Jewish History, Leo Baeck Institute, New York City, pp. 23–24. I am grateful to Jürgen Matthäus for this reference.

44. Summarized in greater detail in Baker, *Days of Sorrow*, 171–174, who called it a lengthy memorandum. Quote is from Geist to Secretary of State, January 23, 1934, most strictly confidential, RG 59, 862.4016/1349, NARA.

45. Geist to Secretary of State, January 23, 1934, most strictly confidential, RG 59, 862.4016/1349, NARA.

46. Baker, *Days of Sorrow*, 174.

47. Messersmith to Secretary of State, March 16, 1934, RG 59, 862.4016/1371, NARA.

48. On the trial, see Louis Anthes, "Publicly Deliberative Drama: The 1934 Mock Trial of Adolf Hitler for 'Crimes against Civilization,'" *American Journal of Legal History* 42, no. 4 (October 1998): 391–410.

49. Messersmith to Secretary of State, March 16, 1934, RG 59, 862.4016/1371, NARA. *Wisconsin Jewish Chronicle*, March 23, 1934.

50. The three primary sources on this meeting are: Dodd's "Memorandum of a Conversation with Chancellor Hitler," undated, William E. Dodd Papers, box 60, Library of Congress; Dodd and Dodd, *Ambassador Dodd's Diary*, 100–101; Arthur Upham Pope interview of "Dr. Sedgwick" (Hanfstaengl's cover name), December 6, 1943, RG 59, 862.00/4499, NARA. Given that Dodd writes that he met with Hitler alone, Hanfstaengl's recollection is based on what Hitler told him. The undated Dodd memo looks to be a fuller and better source than the edited Dodd diary, so I have relied mostly upon that one. There is a good summary of the meeting in Larson, *In the Garden*, 234–237, but his citation of Dodd's memo is incorrect.

51. See Breitman, Stewart, and Hochberg, *Advocate for the Doomed*, 47–48.

52. Arthur Upham Pope interview of "Dr. Sedgwick" (Hanfstaengl's cover name), December 6, 1943, RG 59, 862.00/4499, NARA.

53. According to David Langbart, diplomatic records specialist at the National Archives, there is no indication of how or when this document entered the files of the State Department. Dodd kept a copy for himself—see n. 50.

54. Material on Röhm and the SA from Daniel Siemens, *Stormtroopers: A New History of Hitler's Brownshirts* (New Haven: Yale University Press, 2017), 158–160. Kershaw, *Hitler: 1889–1936*, 506.

55. Geist to Moffat, June 9, 1934, Messersmith Papers, box 4, folder 24, Delaware.

56. Breitman, Stewart, and Hochberg, *Advocate for the Doomed*, 368.

57. Geist to Moffat, June 9, 1934, Messersmith Papers, box 4, folder 24, Delaware.

58. Moffat to Geist, July 2, 1934, Moffat Papers, vol. 5, Houghton Library, Ms Am 1407, Harvard.

59. Geist to Messersmith, June 14, 1934, Messersmith Papers, box 4, folder 24, Delaware.

60. Kershaw, *Hitler: 1889–1936*, 508–510.

61. Geist to Secretary of State, June 20, 1934, RG 59, 862.00/3284, NARA.

62. Browder, *Foundations of the Nazi Police State*, 142–143.

63. Siemens, *Stormtroopers*, 164–170. Kershaw, *Hitler: 1889–1936*, 515. Messersmith to Phillips, August 18, 1934, Messersmith Papers, box 4, folder 25, Delaware.

64. Messersmith to Phillips, July 5, 1934, and August 18, 1934, Messersmith Papers, box 4, folders 24 and 25, Delaware.

65. Dodd to Secretary of State, July 7, 1934, RG 59, 862.00/3311, NARA.

66. Siemens, *Stormtroopers*, 168.

67. Richard J. Evans, *The Third Reich in Power* (New York: Penguin, 2005), 37.

68. Geist to Moffat, August 10, 1934, Messersmith Papers, box 4, folder 25, Delaware.

69. Quoted in Richard Breitman, *The Architect of Genocide: Himmler and the Final Solution* (New York: Alfred A. Knopf, 1991), 5–6.

70. See Reinhard Rürup, ed., *Topography of Terror: Gestapo, SS and Reichs-sicherheitshauptamt on the "Prinz-Albrecht-Terrain": A Documentation*, trans. Werner T. Angress (Berlin: Verlag Willmuth Arenhövel, 1995).

71. Geist to Secretary of State, August 18, 1934, RG 59, 362.1113 Lep-awsky, Albert/2, NARA. It is unlikely that Himmler wrote anything about this meeting, and if he did, it does not survive.

72. Dorothy Thompson, *I Saw Hitler* (New York: Farrar & Rinehart, 1932). Susan Hertog, *Dangerous Ambition: Rebecca West and Dorothy Thomp-son, New Women in Search of Love and Power* (New York: Ballantine Books, 2011), 213–214.

73. "Miss Thompson Not Resentful," Jewish Telegraphic Agency, Septem-ber 16, 1934, www.jta.org/1934/09/16/archive/miss-thompson-not-resentful.

Chapter Six: Immigration and Emigration

1. Ascher, *A Community under Siege*, 85.

2. For example, March 21, 1933: "The situation concerning the Jews in Germany is causing the utmost alarm to the race here. There have been a se-ries of meetings held far and wide over the country and a huge mass meeting is scheduled for Monday next. The reports of outrages reaching the Jews here from their co-religionists who have left Germany are alarming to a degree. Thus far, nothing we have received from the Embassy tends to bear this out." March 23, 1933: "I believe myself that many of the Jewish leaders here are less actuated by what is happening in Germany than by using it as an excuse to lower the bars on our immigration restriction policy in favor of refugees." Moffat Diary, Moffat Papers, Ms Am 1407, Houghton Library, Harvard.

3. This is a very brief summary of events covered in scholarly literature. A concise version in Breitman and Lichtman, *FDR and the Jews*, 67–75; a more detailed version in Breitman and Kraut, *American Refugee Policy*, 11–45.

4. Woodford Report, Trend of German Migratory Movements, Au-gust 7, 1934, RG 59, 862.55/17, NARA.

5. Smolar initially came in to tell Geist about a new Nazi law banning non-Aryans from serving as editors and correspondents, which would put the JTA out of business. "US Consul Gets Orders to Ease Bars on Refugees,"

Jewish Daily Bulletin, January 30, 1934, p. 1; Geist to Secretary of State, February 2 and 5, 1934; RG 59, 150.626J/56 and 60, NARA.

6. The first *Jewish Daily Bulletin* article was datelined January 30; a second article appeared on February 1. Copies in RG 59, 150.626J and quoted in Coulter to Carr, February 1, 1934, RG 59, 150.626J/55, NARA.

7. Kinnicutt to Hull, February 3, 1934, RG 59, 150.626J-. Carr to Trevor, February 21, 1934, RG 59, 150.626J/56, NARA.

8. Geist to Secretary of State, February 5, 1934, RG 59, 150.626J/60, NARA.

9. Edwin Mims Jr., "German Refugees and American Bureaucrats," *Today*, January 20, 1934, and accompanying Moley editorial. Geist's response, Geist to Secretary of State, March 5, 1934, RG 59, 150.626J/74.

10. Messersmith to Carr, July 27, 1933, RG 59, 150.626J/14, NARA. Geist to Secretary of State, March 5, 1934, RG 59, 150.626J/74, NARA.

11. Geist to Secretary of State, July 19, 1934, RG 59, 811.111 Quota 62/456, NARA. About 3,500 received visas at all the German consulates, and just shy of 600 under the German quota outside Germany, so the total usage of the quota from July 1933 through June 1934 was 4,052.

12. On the formation of German Jewish Children's Aid, see Judith Tydor Baumel, *Unfulfilled Promise: Rescue and Resettlement of Jewish Refugee Children in the United States, 1934–1945* (New York: Denali Press, 1990), 16–19.

13. Solomon Lowenstein, German Jewish Children's Aid, to MacCormack, September 4, 1934; Phillips to Geist, September 13, 1934; Razovsky to Simmons, September 18, 1934; MacCormack to Secretary of State, September 24, 1934: RG 59, 150.626J/97-104, NARA.

14. Jenkins to Secretary of State, November 2, 1934, RG 59, 150.626J/117, NARA.

15. Geist Memo, October 16, 1934, attached to Jenkins to Simmons, October 17, 1934; Carr to Jenkins, November 15, 1934, RG 59, 150.626J/115, NARA.

16. Carr to Simmons, November 22, 1934, and Simmons to Carr, November 23, 1934, RG 59, 150.626J/123, NARA. The 350 total is calculated from the data on individuals in the 150.626J file.

17. Carr to Simmons, November 22, 1934, and Simmons to Carr, November 23, 1934, RG 59, 150.626J/123, NARA.

18. Geist to Secretary of State, September 10, 1934; Fletcher note, October 1, 1934; Carr to Jenkins, October 18, 1934: all in RG 59, 811.111 Quota 62/465, NARA.

19. Messersmith to Moffat, December 12, 1934, copy in OPF, NARA-SL. Messersmith to Thomas Wilson, October 29, 1935, copy in OPF, NARA-SL.

20. Moffat to Wilson and Carr, October 15, 1934, and Hull to Geist, November 15, 1934, copies in OPF, NARA-SL.

21. Jenkins to Secretary of State, November 14 and 20, 1934, RG 59, 362.1154/27, and 811.91262/139, NARA.

22. For example, Jenkins to Dunn, July 24, 1935, 862.00/3509 ½, NARA.

23. Jenkins to Secretary of State, July 2, 1936, copy in RG 59, 123 G 271/219 and 224, NARA.

24. This is a summary of many documents in the file 362.1121 Roiderer, Richard, particularly Jenkins to Secretary of State, April 15, 1935, RG 59, 362.1121 Roiderer, Richard/28, NARA.

25. "Roiderer Is Freed in Treason Trial," *New York Times*, April 13, 1935.

26. Jenkins to Secretary of State, June 5, 1935, RG 59, 362.11/7580, excerpt in 362.1121 Roiderer, Richard/32, NARA.

27. Ramsey's undated account, attached to Jenkins to Secretary of State, December 5, 1934, RG 59, 362.1121 Roiderer, Richard/9, NARA.

28. Quoting an account by Geist that is not in the file, Jenkins to Secretary of State, April 15, 1935, RG 59, 362.1121 Roiderer, Richard/28, NARA.

29. Hathaway to Secretary of State, July 5, 1934, RG 59, 362.1121 Roiderer, Richard/8; Jenkins to Secretary of State, June 5, 1935, RG 59, 362.1121 Roiderer, Richard/32; Roiderer's version, written in New York, August 20, 1935, RG 59, 362.1121 Roiderer, Richard/37: all NARA.

30. Jenkins to Secretary of State, April 15, 1935, RG 59, 362.1121 Roiderer, Richard/28, NARA.

31. Richard Breitman, Barbara McDonald Stewart, and Severin Hochberg, eds., *Refugees and Rescue: The Diaries and Papers of James G. McDonald, 1936–1945* (Bloomington: Indiana University Press in association with the United States Holocaust Memorial Museum, 2009), 10.

32. Friedländer, *Nazi Germany and the Jews*, 1: 137–144.

33. Geist's report, The German Economic Situation with Particular Reference to the Political Outlook, November 12, 1935, RG 59, 862.00/3557, NARA. Reprinted in *Fremde Blicke auf das "Dritte Reich": Berichte ausländischer Diplomaten über Herrschaft und Gesellschaft in Deutschland 1933–1945*, eds. Frank Bajor and Christoph Strupp, 440–442.

34. Jenkins to Secretary of State, September 28, 1935; Bannerman to Simmons, October 26, 1935, RG 59, 150.626J/173, NARA.

35. "Is Mr. Geist now in Washington? I should like to see him and hear whether he can give me any news regarding our Endowment Fund." Lewin to Messersmith, November 17, 1939, RG 59, 123 JSW/47, NARA.

36. Larson, *In the Garden*, 216–217, discusses State Department discontent with Dodd as early as 1934.

37. Strictly Confidential Memorandum, September 4, 1935, and Geist to Wilson, September 4, 1935, copies in OPF, NARA-SL.

38. Phillips Diary, December 22, 1935, Phillips Papers, bMs Am 2232, Houghton Library, Harvard.

39. Geist to Moffat, January 26, 1935, Messersmith Papers, box 4, folder 30, Delaware.

40. Messersmith notes, March 21, 1935, Messersmith Papers, box 5, folder 31, Delaware.

41. Geist to My Dear Friend, January 15, 1936, copy in OPF, NARA-SL. Geist's friend was T. H. Wilson, a State Department official.

42. Geist to Dunn, February 15, 1936, Messersmith Papers, box 6, folder 41, Delaware.

43. Geist to Dunn, February 15, 1936, Messersmith Papers, box 6, folder 41, Delaware.

44. Geist struck false notes only in a couple of foreign policy projections. He thought Hitler would not be able to transcend his racial ideology to cooperate with Japan. He also expected Britain and France to resist German expansion earlier and more successfully than they did.

45. Messersmith to Geist, March 3, 1936, Messersmith Papers, box 6, folder 42, Delaware.

46. Geist to Secretary of State, May 15, 1936, RG 59, 862.4016/1630, NARA.

47. David Glick, "Some Were Rescued: Memories of a Private Mission" *Harvard Law School Bulletin*, December 1960, excerpts published in Breitman, Stewart, and Hochberg, *Refugees and Rescue*, 117–118; Jenkins to Secretary of State, June 9,1936, RG 59, 862.4016/1632, NARA. My account of this meeting is a blend of these two sources, one contemporary, the other a detailed recollection. Jenkins was not at the meeting, so Glick's account is superior in some ways. For example, Jenkins does not mention Himmler, but Glick describes him in some detail.

48. In Glick's reconstruction, Heydrich took them into Haselbacher's office. Both Jenkins and Glick spelled his name with two S's, as did Geist in later documents, but the proper spelling is Haselbacher.

49. Haselbacher's card is in the David Glick Papers, Accession Number 2004.320.1, United States Holocaust Memorial Museum, Washington, DC.

50. Friedländer, *Nazi Germany and the Jews*, 1: 206.

Chapter Seven: Post-Olympic Competition

1. See Geist to Secretary of State, December 5, 1933, "The reorganization of German sport and its part in the political scheme of the Hitler Government," RG 59, 862.4063/5, NARA. Geist called the boycotting organization American Athletic Association.

2. Geist to Secretary of State, December 5, 1933, RG 59, 862.4063/5, NARA; David Clay Large, *Nazi Games: The Olympics of 1936* (New York: W. W. Norton, 2007), 69–95.

3. See detailed treatment in Large, *Nazi Games*, 69–94.

4. Dodd to Secretary of State, October 11, 1935, RG 59, 862.4063 Olympic Games/49, NARA.

5. Large, *Nazi Games*, 94–99.

6. Friedländer, *Nazi Germany and the Jews*, 1: 181.

7. "Hope and Despair: The Curse of the Diamond," *Washington Post*, September 29, 1997.

8. "Hope and Despair," *Washington Post*, September 29, 1997. Reynolds said, "I would today build a wall about the United States so high and so secure that not a single alien or foreign refugee from any country upon the face of the earth could possibly scale or ascend it." See Sarah Wildman, "Meet Robert Reynolds, the Senator who Wanted to 'Build a Wall' 70 Years before Trump," *Vox*, April 4, 2017.

9. "Hope and Despair," *Washington Post*, September 29, 1997.

10. Wilson to Geist, June 22, 1936, copy in OPF, NARA-SL. On the Adlon, Hertog, *Dangerous Ambition*, 213.

11. Large, *Nazi Games*, 208–212: quote on 212.

12. Weinberg, *Diplomatic Revolution in Europe, 1933–1936*, 239–264. Kershaw, *Hitler: 1889–1936*, 582–589.

13. "Seven Years of Socialism under Adolf Hitler," Text of 1940 Speech. Raymond Geist Papers, Franklin D. Roosevelt Library.

14. Evans, *The Third Reich in Power*, 357–368.

15. Geist to Messersmith, January 11, 1937, Messersmith Papers, box 7, folder 51, Delaware.

16. Franklin D. Roosevelt, "Address before the Inter-American Conference for the Maintenance of Peace, Buenos Aires, Argentina," December 1, 1936, American Presidency Project, www.presidency.ucsb.edu/ws/index.php?pid=15238.

17. On Welles and Messersmith, see Irwin F. Gellman, *Secret Affairs: Franklin Roosevelt, Cordell Hull, and Sumner Welles* (Baltimore: Johns Hopkins University Press, 1995), 120–139. See also, Stiller, *George S. Messersmith*, 95.

18. Breitman and Lichtman, *FDR and the Jews*, 67–80; on the ten thousand Jews, 71.

19. Breitman and Lichtman, *FDR and the Jews*, 89–94.

20. Messersmith to Secretary of State, November 13, 1936, RG 59, 150.01/1458, quoted in Breitman and Kraut, *American Refugee Policy*, 48–49.

21. Messersmith later told Geist that the president had read some of his recent letters. Messersmith to Geist, February 10, 1937, Messersmith Papers, box 8, folder 53, Delaware.

22. Breitman and Kraut, *American Refugee Policy*, 48.

23. Visa Instruction, January 5, 1937, RG 59, 150.626J/242, NARA.

24. Wiley to Hodgdon, January 6, 1937, and Hodgdon to Wiley, January 11, 1937, John C. Wiley Papers, box 7, general correspondence H, Franklin D. Roosevelt Library.

25. Breitman and Kraut, *American Refugee Policy*, 50.

26. Messersmith to Geist, November 27, 1937, Messersmith Papers, box 8, folder 57, Delaware.

27. Friedrich Brodnitz to Heinz and Susi Brodnitz, March 24, 1937, US Holocaust Memorial Museum Archive, Acc 189.1. I am grateful to Jürgen Matthäus for this reference.

28. Friedrich Brodnitz, interview by Herbert Strauss and Joan Lessing, June 21, 1977, AR 25385, Center for Jewish History, Leo Baeck Institute, New York City, p. 23. I am grateful to Jürgen Matthäus for this reference.

29. Huddle's June 30, 1937, report on Geist, copy in OPF, NARA-SL. The next three paragraphs are all based on this report.

30. Messersmith to Gilbert, October 25, 1937, Messersmith Papers, box 8, folder 57, Delaware. Secretary of State to Geist, November 1, 1937, RG 59, 123 G 271/241, NARA.

31. Geist to Messersmith, January 11, 1937, Messersmith Papers, box 7, folder 51, Delaware.

32. Geist to Secretary of State, November 9, 1937, RG 59, 150.626J/328, NARA.

33. Glick's report attached to Jenkins to Secretary of State, August 3, 1936, RG 59, 862.4016/1638, NARA. Also, Glick, "Some Were Rescued."

34. "Nazis Dissolve B'nai B'rith, Seize All Property," Jewish Telegraphic Agency, April 21, 1937, www.jta.org/1937/04/21/archive/nazis-dissolve-bnai-brith-seize-all-property. Martin Dean, *Robbing the Jews: The Confiscation of Jewish Property in the Holocaust, 1933–1945* (New York: Cambridge University Press in association with the United States Holocaust Memorial Museum, 2008), 46, but with the incorrect date, April 10.

35. Geist to Secretary of State, April 26, 1937; Jenkins to Secretary of State, April 28, 1937; Jenkins to Secretary of State, May 5, 1937: RG 59, 862.4016/1662, 1663, and 1669, NARA.

36. Dodd to Secretary of State, April 29, 1937, RG 59, 862.4016/1664, NARA. Glick, "Some Were Rescued."

37. Memorandum, May 19, 1937, copy in Glick Papers, Leo Baeck Institute Archive, New York. See brief discussion in Mordecai Paldiel, *Saving One's Own: Jewish Rescuers during the Holocaust* (Philadelphia: Jewish Publication Society of America, 2017), 17.

38. Herbert, *Best*, 42–107.

39. Sackett to Secretary of State, December 1, 1931, RG 59, 862.00/2644, NARA.

40. Herbert, *Best*, 112–118. Sackett to Secretary of State, December 1, 1931, RG 59, 862.00/2644, NARA.

41. Herbert, *Best*, 117.

42. Herbert, *Best*, 205–206.

43. Herbert, *Best*, 196, 660–662.

44. "Grundfragen einer deutschen Grossraum-Verwaltung," in *Festgabe für Heinrich Himmler* (Darmstadt: L. C. Wittich, 1941).

45. David Glick Papers, AR 1239, Center for Jewish History, Leo Baeck Institute, New York City.

46. "Introduction," Helmut Hirsch Exhibit, https://lts.brandeis.edu/research/archives-speccoll/exhibits/hirsch/introduction.html. Division of Western European Affairs Memorandum, June 9, 1937, RG 59, 362.1121 Hirsch, Helmuth/74, NARA.

47. Jenkins to Secretary of State, June 9, 1937, RG 59, 362.1121 Hirsch, Helmuth/71, NARA. Sigrid Schultz, "Nazis Behead Jewish Youth, Citizen of the US," *Chicago Tribune*, June 5, 1937.

48. Geist to Messersmith, October 24, 1937, Messersmith Papers, box 8, folder 56, Delaware.

49. Geist to Messersmith, October 24, 1937, November 1, 1937, and December 5, 1937; information from Susan Cooper. Messersmith to Geist, November 27, 1937: all in Messersmith Papers, box 8, folder 57, Delaware. On Mainz's sick leave, January 8, 1938, RG 59, entry 199, box 67, source card for 125.1953/724, NARA. The document itself is not present in the files.

50. Ron Grossman, "Chicago's First Cardinal Not Afraid to Lead in City—and the World," *Chicago Tribune*, July 20, 2014, www.chicagotribune.com/news/ct-cardinal-mundelein-flashback-0720-20140720-story.html.

51. *Cleveland Plain Dealer*, October 6, 1933, p. 1.

52. *Cleveland Plain Dealer*, October 6, 1937, pp. 1, 4.

53. Robert Dallek, *Franklin D. Roosevelt: A Political Life* (New York: Viking, 2017), 289–291.

54. Dodd and Dodd, *Ambassador Dodd's Diary*, 430–431.

55. Larson, *In the Garden*, 342–347. Geist to Messersmith, October 24, 1937, Messersmith Papers, box 8, folder 56, Delaware.

56. Larson, *In the Garden*, 346–47. Fromm, *Blood and Banquets*, 260. Heald, *Journalist at the Brink*, 287.

57. Geist to Messersmith, October 24, 1937, and November 1, 1937, Messersmith Papers, box 8, folder 56, Delaware.

58. Glick to Baerwald, October 11, 1937, reprinted in "Gestapo Is Germany's Government De Facto," *Pittsburgh Jewish Chronicle*, July 12, 1963.

59. Messersmith to Geist, November 27, 1937, Messersmith Papers, box 8, folder 57, Delaware.

60. Rosenbluth to Landauer, October 27, 1937, Glick Papers, Leo Baeck Institute Archives, New York.

61. Geist to Secretary of State, November 16, 1937, RG 59, 362.1154 Jewish Telegraphic Agency/50, NARA.

62. Geist to Secretary of State, December 14, 1937, and January 4, 1938, RG 59, 362.1154 Jewish Telegraphic Agency/56 and 58, NARA.

63. Geist to Secretary of State, December 14, 1937, RG 59, 362.1154 Jewish Telegraphic Agency/56, NARA.

64. Geist to Messersmith, December 5, 1937, Messersmith Papers, box 8, folder 57, Delaware. Geist misspelled Bömer.

65. Geist to Messersmith, December 5, 1937, Messersmith Papers, box 8, folder 57, Delaware.

66. See chapter eight.

67. Geist to Messersmith, December 5, 1937, Messersmith Papers, box 8, folder 57, Delaware.

Chapter Eight: Austria and Freud

1. Max Domarus, *Hitler: Speeches and Proclamations, 1932–1945*, vol. 2, *1935–1938*, trans. Chris Wilcox and Mary Fran Gilbert (Wauconda, IL: Bolchazy-Carducci, 1990), 1023.

2. Heald, *Journalist at the Brink*, 308.

3. Heald, *Journalist at the Brink*, 13–23.

4. Heald, *Journalist at the Brink*, 328.

5. Lochner kept a handwritten daily diary in 1939, which suggests their relationship. See also n. 14.

6. Informal handwritten distribution list on Geist to Messersmith, April 23, 1938, Messersmith Papers, box 9, folder 62, Messersmith Papers, Delaware.

7. See concise treatment in Gerhard L. Weinberg, *The Foreign Policy of Hitler's Germany: Starting World War II, 1937–1939* (Chicago: University of Chicago Press, 1980), 35–42. Kershaw, *Hitler: 1936–1945*, 46–51. Evans, *The Third Reich in Power*, 370, 642. Hayes, *Why?*, 79–81.

8. Kershaw, *Hitler: 1936–1945*, 51–53.

9. Peter Longerich, *Heinrich Himmler* (New York: Oxford University Press, 2012), 398–400. Robert Gerwarth, *Hitler's Hangman: The Life of Heydrich* (New Haven: Yale University Press, 2012), 116–118.

10. Gerwarth, *Hitler's Hangman*, 118.

11. See Weinberg, *Starting World War II*, 43–45. Geist to Messersmith, February 7, 1938, Messersmith Papers, box 8, folder 59, Delaware.

12. Geist to Messersmith, February 15, 1938, and Geist to Moffat, March 1, 1938, Messersmith Papers, box 8, folders 59–60, Delaware.

13. Summary in Evans, *The Third Reich in Power*, 648–653.

14. Based on information from Lochner, Geist had initially predicted a Nazi putsch in Austria. Geist to Messersmith, January 27, 1938, Messersmith Papers, box 8, folder 58; Geist to Messersmith, March 23, 1938, box 9, folder 61, Delaware.

15. Breitman and Lichtman, *FDR and the Jews*, 119–120.

16. Messersmith to Wilson, March 4, 1938, Hugh R. Wilson Papers, box 3, Messersmith folder, Hoover Library.

17. Wilson to Messersmith, March 13, 1938; Messersmith to FP and Shaw, March 28, 1938; Shaw to FA, March 31, 1938: all in OPF, NARA-SL. There were two other first secretaries. It appears that Wilson ratified Geist's rank, which he held earlier.

18. Geist to Messersmith, March 1, 1938, Messersmith Papers, box 8, folder 60, Delaware.

19. On the car, see Morris to Secretary of State, October 30, 1940, RG 59, 123 G 271/331, NARA. On the location, Affidavit of August 28, 1945, Office of the United States Chief of Counsel for Prosecution of Axis Criminality, *Nazi Conspiracy and Aggression*, vol. 4 (Washington, DC: United States Printing Office, 1946),1759-PS. On Geist finding the Wilsons a house there, Geist to Messersmith, June 5, 1938, Messersmith Papers, box 9, folder 63, Delaware.

20. Annual Efficiency Report of August 1, 1938, copy in OPF, NARA-SL.

21. Entries of March 25, April 9, May 26, July 8, Wilson Diary 1938, Wilson Papers, box 4, Hoover Library.

22. Wilson Diary, June 15, 1938, Wilson Papers, box 4, 1938 folder, Hoover Library. Mayers, *FDR's Ambassadors*, 54–55.

23. Geist to Messersmith, April 20, 1938, Messersmith Papers, box 9, folder 62, Delaware.

24. Geist to Messersmith, March 23, 1938, and Messersmith to Geist, April 5, 1938, Messersmith Papers, box 9, folder 61, Delaware.

25. Rosenman to Welles, March 11, 1938; Welles to Messersmith, March 12, 1938; Messersmith to Rosenman, March 15, 1938; Messersmith to Geist, March 14, 1938: all in RG 59, 811.111 Laband, Paul, NARA.

26. Geist to Messersmith, April 4, 1938, RG 59, 811.111 Laband, Paul, NARA. I found no new instruction, but the policy did change.

27. Geist to Secretary of State, July 2, 1938, RG 59, 811.111 Auernheimer, Raoul, NARA.

28. Quoted in Peter Gay, *Freud: A Life for Our Time* (New York: W. W. Norton, 2006), 619.

29. Hans Safrian, *Eichmann's Men*, trans. Ute Stargardt (New York: Cambridge University Press in association with the United States Holocaust Memorial Museum, 2010), 21–22. Gardner Richardson Memo, Persecution

of Jews in Vienna, March 25, 1938, Messersmith Papers, box 9, folder 61, Delaware.

30. Gay, *Freud*, 621, has an estimate of five hundred, but later studies have reduced this number.

31. Geist to Messersmith, April 20, 1938, Messersmith Papers, box 9, folder 62, Delaware.

32. Evans, *The Third Reich in Power*, 657.

33. Letter of April 14, 1938, in Heald, *Journalist at the Brink*, 312–313.

34. Welles to Wilson, March 16, 1938, RG 59, 363.6315/8B, NARA. Gay, *Freud*, 548–551, 592–93.

35. Gay, *Freud*, 622–623. Welles to Wilson, March 16, 1938, RG 59, 363.6315/8B, NARA. Since Roosevelt had no official standing to intervene and was himself a frequent target of vitriolic Nazi propaganda, Undersecretary Welles suggested that Wiley simply say to Nazi officials that generous treatment of Freud would create a favorable impression in the United States.

36. Gay, *Freud*, 623–624.

37. Gay, *Freud*, 624.

38. Harvard Medical School professor Walter B. Cannon wrote Felix Frankfurter about Loewi. Frankfurter wrote FDR, who asked Sumner Welles what could be done. Welles wrote Ambassador Wilson, asking him to meet with the proper officials at the Consulate General (i.e., Geist) to see what could be done. Welles suggested that Geist take the line that giving Loewi and another scientist permission to leave Germany would favorably affect public opinion in the United States. See the mid-April 1938 documents in RG 59, 363.6315/91 ½, NARA.

39. Geist to Secretary of State, March 29, 1938, RG 59, 363.6315/45, NARA. Wilson to Secretary of State, April 27, 1938, RG 59, 362.1113/37, NARA. Geist to Messersmith, May 8, 1938, Messersmith Papers, box 9, folder 62, Delaware. (Most of the B'nai B'rith men were released in August. Bisgyer to Davis, August 12, 1938, RG 59, 363.6315/117, NARA.)

40. Geist to Messersmith, May 8, 1938, Messersmith Papers, box 9, folder 62, Delaware.

41. Geist to Messersmith, May 8, 1938, Messersmith Papers, box 9, folder 62, Delaware.

42. Geist to Messersmith, October 21, 1938, Messersmith Papers, box 9, folder 67, Delaware.

43. Wilson to Secretary of State, May 6, 1938, RG 59, 363.6315/102, NARA. Gay, *Freud*, 627–628.

44. All material on Heller in the following paragraphs comes from Wiley to Secretary of State, May 12, 1938, RG 59, 362.1113/44, NARA, and Geist to Messersmith, May 8, 1938, Messersmith Papers, box 9, folder 62, Delaware.

45. Geist to Messersmith, May 8, 1938, Messersmith Papers, box 9, folder 62, Delaware.

46. Gay, *Freud*, 628.

47. Erhardt to Secretary of State, July 15, 1938, RG 59, 811.111 Quota 62/588, NARA.

48. Geist to Secretary of State, May 19 and June 9, 1938, RG 59, entry 199, file card for 125.1952/38, NARA. The document is not present in the files. On another officer and more clerks, Geist to Secretary of State, June 21, 1938, RG 59, 125.1953/735, NARA. On the forms, Geist to Secretary of State, August 16, 1938, RG 59, 811.111 Quota 62/591, NARA.

49. Erhardt to Secretary of State, July 15, 1938, RG 59, 811.111 Quota 62/588, NARA.

50. Wiley Memorandum for Inspector Erhardt, July 6, 1938, RG 59, 811.111 Quota 62/588, NARA. Wiley to Geist, August 4, 1938, John Cooper Wiley Papers, box 7, folder General Correspondence G, Franklin D. Roosevelt Library. On Wiley generally, see Melissa Jane Taylor, "Bureaucratic Response to Human Tragedy: American Consuls and the Jewish Plight in Vienna, 1938–1941," *Holocaust and Genocide Studies* 21, no. 2 (2007): 243–267. Geist to Wiley, July 23, 1938, Wiley Papers, box 7, folder General Correspondence G, Franklin D. Roosevelt Library. Geist to Messersmith, October 21, 1938, Messersmith Papers, box 9, folder 67, Delaware.

51. Geist to Messersmith, May 16, 1938, Messersmith Papers, box 9, folder 63, Delaware.

Chapter Nine: *The Refugee Crisis*

1. Evans, *The Third Reich in Power*, 664. Kershaw, *Hitler: 1936–1945*, 92.

2. Geist to Messersmith, April 23, 1938, Messersmith Papers, box 9, folder 62, Delaware.

3. Geist to Messersmith, June 12, 1938; Messersmith to Hull, June 24, 1938; Messersmith to Welles, July 7, 1938; Messersmith Papers, box 9, folder 64, Delaware.

4. Evans, *The Third Reich in Power*, 669–672.

5. Messersmith to Pittman, September 1, 1938, Messersmith Papers, box 9, folder 65, Delaware.

6. Geist to Messersmith, October 21, 1938, Messersmith Papers, box 9, folder 67, Delaware.

7. Evans, *The Third Reich in Power*, 672–674.

8. Geist to Messersmith, October 21, 1938, Messersmith Papers, box 9, folder 67, Delaware.

9. Weinberg, *Starting World War II*, 467.

10. Messersmith to Hull, September 29, 1938, Messersmith Papers, box 9, folder 65, Delaware. Weinberg, *Starting World War II*, 462.

11. Breitman and Lichtman, *FDR and the Jews*, 102–106, 108–109.

12. Breitman and Lichtman, *FDR and the Jews*, 108–109.

13. Breitman and Lichtman, *FDR and the Jews*, 106–107. Breitman, Stewart, and Hochberg, *Refugees and Rescue*, 135–136.

14. On Messersmith, see Breitman, Stewart, and Hochberg, *Refugees and Rescue*, 137. Geist to Taylor, June 24, 1938, RG 59, entry 199, file card for 840.48 Refugees/483. The document itself is not present in the files.

15. Wiley to Messersmith, July 18, 1938, Messersmith Papers, box 9, folder 64, Delaware.

16. Naomi Shepherd, *A Refuge from Darkness: Wilfrid Israel and the Rescue of the Jews* (New York: Pantheon, 1984), 134–135.

17. On the conference as a whole, Diane Afoumado, *Indésirables: 1938: la Conférence d'Évian et les réfugiés juifs* (Paris: Calmann-Lévy, 2018). S. Adler-Rudel, "The Evian Conference on the Refugee Question," *Leo Baeck Institute Year-Book* 13 (1968): 235–260. On the US objectives, Breitman, Stewart, and Hochberg, *Refugees and Rescue*, 139.

18. Wilson to Taylor, July 27, 1938, Wilson Papers, box 3, Taylor folder, Hoover Library.

19. Geist to Secretary of State, August 3, 1938, copy in RG 59, 123 G 271/260, NARA. He is listed among the dinner guests at Claridge's on the evening of August 4, 1938. Myron Taylor Papers, box 5, Intergovernmental Committee on Political Refugees, 1938 Correspondence folder, Franklin D. Roosevelt Library. Geist to Secretary of State, August 9, 1938, RG 59, 123 G 271/261, NARA.

20. Wilson Diary, August 10, 1938, Wilson Papers, box 4, Hoover Library.

21. Geist to Wilson, December 5, 1938, Wilson Papers, box 2, Geist folder, Hoover Library.

22. Johnson (Taylor) to Secretary of State, August 12, 1938, RG 59, 840.48 Refugees/657, NARA.

23. Details are to be found, among other places, in the minutes of the meeting of the President's Advisory Committee on Political Refugees, September 30, 1938, RG 59, Lot File 52D408, box 9, PACPR minutes, NARA.

24. George L. Brandt report, July 30, 1938, copy in Myron Taylor Papers, box 5, Intergovernmental Committee on Refugees 1938, Franklin D. Roosevelt Library.

25. Freudenthal to Secretary of State, August 29, 1938, copy in RG 59, 123 G 271/263, NARA.

26. Geist to Secretary of State, September 8, 1938, and Hull to Geist, September 13, 1938, RG 59, 150.626J/482, NARA.

27. Geist to Secretary of State, September 8, 1938, RG 59, 150. 626J/482, NARA. Journal of Trip to Europe 1938, September 14–19, 1938, Clarence Pickett Papers, American Friends Service Committee Archives, Philadelphia. On the Nazi measures, Friedländer, *Nazi Germany and the Jews*, 1: 258. Geist to Messersmith, October 21, 1938, Messersmith Papers, box 9, folder 67, Delaware.

28. Geist to Secretary of State, October 8 and 10, 1938, RG 59, 150.626J/506 and 522, NARA. Geist to Secretary of State, October 10, 1938, RG 59, 862.4016/1793, NARA.

29. Friedländer, *Nazi Germany and the Jews*, 1: 264.

30. Best's acceptance in the Raymond Geist Papers, Franklin D. Roosevelt Library. See also, Best's daily calendar, October 15, 1938, Nachlass 1023, Microfilm 1157 K, Bundesarchiv Koblenz. I am grateful to Melanie Hembera for tracking down this document.

31. Geist to Messersmith, October 21, 1938, Messersmith Papers, box 9, folder 67, Delaware.

32. Herbert, *Best*, 191–193, 230–233; Katrin Paehler, *The Third Reich's Intelligence Services: The Career of Walter Schellenberg* (New York: Cambridge University Press, 2017), 52–53. Gerwarth, *Hitler's Hangman*, 163–165.

33. There is no surviving summary of their conversation.

34. Geist to Messersmith, October 21, 1938, Messersmith Papers, box 9, folder 67, Delaware. Longerich, *Heinrich Himmler*, 408.

35. Geist to Messersmith, October 21, 1938, Messersmith Papers, box 9, folder 67, Delaware.

36. See Nikolaus Wachsmann, *A History of the Nazi Concentration Camps* (New York: Farrar, Strauss and Giroux, 2015), 57–60, 83–86; Charles W. Sydnor Jr., *Soldiers of Destruction: The SS Death's Head Division, 1933–1945* (Princeton, NJ: Princeton University Press, 1977), esp. 3, 17, 30–31.

37. Geist to Messersmith, October 21, 1938, Messersmith Papers, box 9, folder 67, Delaware.

38. Geist later mentioned a conversation with the Dutch consul general on November 16 in which he told the official about the arrangement he already had with both the British and French to give visitors' visas to those near the top of the US waiting list. Geist to Secretary of State, December 12, 1938, RG 59, 840.48 Refugees/1137 (microfilm M-1284, R 23), NARA. On Foley, see Michael Smith, *Foley: The Spy Who Saved 10,000 Jews* (London: Coronet Books, 1999). But Smith does not mention Foley's cooperation with Geist.

39. Minutes of the Meeting of the President's Advisory Committee on Political Refugees, September 30, 1938, RG 59, Lot File 52D408, box 9, PACPR minutes, NARA. Kennedy (Rublee) to Secretary of State, October 12, 1938, copy in RG 59, Lot File 52D408, Alphabetical Subject File, box 7, 2nd Officer's Meeting, NARA.

40. Geist to Messersmith, October 21, 1938, Messersmith Papers, box 9, folder 67, Delaware.

41. These items are part of an exhibition called *Americans and the Holocaust* at the US Holocaust Memorial Museum. It opened in 2018.

42. Charles A. Lindbergh, *The Wartime Journals of Charles A. Lindbergh* (New York: Harcourt Brace Jovanovich, 1970), 101–103.

43. Geist to Messersmith, October 21, 1938, Messersmith Papers, box 9, folder 67, Delaware.

44. Wilson Diary, October 25, 1938, Wilson Papers, box 4, 1938 folder, Hoover Library.

45. See Lynne Olson, *Those Angry Days: Roosevelt, Lindbergh and America's Fight over World War II, 1939–1941* (New York: Random House, 2013).

46. Longerich, *Heinrich Himmler*, 408. Friedländer, *Nazi Germany and the Jews*, 1: 267.

47. Himmler's calendar of appointments, copy in Hoover Institution Microfilm T-501, R 37A, NARA. The one additional document about this meeting identifies Geist but does not identify Himmler, and it probably does not give all the topics they covered.

48. Wilson to Secretary of State, October 29, 1938, RG 59, 862.4016/1802, NARA.

49. Friedländer, *Nazi Germany and the Jews*, 1: 267–268.

50. Kennedy (Rublee) to Secretary of State, November 3, 1938, RG 59, 840.48 Refugees/868, NARA.

51. Geist to Eugenia, September 25, 1933, postcard collection, Raymond Geist Papers, Franklin D. Roosevelt Library.

52. Geist Affidavit, August 28, 1945, *Nazi Conspiracy and Aggression*, vol. 4, 1759-PS.

53. Geist to Messersmith, October 21, 1938, Messersmith Papers, box 9, folder 67, Delaware.

54. Geist to Messersmith, October 21, 1938, Messersmith Papers, box 9, folder 67, Delaware.

55. Geist to Messersmith, October 21, 1938, Messersmith Papers, box 9, folder 67, Delaware.

56. Geist to Messersmith, October 21, 1938, Messersmith Papers, box 9, folder 67, Delaware.

Chapter Ten: Kristallnacht

1. Interview with Ralph Rehbock, November 9, 2016. Rehbock emails of November 2016.

2. Charles W. Thayer, *The Unquiet Germans* (New York: Harper and Brothers, 1957), 162.

3. In his postwar affidavit, Geist misdated Kristallnacht as November 8–9. I have corrected the date. He specifically stated that he did not witness the destruction itself because he was en route to Eisenach. Affidavit of August 28, 1945, *Nazi Conspiracy and Aggression*, vol. 4, 1759-PS.

4. Alan E. Steinweis, *Kristallnacht 1938* (Cambridge, MA: Belknap Press of Harvard University Press, 2009), esp. 42–53. Beate Meyer, Hermann Simon, and Chana Schütz, eds., *Jews in Nazi Berlin: From Kristallnacht to Liberation* (Chicago: University of Chicago Press, 2009), 9.

5. Thayer, *The Unquiet Germans*, 162–163.

6. Longerich, *Himmler*, 409–410.

7. Affidavit of August 28, 1945, *Nazi Conspiracy and Aggression*, vol. 4, 1759-PS. Geist to Secretary of State, November 10, 1938, RG 59, 862.422/3, NARA.

8. Interview with Ralph Rehbock, November 9, 2016, and email exchanges afterward. Ralph Rehbock heard the story of these events from his mother, who began to talk about them only in 1983. He learned the identity of the man in charge at the Consulate General only when I told him in 2016.

9. Steinweis, *Kristallnacht 1938*, 95–96.

10. Diary entries of November 10–12, 1938, Wilson Papers, box 4, 1938 folder, Hoover Library.

11. Thayer, *The Unquiet Germans*, 162–163.

12. Geist's inquiries with Nazi officials about specific individuals are mentioned in Sigrid Schultz, "Wilson Sees Ribbentrop," *Chicago Tribune*, November 16, 1938; also, "Arrested Jews with Emigration Prospects to be Released, U.S. Envoy Told by Nazis," Jewish Telegraphic Agency, November 17, 1938. On the crowd of 1,500 at the Consulate General, Geist to Secretary of State, November 14, 1938, RG 59, 811.111 Quota 62/635, NARA. On the waiting list, "Reichsverband Reopens: Munich Ban on Religious Services Lifted: Arrests Total 60,000," Jewish Telegraphic Agency, November 30, 1938.

13. Best's list of appointments, November 15, 1938, Nachlass Best, NL 1023, Microfilm 1157 K, Bundesarchiv Koblenz. I am grateful to Jürgen Matthäus for locating this document. Affidavit of August 28, 1945, *Nazi Conspiracy and Aggression*, vol. 4, 1759-PS.

14. On Best's meeting with Heydrich and with Geist, Best's list of appointments, November 14 and 15, Nachlass Best, NL 1023, Microfilm

1157 K, Bundesarchiv Koblenz. I am indebted to Melanie Hembera and Jürgen Matthäus for tracking down these documents.

15. Affidavit of August 28, 1945, *Nazi Conspiracy and Aggression*, vol. 4, 1759-PS. Geist wrote that he obtained the release of about twenty people from Sachsenhausen.

16. Eugene Garbáty was co-owner of the Garbáty concern with his brother Moritz. Moritz also had dealings with Helldorff, got an exit permit in December 1938, and went to the United States, but managed to avoid a concentration camp. See Beate Meyer, "'Aryanized' and Financially Ruined: The Case of the Garbáty Family," in *Jews in Nazi Berlin*, eds. Meyer, Simon, and Schütz, 68–73.

17. Affidavit of August 28, 1945, *Nazi Conspiracy and Aggression*, vol. 4, 1759-PS. *Bull*, Italian Renaissance about 1600, bronze, Museum of Fine Arts Boston, www.mfa.org/collections/object/bull-53591. W. E. Cyrenius, *Landscape*, 1925, watercolor and gouache, 7 1/16 x 9 3/8 in. (17.9 x 23.8 cm), www.metmuseum.org/art/collection/search/335325.

18. Geist to Messersmith, December 12, 1938, Messersmith Papers, box 10, folder 71, Delaware. "Fritz M. Warburg of Banking House; Last of 5 Brothers in Noted German Family Is Dead," *New York Times*, October 15, 1964, www .nytimes.com/1964/10/15/fritz-m-warburg-of-banking-house.html.

19. Most of the original sources in RG 59, 811.111 Bettelheim, Bruno, NARA. The critical document is Geist to Secretary of State, November 26, 1938. But Bettelheim himself credited Avra Warren for his release. See, Nina Sutton, *Bettelheim: A Life and a Legacy* (Boulder, CO: Westview Press, 1996), 131–132, 176–180.

20. Documents in RG 59, 362.1121 Schick, Herbert, NARA. The critical document is Geist to Secretary of State, November 23, 1938, RG 59, 362.1121 Schick, Herbert/7, NARA.

21. Geist to Secretary of State, December 12, 1938, RG 59, 840.48 Refugees/1187, NARA.

22. Geist to Messersmith, December 12, 1938, Messersmith Papers, box 10, folder 71, Delaware.

23. This is the opinion of Danny Greene, curator of the *Americans and the Holocaust* exhibition at the US Holocaust Memorial Museum. Greene presentation on May 7, 2018, at the US Holocaust Memorial Museum, Washington, DC. Heald, *Journalist at the Brink*, 328–329. Breitman and Lichtman, *FDR and the Holocaust*, 114–116.

24. *Franklin D. Roosevelt "Day by Day" Project* (Hyde Park, NY: Pare Lorentz Center at the Franklin D. Roosevelt Library, 2011), www.fdrlibrary .marist.edu/daybyday/. There is no account of their conversation from November 14, 1938.

25. Harold L. Ickes, *The Secret Diary of Harold L. Ickes*, vol. 2, *The Inside Struggle, 1936–1939* (New York: Simon & Schuster, 1954), 505. "Text of the Protests by Leaders in U.S. against Reich Persecution," *New York Times*, November 15, 1938, p. 4.

26. Ickes, *Secret Diary of Harold L. Ickes*, 2: 504. Breitman and Lichtman, *FDR and the Jews*, 115–116.

27. Wilson conveyed it at his meeting with FDR either on November 28 or December 6–7.

28. Sigrid Schultz, "Wilson Sees Ribbentrop," *Chicago Tribune*, November 16, 1938. "December 7th, 1938," in *Franklin D. Roosevelt "Day by Day" Project* (Hyde Park, NY: Pare Lorentz Center at the Franklin D. Roosevelt Library, 2011), www.fdrlibrary.marist.edu/daybyday/daylog /december-7th-1938/. FDR to Secretary of State, December 10, 1938, RG 59, 840.48 Refugees/1072 Confidential File, NARA.

29. Steinweis, *Kristallnacht 1938*, 135.

30. Steinweis, *Kristallnacht 1938*, 104–107. Dan Michman, *The Emergence of Jewish Ghettos during the Holocaust*, trans. Lenn J. Scramm (New York: Cambridge University Press, 2014), 45–60. Best's list of appointments, November 14 and 17, Nachlass Best, NL 1023, Microfilm 1157 K, Bundesarchiv Koblenz. I am indebted to Melanie Hembera and Jürgen Matthäus for this source.

31. Gilbert to Secretary of State, December 5, 1938, RG 59, 862.00/3806 and 711.62/174, NARA.

32. Gilbert to Secretary of State, December 5, 1938, RG 59, 862.00/3806, NARA.

33. "Juden, was nun?" *Das Schwarze Korps*, November 24, 1938.

34. Geist to Messersmith, December 5, 1938, Messersmith Papers, box 10, folder 70, Delaware.

35. Geist to Messersmith, December 5, 1938, Messersmith Papers, box 10, folder 70, Delaware. Wilson to Rublee, November 9, 1938, and Rublee to Wilson, November 10, 1938, Wilson Papers, box 3, Rublee folder, Hoover Library.

36. Geist to Wilson, December 5, 1938, Wilson Papers, box 2, Geist folder, Hoover Library. Getting the embassy work done was another of Geist's many jobs. See appendix.

37. Affidavit of August 28, 1945, *Nazi Conspiracy and Aggression*, vol. 4, 1759-PS. See Haselbacher's SS Personnel File, RG 242-Berlin Document Center, R 067A, NARA.

38. This was the standard address for a report to the State Department.

39. Geist to Secretary of State, December 12, 1938, RG 59, 840.48 Refugees/1187, NARA.

40. Geist to Messersmith, December 12, 1938, Messersmith Papers, box 10, folder 71, Delaware.

41. Geist to Messersmith, December 12, 1938; Geist to Messersmith, May 10, 1939, Messersmith Papers, box 10, folder 71; box 11, folder 80, Delaware.

42. Geist to Messersmith, December 12, 1938, Messersmith Papers, box 10, folder 71, Delaware.

43. Messersmith to Geist, December 8, 1939, Messersmith Papers, box 10, folder 70, Delaware.

44. Messersmith to Geist, December 8, 1939, Messersmith Papers, box 10, folder 70, Delaware.

45. Messersmith to Geist and Messersmith to Warren, December 9, 1938, RG 59, 811.111 Quota 62/662a and 662b, NARA.

46. On Warren and Messersmith, see n. 45. Reynolds to Messersmith, January 16, 1939, and Messersmith to Reynolds, January 19, 1939, RG 59, 150.626J/593, NARA.

47. On Messersmith, see n. 44. Gilbert to Moffat, December 10, 1938, vol. 13, Moffat Papers, Ms Am 1407, Houghton Library, Harvard.

48. Geist to Secretary of State, December 15, 1938, RG 59, 811.111 Quota 62/659, NARA.

49. Factual notes on Trip to Germany by Robert Yarnall, Refugee Service 1938, American Friends Service Committee Archives, Philadelphia. *The Holocaust Encyclopedia*, s.v. "Quakers," US Holocaust Memorial Museum, www.ushmm.org/wlc/en/article.php?ModuleId=10005212.

50. Factual notes on Trip to Germany by Robert Yarnall, Refugee Service 1938, American Friends Service Committee Archives, Philadelphia.

51. Gilbert to Secretary of State, February 2, 1939, RG 59, 762.00/237 Confidential File, NARA.

52. Geist to Messersmith, January 22, 1939, Messersmith Papers, box 10, folder 73, Delaware.

53. Gilbert to Secretary of State, February 2, 1939, RG 59, 762.00/237, NARA.

54. *Rede des Führers und Reichkanzlers Adolf Hitler vor dem Reichstag am 30. Januar 1939* (Berlin: M. Müller & Sohn, 1939), partial translation by Thomas Dunlap in "Excerpts from Hitler's Speech before the First 'Greater German Reichstag' (January 30, 1939)," German History in Documents and Images, http://germanhistorydocs.ghi-dc.org/docpage .cfm?docpage_id=2925.

55. Kershaw, *Hitler: 1936–1945*, 152.

56. Along these lines, Jeffrey Herf, *The Jewish Enemy: Nazi Propaganda during World War II and the Holocaust* (Cambridge, MA: Belknap Press of Harvard University Press, 2008).

Chapter Eleven: Testing Göring

1. Nazi officials spread the rumor that its director, George Rublee, was Jewish. Rublee's ancestors were actually French Huguenots, he wrote Wilson. Wilson to Rublee, November 9, 1938, and Rublee to Wilson, November 10, 1938, Wilson Papers, box 3, Rublee folder, Hoover Library.

2. See Shepherd, *A Refuge from Darkness*, 153–155; Breitman and Kraut, *American Refugee Policy*, 67–68.

3. Kennedy (Rublee) to Secretary of State, Strictly Confidential for the Secretary and Undersecretary, October 12, 1938, RG 59, Lot File 52D408, Alphabetical Subject File, box 7, second officers meeting, December 2, 1938, NARA.

4. Geist to Messersmith, January 4, 1939, Messersmith Papers, box 10, folder 72, Delaware. The source, identified as one of Messersmith's friends, was quite possibly Dannie Heinemann, Belgian American engineer and businessman who held a controlling interest in the multinational corporation Sofina. There is extensive correspondence between the two in the Messersmith Papers.

5. On the Esplanade, Lochner Diary, January 10, 1939, Lochner Papers, box 11, diaries folder, Wisconsin Historical Society.

6. Geist to Messersmith, April 12, 1939, Messersmith Papers, box 11, folder 77, Delaware. Geist to Secretary of State, March 7, 1939, RG 59, 124.621/478, NARA. The move took place in the late winter of 1938–1939 and the spring.

7. Gilbert (Rublee) to Secretary of State, January 11, 1939, RG 59, 840.48 Refugees/258, NARA.

8. This account of Geist's activity is based on two very detailed, consistent, but slightly different contemporary sources, which I have blended together: Geist to Messersmith, January 22, 1939, Messersmith Papers, box 10, folder 73, Delaware; and Lochner Diary, January 25, 1939, Lochner Papers, box 11, diaries folder, Wisconsin Historical Society. Rublee's account of the discussion with Göring is in Gilbert (Rublee) to Secretary of State, January 21, 1939, RG 59, 840.48 Refugees/328. Rublee intentionally did not mention Geist for reasons explained in the text.

9. Gilbert (Rublee) to Secretary of State, January 21, 1939, RG 59, 840.48 Refugees/1328, NARA.

10. Messersmith to Hull, Welles, and Moffat, March 27, 1939, RG 59, 862.4016/2100, NARA.

11. Messersmith to Geist, February 16, 1939, personal and strictly confidential, Messersmith Papers, box 10, folder 74, Delaware.

12. Franklin D. Roosevelt, "Annual Message to Congress," January 4, 1939, American Presidency Project, www.presidency.ucsb.edu/ws/index.php?pid=15684.

13. Dobbs, *The Unwanted*, 41, 81. Honaker to Secretary of State, December 31, 1938, RG 59, 125.8853/497, NARA. On the bribery of Vice Consul Stephen Vaughan in Breslau, see Ascher, *A Community under Siege*, 135–136. The State Department ordered an investigation in late April 1939, but accusations against Vaughan surfaced early in 1939. See Hull (Warren) to American Embassy (Geist), April 27, 1939, RG 59, 125.2316/35A, NARA; Morris to Secretary of State, June 14, 1939, RG 59, 123 M 83/466, NARA.

14. Messersmith to Geist, February 16, 1939, Messersmith Papers, box 10, folder 74, Delaware.

15. The portion of his letter to Messersmith spelling out his thoughts on visitors' visas is torn off, so that it is not possible to determine exactly what he wrote.

16. Foley to Jeffes, January 17, 1939, and Cooper to Reilly, January 26, 1939, HO 213/115, National Archives, UK. I am grateful to Michael Dobbs for a copy of these documents.

17. Lochner Diary, January 17, 1939, Lochner Papers, box 11, diaries folder, Wisconsin Historical Society.

18. Geist to Messersmith, January 22, 1939, Messersmith Papers, box 10, folder 73, Delaware.

19. Geist to Messersmith, January 22, 1939, Messersmith Papers, box 10, folder 73, Delaware.

20. See Pell's analysis in Breitman, Stewart, and Hochberg, *Refugees and Rescue*, 164–165. Also, Shepherd, *A Refuge from Darkness*, 156.

21. Lochner Diary, February 2 and 7, 1939, Lochner Papers, box 11, diaries folder, Wisconsin Historical Society.

22. Geist to Messersmith, April 4, 1939, Messersmith Papers, box 11, folder 77, Delaware.

23. Confidential Report by the Jewish Telegraphic Agency, March 6, 1939, copy in Messersmith Papers, box 10, folder 75, Delaware.

24. Geist to Messersmith, April 4, 1939, Messersmith Papers, box 11, folder 77, Delaware.

25. Geist to Messersmith, April 4, 1939, Messersmith Papers, box 11, folder 77, Delaware.

26. Geist used the phrase "some degree of moderation will at least be exercised by the Germans." Geist to Messersmith, April 4, 1939, Messersmith Papers, box 11, folder 77, Delaware. Also, Geist commented to Lochner on March 1: "We should be very careful to see the Rublee committee work." Lochner Diary, March 1, 1939, Lochner Papers, box 11, Wisconsin Historical Society.

27. Lochner Diary, February 25, 1939, Lochner Papers, box 11, diaries folder, Wisconsin Historical Society.

28. Geist to Secretary of State, March 1, 1939, RG 59, 362.1121 Weyl, Henry/7; Alfred Block to Secretary of State, c/o Moffat, March 30, 1939; Weyl, Henry/12, NARA. On the Jewish community of Kippenheim, see Dobbs, *The Unwanted*.

29. Geist to Secretary of State, March 8, 1939, RG 59, Lot File 52D408, country file, box 5, Germany 1939, NARA.

30. Detailed treatment in Weinberg, *Starting World War II*, 467–534; Kershaw, *Hitler: 1936–1945*, 163–171.

31. Friedländer, *Nazi Germany and the Jews*, 1: 302–305. Detailed treatment in Wolf Gruner, *Die Judenverfolgung im Protektorat Böhmen und Mähren: Lokale Initiativen, zentrale Entscheidungen, jüdische Antworten 1939–1945* (Göttingen, Germany: Wallstein Verlag, 2016), 44–74. Geist to Secretary of State, March 17, 1939, RG 59, 860f.48/56a, NARA.

32. For detailed treatment, Weinberg, *Starting World War II*, 540–560. Also, Lochner Diary, March 31, 1939, Lochner Papers, box 11, diaries folder, Wisconsin Historical Society. Geist to Secretary of State, April 6, 1939, RG 59, 740.00/742, NARA. The source was General Erhard Milch.

33. Geist to Secretary of State, April 13, 1939, RG 59, 740.00/794, NARA.

34. See Achilles to Messersmith and Welles, March 14, 1939, RG 59, Lot File 52D408, Alphabetical Subject File, box 9, President's Advisory Committee 1939, NARA. Breitman, Stewart, and Hochberg, *Refugees and Rescue*, 167–171.

35. Geist to Messersmith, April 4, 1939, Messersmith Papers, box 11, folder 77, Delaware.

36. Geist to Messersmith, April 12, 1939, Messersmith Papers, box 11, folder 77, Delaware. [Jones?] to Pickett, April 5, 1939, American Friends Service Committee Archive, Refugee Service 1939, Letters from Germany, Philadelphia.

37. Kennedy (Pell) to Secretary of State, April 25, 1939; Kennedy (Pell) to Secretary of State, April 28, 1939, RG 59, 840.48 Refugees/1570 and 1587, NARA.

38. Geist to Secretary of State, May 3, 1939, RG 59, 840.48 Refugees/1597, NARA.

39. Shepherd, *A Refuge from Darkness*, 161–162.

40. *Franklin D. Roosevelt "Day by Day" Project* (Hyde Park, NY: Pare Lorentz Center at the Franklin D. Roosevelt Library, 2011), www.fdrlibrary.marist.edu/daybyday/. Roosevelt sent a similar telegram to Mussolini, April 7, 1939.

41. Geist to Secretary of State, April 17, 1939, RG 59, 740.00/911; Lochner Diary, April 22 and 26, 1939, Lochner Papers, box 11, diaries folder, Wisconsin Historical Society.

42. Geist to Secretary of State, April 16, 1939, RG 59, 740.00/839, NARA.

43. Geist to Secretary of State, April 27 and 28, 1939, RG 59, 740.00/1181 and 1206, NARA.

44. Lochner Diary, May 9, 1939, Lochner Papers, box 11, diaries folder, Wisconsin Historical Society. Photo in *Historische Stunden* Unidentified photo collection from a German newspaper or brochure, Raymond Geist Papers, Franklin D. Roosevelt Library.

45. Domarus, *Hitler*, vol. 2, *1935–1938*, 1583–1590; Kershaw, *Hitler: 1936–1945*, 189. Klaus P. Fischer, *Hitler and America* (Philadelphia: University of Pennsylvania Press, 2011), 104–105.

46. Quoted by Fischer, *Hitler and America*, 106.

47. Geist to Secretary of State, April 28, 1939, RG 59, 740.00/1212, NARA.

48. Geist to Secretary of State, May 4, 1939, RG 59, 740.00/1454, NARA. Lochner Diary, May 4, 1939, Lochner Papers, box 11, diaries folder, Wisconsin Historical Society.

49. Geist to Secretary of State, May 3, 1939, RG 59, 840.48 Refugees/1597, NARA. See related documents on the meeting in Breitman, Stewart, and Hochberg, *Refugees and Rescue*, 170–174.

50. Geist to Messersmith, October 21, 1938, Messersmith Papers, box 9, folder 67, Delaware.

51. Moffat Journal, May 4, 1939, Moffat Papers, vol. 42, Ms Am 1407, Houghton Library, Harvard University. By permission of Houghton Library, Harvard University. Also, Breitman and Lichtman, *FDR and the Jews*, 155.

Chapter Twelve: Children

1. Journalist Steven Pressman already has narrated this fascinating rescue from the perspective of the Krauses, his wife's grandparents. Eleanor Kraus wrote a memoir from which Pressman drew heavily. An afterword, written by Paul Shapiro of the US Holocaust Memorial Museum, acknowledges the role of Messersmith and Geist. Steven Pressman, *50 Children: One Ordinary American Couple's Extraordinary Rescue Mission into the Heart of Nazi Germany* (New York: Harper Perennial, 2015), 256–257.

2. See Breitman and Lichtman, *FDR and the Jews*, 147.

3. Breitman and Lichtman, *FDR and the Jews*, 147–149. The poll results of the National Center for Public Opinion, presented in the US Holocaust Memorial Museum exhibition *Americans and the Holocaust*.

4. Pressman, *50 Children*, 4–5.

5. On the acquaintanceship, Pressman, *50 Children*, 57. On Sacks's visits: "Congressman Leo Sacks of Pennsylvania has been in to see me a number of times together with Mr. Kraus and his associates." Messersmith to Warren and Coulter, February 7, 1939, RG 59, 150.626J/610, NARA.

6. Messersmith to Geist, February 3 and 6, 1939, RG 59, 150.626J/610, NARA.

7. Messersmith to Geist, February 3, 1939, RG 59, 150.626J/610, NARA. Also discussed by Pressman, *50 Children*, 61. Geist to Messersmith, February 20, 1939, RG 59, 150.626J/612, NARA.

8. See Pressman, *50 Children*, 84–85.

9. See chapter six above.

10. Geist to Secretary of State, October 10, 1938, and Razovsky to Warren, October 27, 1938, RG 59, 150.626J/523-524, NARA.

11. Pressman, *50 Children*, 55–62.

12. Messersmith to Geist, February 6, 1939, RG 59, 150.626J/610, NARA.

13. Messersmith to Kraus, February 6, 1939, RG 59, 150.626J/610, NARA.

14. Messersmith to Kraus, February 6, 1939, RG 59, 150.626J/610, NARA.

15. Geist to Secretary of State, March 21, 1939, RG 59, 150.626J/621; Warren to Messersmith, March 24, 1939, RG 59, 150.626J/621, NARA.

16. Pressman, *50 Children*, 76–80. Warren to Blanche Goldman, German Jewish Children's Aid, March 2, 1939, RG 59, 150.626J/604, NARA.

17. See discussion in Breitman and Lichtman, *FDR and the Jews*, 149–150.

18. Pressman, *50 Children*, 88–92.

19. Messersmith to Geist, March 29, 1939, RG 59, 150.626J/625A, NARA.

20. Pressman, *50 Children*, 100–101.

21. Geist to Messersmith, May 4, 1939, RG 59, 150.626J/649, NARA. This differs somewhat from the account in Pressman, *50 Children*, 102, that Geist said time was running out for the Jews of Vienna. On the situation of Jews in Vienna, see Ilana Fritz Offenberger, *The Jews of Nazi Vienna, 1938–1945: Rescue and Destruction* (New York: Palgrave Macmillan, 2017).

22. Pressman, *50 Children*, 120–121. Most Famous Hotels in the World, s.v. "Bristol Vienna," https://famoushotels.org/hotels/bristol-vienna.

23. Pressman, *50 Children*, 102–110, 115–120.

24. Geist to Messersmith, May 4, 1939, RG 59, 150.626J/649, NARA. Pressman, *50 Children*, 123–134.

25. Geist to Secretary of State, May 26, 1939, 811.111 Quota 62/699, NARA. The system was complicated. The consulates general in Berlin, Vienna, Hamburg, and Stuttgart each had an allotment from the quota for

Germany. For the first ten months of the year, they could not exceed 10 percent of their allotment in each month. If everyone actually used their visas, nothing was left over for May and June, but now those who had registered early enough could recycle the unused visas.

26. Pressman, *50 Children*, 134–135. There is no trace of this addition in visa records.

27. Geist to Messersmith, May 4, 1939; Hull (Warren) to Morris, May 16, 1939; Hull (Messersmith) to Geist, May 18, 1939, RG 59, 811.111 Quota 62/649–650, NARA.

28. Pressman, *50 Children*, 137–138, 142.

29. Geist to Secretary of State, May 19, 1939, RG 59, 150.626J/651, NARA.

30. Pressman, *50 Children*, 142–144.

31. Geist to Messersmith, May 11, 1939, RG 59, 150.626J/654, NARA.

32. Pressman, *50 Children*, 199–202. *New York Times* article reprinted in Pressman, photo section after 160.

33. See Breitman and Lichtman, *FDR and the Jews*, 150–151.

34. Kraus to Messersmith, June 8, 1939, RG 59, 150.626J/657, NARA.

35. Holman to Secretary of State, June 6, 1939, RG 59, 150.626J/656, NARA.

36. Geist to Secretary of State, June 20, 1939, RG 59, 811.111 Quota 62/702, NARA.

37. Contemporary records show data for the calendar year 1938 as 84 percent Jewish. See undated immigration chart [June 1939], RG 59, 811.111 Quota 62/706, NARA.

Chapter Thirteen: Toward War

1. Hull to Geist, April 13, 1939, RG 59, 123 G 271/282, NARA.

2. Efficiency Rating—Political Work, copy in OPF, NARA-SL.

3. Wikipedia, s.v. "Alexander Comstock Kirk," last modified November 6, 2018, 16:50, https://en.wikipedia.org/wiki/Alexander_Comstock_Kirk.

4. Kirk signed most of the political reports to Washington after mid-May. See RG 59, 740.00/1371ff, NARA.

5. Lochner Diary, August 17, 1939, Lochner Papers, box 11, diaries folder, Wisconsin Historical Society.

6. Lochner Diary, May 13, 1939, Lochner Papers, box 11, diaries folder, Wisconsin Historical Society. Jochen Thies, *Hitler's Plans for Global Domination: Nazi Architecture and Ultimate War Aims*, trans. Ian Cooke and Mary-Beth Friedrich (New York: Berghahn Books, 2012), 119. Hitler frequently stated that he might die young.

7. Lochner Diary, May 20, 1939, Lochner Papers, box 11, diaries folder, Wisconsin Historical Society.

8. Geist to Messersmith, January 22, 1939, Messersmith Papers, box 10, folder 73, folder, Delaware.

9. Lochner Diary, May 1939, Lochner Papers, box 11, diaries folder, Wisconsin Historical Society. Heald, *Journalist at the Brink*, 366–369.

10. Otto Tolischus, "Trouble-Shooter in Berlin," *New York Times Magazine*, July 23, 1939. Howard K. Smith, *Last Train from Berlin* (New York: Alfred A. Knopf, 1942), 52.

11. Geist to Wiley, May 16, 1939; Geist to Sussdorff Jr., May 16, 1939; Wiley to Geist, May 18, 1939, John C. Wiley Papers, box 7, General Correspondence G, Franklin D. Roosevelt Library.

12. For more details, see Breitman, Stewart, and Hochberg, *Refugees and Rescue*, 175–177.

13. Kennedy (Pell) to Secretary of State, June 3, 1939, RG 59, 840.48 Refugees/1647, NARA.

14. Messersmith to Shaw, August 15, 1939, OPF, NARA-SL.

15. Geist to Secretary of State, June 14, 1939, RG 59, 123 G 271/286, NARA. On Davenport, Davenport to Roosevelt, September 26, 1939, Adolf Berle Papers, box 66, Memoranda to FDR, April–December 1939, Franklin D. Roosevelt Library.

16. Daniel Scroop, *Mr. Democrat: Jim Farley, the New Deal, and the Making of Modern American Politics* (Ann Arbor: University of Michigan Press, 2006), 177–178.

17. Lochner Diary, August 17, 1939, Lochner Papers, box 11, diaries folder, Wisconsin Historical Society.

18. Farley's "Notes on Trip to Europe, July–September 1939," James A. Farley Papers, microfilm R 4, Franklin D. Roosevelt Library.

19. Geist's speech, "Seven Years of Socialism under Adolf Hitler" (1940), Raymond Geist Papers, Franklin D. Roosevelt Library.

20. Lochner Diary, August 17, 1939, Lochner Papers, box 11, diaries folder, Wisconsin Historical Society. Lochner referred to the camp by the name of Oranienburg. On the view, Günter Morsch and Astrid Ley, eds., *Sachsenhausen Concentration Camp, 1936–1945: Events and Developments* (Berlin: Metropol, 2013), 58. Farley thanked Geist later. Farley to Geist, OPF, NARA-SL.

21. Morsch and Ley, *Sachsenhausen Concentration Camp*, 54–55, 70–71.

22. Lochner Diary, August 21, 1939, Lochner Papers, box 11, diaries folder, Wisconsin Historical Society.

23. Lochner Diary, August 21, 1939, Lochner Papers, box 11, diaries folder, Wisconsin Historical Society.

24. See Gerhard L. Weinberg, *A World at Arms: A Global History of World War II* (New York: Cambridge University Press, 1994), 87; Fischer, *Hitler and America*, 106–107.

25. Lochner Diary, August 27, 1939, Lochner Papers, box 11, diaries folder, Wisconsin Historical Society.

26. Farley's "Notes on Trip to Europe, July–September 1939," Farley Papers, Roll 4, Franklin D. Roosevelt Library. Benjamin Welles, *Sumner Welles: FDR's Global Strategist* (New York: St. Martin's Press, 1997), 248.

27. Lochner Diary, September 1939, Lochner Papers, box 11, diaries folder, Wisconsin Historical Society.

28. Herbert, *Best*, 239.

29. Herbert, *Best*, 239.

30. Alexander B. Rossino, *Hitler Strikes Poland: Blitzkrieg, Ideology, and Atrocity* (Lawrence: University Press of Kansas, 2003), 78–84.

31. Herbert, *Best*, 239–243.

32. Michael Wildt, *An Uncompromising Generation: The Nazi Leadership of the Reich Security Main Office*, trans. Tom Lampert (Madison: University of Wisconsin Press, 2009), 155–169.

33. The basic source, Kirk to Secretary of State, October 10, 1939, confidential for Howland Shaw, RG 59, 123 G 271/291, NARA, does not specify when Geist's problems—compounded by nervous exhaustion—first arose, but suggests that they started in early September, got better for a short while, then deteriorated in early October. I found in Lochner's diary no direct contacts between Lochner and Geist from the end of August until October 3. But the two could have passed messages through Lochner's daughter, Rosemarie, who now worked at the Embassy.

34. On the evacuations, for example, Geist to Secretary of State, September 22, 1939, RG 59, 125.0062/268, NARA. On the currency smuggling case involving Frederich Wirth Jr., see Kirk to Secretary of State, September 16 and October 3, 1939, RG 59, 362.1121 Wirth Jr., NARA. On Wohlthat, Kirk to Secretary of State, September 28, 1939, confidential for Achilles, RG 59, 840.48 Refugees/1872, NARA.

35. Casualties from Weinberg, *A World at Arms*, 57. Lochner Diary, October 3, 1939, Lochner Papers, box 11, diaries folder, Wisconsin Historical Society.

36. Davenport to Roosevelt, September 26, 1939, Adolf Berle Papers, box 66, Franklin D. Roosevelt Library.

37. Lochner Diary, October 11, 1939, Lochner Papers, box 11, diaries folder, Wisconsin Historical Society.

38. Geist to Secretary of State, November 30, 1939, with medical opinion by Dr. Jürg Zutt, RG 59, 123 G 271/300, NARA.

39. Geist to Messersmith, November 9, 1939, copy in OPF, NARA-SL.

40. Adolf Berle Diary, November 28, 1939, Berle Papers, Franklin D. Roosevelt Library.

41. Geist to Messersmith, June 12, 1940, Messersmith Papers, box 12, folder 90, Delaware.

42. Weinberg, *A World at Arms*, 94.

43. Kirk to Secretary of State, October 10, 1939, RG 59, 123 G 271/291, NARA.

44. Wikipedia, "SS *Conte di Savoia*," last updated April 2, 2019, 14:00, https://en.wikipedia.org/wiki/SS_Conte_di_Savoia.

45. Geist to Shaw, October 21, 1939, copy in OPF, NARA-SL.

46. For example, Lewin to Messersmith, October 17, 1939, and Messersmith to Lewin, November 14, 1939. Emil Baerwald wanted to see Geist, too. Baerwald to Secretary of State, November 2, 1939, all in RG 59, 123 G 271/293, NARA.

47. Petition for Naturalization, February 1941, with reference to November 24, 1939, declaration, USCIS FOIA for Erich Kurt Mainz, GEN 2108002206. Mainz's visa case file does not survive. The details of how he received an immigration visa are unknown, but we may infer that Geist had encouraged him to apply early enough and sponsored him with an affidavit of support.

48. Blinded assessments, November 28-29, 1939, copies in OPF, NARA-SL.

49. Adolf Berle Diary, November 28–29, 1939, Berle Papers, Franklin D. Roosevelt Library. The addition is reprinted in Beatrice Bishop Berle and Travis Beal Jacobs, eds., *Navigating the Rapids, 1918–1971: From the Papers of Adolf A. Berle* (New York: Harcourt Brace Jovanovich, 1973), 273.

50. Roosevelt to Welles, November 21, 1939, Official File 67, Foreign Service 1939, Franklin D. Roosevelt Library: "Geist, Con. Gen. Berlin: I want to see him. FDR."

51. Correspondence from December 1, 1939. "December 1st, 1939," in *Franklin D. Roosevelt "Day by Day" Project* (Hyde Park, NY: Pare Lorentz Center at the Franklin D. Roosevelt Library, 2011), www.fdrlibrary.marist.edu/daybyday/december-1st-1939/.

52. Henry Ashby Turner Jr., *General Motors and the Nazis: The Struggle for Control of Opel, Europe's Biggest Carmaker* (New Haven: Yale University Press, 2005), 114. Mooney is listed as having met FDR on December 22, 1939. *Franklin D. Roosevelt "Day by Day" Project* (Hyde Park, NY: Pare Lorentz Center at the Franklin D. Roosevelt Library, 2011), http://www.fdrlibrary.marist.edu/daybyday/.

Chapter Fourteen: From Afar

1. Mainz's Alien Registration Form [1940], Mainz FOIA, GEN20180 02206. The house at 3501 Davis Street NW still exists.

2. 5201 Edgemoor Lane address from census data. Morris to Secretary of State, October 30, 1940, RG 59, 123 G 271/331, NARA. But the car had been shipped months earlier.

3. Anna is listed as resident in Bethesda in the 1940 census. Erick is listed as resident in Bethesda in his February 1941 petition for naturalization. Efforts to trace ownership of the house, which no longer exists, have been unsuccessful. See photo.

4. William Offutt, *Bethesda: A Social History of an Area through World War II* (Bethesda, MD: The Innovation Game, 1995), 298–304, 314, 457. On the restrictive covenant, email from Eron Sodie, April 9, 2019.

5. Secretary of State to Geist, March 27, 1940, RG 59, 123 G 271/311, NARA. The salary increase took effect upon Senate confirmation.

6. "1940–1949," Administrative Timeline of the Department of State, Office of the Historian, US Department of State, https://history.state.gov /departmenthistory/timeline/1940-1949.

7. RG 59, press releases, State Department press release #133, April 2, 1940.

8. Charles A. Lindbergh, "Our National Safety: Let Us Turn Our Eyes to Our Own Nation," delivered over radio, May 19, 1940, www.ibiblio.org /pha/policy/1940/1940-05-19a.html.

9. Lindbergh, *Wartime Journals*, 350.

10. Quoted by Susan Dunn, *1940: FDR, Willkie, Lindbergh, Hitler—the Election amid the Storm* (New Haven: Yale University Press, 2013), 56.

11. Long to Geist, May 18, 1940, RG 59, 123 G 271/318, NARA.

12. Copy of text and notes in Raymond Geist Papers, Franklin D. Roosevelt Library. "Foreign Trade Week Starts," *Charleston Gazette*, May 20, 1940.

13. There was much more in Geist's text and notes, but other portions repeat incidents described earlier in this book.

14. Weinberg, *A World at Arms*, 122–131.

15. Francis MacDonnell, *Insidious Foes: The Axis Fifth Column and the American Home Front* (New York: Oxford University Press, 1995), 116–121.

16. MacDonnell, *Insidious Foes*, 30–32, 49–65.

17. Breitman and Lichtman, *FDR and the Jews*, 166–167. Long Diary, May 17, 1940, Breckinridge Long Papers, box 5, Library of Congress.

18. Cited by Dunn, *1940*, 58.

19. MacDonnell, *Insidious Foes*, 119–121. Seventy percent poll in US Holocaust Memorial Museum exhibition *Americans and the Holocaust*.

20. Geist's "Nazi Propaganda in the United States," January 5, 1934; Dodd to Secretary of State, January 15, 1934; Coulter to Carr, February 8, 1934: RG 59, 811.00 Nazi/50-54, NARA.

21. Breitman and Lichtman, *FDR and the Jews*, 168.

22. Breitman and Lichtman, *FDR and the Jews*, 177.

23. State Department reorganizations in 1940 made the position of the Division of Commercial Affairs ambiguous. Whether reorganization or personal factors induced Geist to work more with Berle is unclear. I am grateful to Melissa Jane Taylor, a State Department historian, for her information on this subject.

24. Long Diary, December 11–12, 1940, Long Papers, box 5, Library of Congress.

25. Berle Diary, August 28, 1940, reprinted in Berle and Jacobs, *Navigating the Rapids*, 332.

26. Geist Memo, July 5, 1940; Bannerman Memo, July 27, 1940; Geist to Warren, August 19, 1940, RG 59, 800.20211 Goldschmidt, Jakob/3-7, NARA.

27. Geist to Wilson, May 19, 1942, RG 226, entry 168A, box 1, folder 14, NARA. Sherman subsequently worked for the Office of Strategic Services.

28. Hoover to Berle, June 17, 1940; Geist Memo of Conversation, June 29, 1940, RG 59, 811.111 Stennes [*sic*], Edmund, NARA.

29. The unsigned background memo on Stinnes, giving the correct spelling of his name, is in RG 59, 811.111 Stennes, Edmund Jr., NARA. See also Walter Laqueur and Richard Breitman, *Breaking the Silence: The German Who Exposed the Final Solution* (Hanover, NH: University Press of New England, 1994), 61–62.

30. Geist to Fletcher Warren, and Geist's Confidential Memorandum of German Propaganda, July 12, 1940. RG 59, 800.01, Registration—German Library of Information/112ff, NARA.

31. Geist to Fletcher Warren, and Geist's Confidential Memorandum on German Propaganda, July 12, 1940; Hoover to Berle, July 24, 1940; Kleinfeld to Hull, September 16, 1940; Price Memo, September 19, 1940: all in RG 59, 800.01 Registration—German Library of Information/112-196, NARA.

32. Geist report on Rauber, September 30, 1940, RG 59, 862.20211 Rauber/1-7, NARA. On von Gienanth and Wagner, Geist to Berle, September 30, 1940; Berle to Hoover, September 30, 1940, RG 59, 701.6211/1200-1202, NARA.

33. Hoover to Berle, November 12, 1941, RG 59, 701.6211/1432 CF, NARA.

34. Geist to Berle, October 11, 1940, RG 59, 701.6211/1324 CF, NARA. November 6, 1935, Memo to Himmler's Personal Chancellery; Heydrich to

von Gienanth, November 9, 1935; and von Gienanth Lebenslauf, in RG 242, Berlin Document Center, SSO, roll A12, NARA.

35. Matt Lebovic, "When Boston Was America's 'Capital' of Anti-Semitism," *Times of Israel*, September 4, 2017, www.timesofisrael.com/when -boston-was-the-capital-of-anti-semitism-in-america/. Geist to Berle, October 11, 1940; Berle to War Department, FBI, and ONI, October 16, 1940, RG 59, 701.6211/1324 CF, NARA. On Thomsen, MacDonnell, *Insidious Foes*, 27. Memo to the SS-Hauptamt, August 22, 1935, RG 242, Berlin Document Center, SSO, roll B98, NARA.

36. Harold Ross and E. J. Kahn Jr., "Ex-Consul," *New Yorker*, July 20, 1940, www.newyorker.com/magazine/1940/07/20/ex-consul. Breitman, Stewart, and Hochberg, *Advocate for the Doomed*, 255.

37. "Through Mr. Geist, Dr. Schwarz has been supplying very confidential political information to Mr. Berle regarding the Transocean Press Service and on other matters." Summary of Conversation, Geist, Atherton, December 31, 1940, RG 59, 862.20210 Schwarz, Paul/5, NARA.

38. REM to Long, October 9, 1940, 862.20210 Transocean News Agency/10-940 CF; Welles to All American Diplomatic Missions in the other American Republics, August 19, 1941, RG 59, 862.20210 Transocean News Agency/93, NARA. On Schwarz, n. 37 above.

39. Summary of Conversation, Geist, Atherton, December 31, 1940; Atherton to Berle, December 31, 1940, RG 59, 862.20210 Schwarz, Paul/ 5-6, NARA.

40. See Geist's Memo of Conversation with George Riedel of GM, December 19, 1940, RG 59, 164.12 General Motors Export Co/9, NARA, and subsequent documents in this file.

41. Geist to Warren, March 5, 1941, RG 59, 862.20211 Mooney, James D./1-2, NARA.

42. Messersmith to Stewart, March 4, 1941, and Messersmith to Warren, March 5, 1941, RG 59, 862.20211 Mooney, James D./3, NARA. Turner, *General Motors*, 105–126.

43. Breitman and Lichtman, *FDR and the Jews*, 191.

44. Michael Dobbs, *Saboteurs: The Nazi Raid on America* (New York: Vintage, 2005).

45. Attorney General Francis Biddle to Secretary of State, July 21, 1943, copy in OPF, NARA-SL.

46. Harrison to Secretary of State, December 5, 1942; Harrison to Secretary of State, January 7, 1943, secret for Berle; Neal to Geist, January 12, 1943; Geist to Neal, January 13, 1943, RG 59, 862.20200 Goerdeler, Karl [*sic*], CF, NARA. For a good historical assessment of Goerdeler, see Peter Hoffmann, *Carl Goerdeler gegen die Verfolgung der Juden* (Cologne: Bohlau Verlag, 2013).

47. Copy of Geist's text "Some Economic Aspects of Our Foreign Relations," October 8, 1942, in RG 59, 123 G 271/382, NARA.

48. RG 59, Press Releases, #239, May 21, 1942, NARA.

49. Breitman and Lichtman, *FDR and the Jews*, 198.

50. Morris to Secretary of State, September 8, 26, 30, 1941; October 14, 18, 20, 27, 1941, RG 59, 862.4016/2202-2208; Morris to Secretary of State, November 1, 1941, RG 59, 862.4016/2209, NARA.

51. Morris to Secretary of State, November 16, 1941, RG 59, 862. 4016/2212, NARA.

Chapter Fifteen: Indirect Influence

1. See Henry Friedlander, *The Origins of Nazi Genocide: From Euthanasia to the Final Solution* (Chapel Hill: University of North Carolina Press, 1997); LeRoy Walters, "Paul Braune Confronts the National Socialists' 'Euthanasia' Program," *Holocaust and Genocide Studies* 21, no. 3 (2007): 454–487.

2. Thorsten Noack, "William L. Shirer and International Awareness of the Nazi 'Euthanasia' Program," *Holocaust and Genocide Studies* 30, no. 3 (2016): 439–448.

3. All of the following related reports were stamped by the Division of Commercial Affairs: Morris to Secretary of State, December 20, 1940; Stewart to Secretary of State, December 23, 1940; Morris to Secretary of State, March 23, 1941; RG 59, 862.1241/13, /14, /15, NARA.

4. Two letters from Schultz to Geist survive, but none from Geist to her. See Schultz to Geist, December 21, 1939, and February 18, 1940, Sigrid Schultz Papers, box 11, folder Correspondence Personal General 1939–1940, Wisconsin Historical Society.

5. Noack, "William L. Shirer," 442.

6. Geist's undated cover letter to Honaker to Morris, February 7, 1941, RG 59, 862.12/33, NARA. Wurm's letter is attached.

7. Alfred M. Beck, *Hitler's Ambivalent Attaché: Lt. Gen. Friedrich von Boetticher in America, 1933–1941* (Washington, DC: Potomac Books, 2005), 103, 192, 262n28.

8. Notes of cabinet, 19 December 1941, Francis Biddle Papers, box 1, cabinet meetings 1941, Franklin D. Roosevelt Library. Boetticher's son remained in the United States and joined the US Army Air Force upon his release from treatment in 1944. Beck, *Hitler's Ambivalent Attaché*, 192.

9. Noack, "William L. Shirer," 436–437, 445.

10. Morris to Secretary of State, September 8, 26, 30, 1941; October 14, 18, 20, 27, 1941, RG 59, 862.4016/2202–2208; Morris to Secretary of State, November 1, 1941, RG 59, 862.4016/2209, NARA. Most of these

reports went only to the Division of European Affairs and Division of Communications and Records; one went to the Visa Division as well, another to the Division of Current Information.

11. The story of how Riegner obtained this information, once a secret, then disputed, is now well known and confirmed by Riegner. Laqueur and Breitman, *Breaking the Silence*. On Riegner's reports from Geneva, Jürgen Matthäus, *Predicting the Holocaust: Jewish Organizations Report from Geneva on the Emergence of the "Final Solution," 1939–1942*, Documenting Life and Destruction: Holocaust Sources in Context 13 (Lanham, MD: Rowman & Littlefield, 2018).

12. Breitman interview with Gerhart M. Riegner, April 20, 1992, RG 50.030*0189, United States Holocaust Memorial Museum.

13. Harrison to Secretary of State, August 11, 1942, strictly confidential, RG 59, 862.4016/2233, NARA.

14. Hull to American Legation, Bern, August 17, 1942, RG 59, 862.4016/2233, NARA.

15. Durbrow Memorandum, August 13, 1942, RG 59, 862.4016/2235, NARA.

16. Shorter version of cable. Breitman and Lichtman, *FDR and the Jews*, 199–200.

17. See Jeffrey Herf, *The Jewish Enemy: Nazi Propaganda during World War II and the Holocaust* (Cambridge, MA: Belknap Press of Harvard University Press, 2008).

18. Breitman and Lichtman, *FDR and the Jews*, 197–206. Breitman and Kraut, *American Refugee Policy*, 157 and 281n48.

19. Breitman and Kraut, *American Refugee Policy*, 157.

20. Harrison to Secretary of State, for the Undersecretary, January 21, 1943, RG 59, 740.00116 E.W. 1939/753, NARA.

21. Hull to American Legation, Bern, February 10, 1943, RG 59, 740.00116 E.W. 1939/753, CF, NARA.

22. Breitman and Lichtman, *FDR and the Jews*, 216–225.

23. Breitman and Lichtman, *FDR and the Jews*, 231–232.

24. See "Records of the Department of State 1921–1958," attached to Anderson to Trone, March 30, 1959, RG 59, Central Decimal File 1955–1959, 114/3-3159, NARA. I am grateful to David Langbart for this document. Berle to Messersmith, November 17, 1943, and Messersmith to Berle, December 20, 1943, Berle Papers, box 43, Correspondence, Messersmith folder, Franklin D. Roosevelt Library. Also, Duvall to Gray, September 19, 1943, with praise of Geist, copy in OPF, NARA-SL. In this position, Geist reported to Assistant Secretary of State Dean Acheson, who rated him very good. Performance evaluations in OPF, NARA-SL.

25. See the epilogue.

26. OSS, Washington to Bern, March 20, 1944, RG 226, entry 210, box 442, folder wn 16644–16648, NARA. It is clear from this document that Geist had already done earlier work for OSS. On Kolbe, see Greg Bradsher, "A Time to Act: The Beginning of the Fritz Kolbe Story, 1900–1943," *Prologue* 34, no. 1 (Spring 2002), www.archives.gov/publications/prologue /2002/spring/fritz-kolbe-2.html.

27. See discussion in Breitman and Lichtman, *FDR and the Jews*, 205–212.

28. Herbert, *Best*, 354–359; Bo Lidegaard, *Countrymen*, trans. Robert Maass (New York: Alfred A. Knopf, 2013), 40–45.

29. Herbert, *Best*, 362–365. Lidegaard, *Countrymen*, 44–45.

30. Hans Kirchhoff, *Georg Ferdinand Duckwitz: Die Rettung der dänischen Juden* (Berlin: Auswärtiges Amt, 2013), 56–61.

31. Lidegaard, *Countrymen*, 44–95.

32. Lidegaard, *Countrymen*, 70–73. Herbert, *Best*, 369–372.

33. That figure includes non-Jewish spouses and some others. Therkel Straede told me on November 2, 2018, that, since the publication of Ulrich Herbert's biography of Best, this is the consensus among Danish experts on the subject.

34. Taylor (Tikander), Stockholm to OSS Director, Washington (Donovan), February 24, 1945, RG 226, entry 210, box 365, folder 14287–14300, NARA. The key part of the telegraph reads: "Cutout to Himmler is Doctor Best, who is still in close contact with Himmler. Best will, on short notice, send trustworthy official to Stockholm if there is any message for Himmler. No one else will see message." On the general situation, see Meredith Hindley, "Negotiating the Boundary of Unconditional Surrender: The War Refugee Board in Sweden and Nazi Proposals to Ransom Jews, 1944–1945," *Holocaust and Genocide Studies* 10, no. 1 (Spring 1996): 52–77. Hindley does not mention Best's effort, as the document naming him was declassified after her article was published.

Epilogue

1. T. Rees Shapiro, "German-Born U.S. Soldier Found Hitler's Last Will and Testament," *Washington Post*, December 10, 2010, www.washington post.com/wp-dyn/content/article/2010/12/09/AR2010120906180.html.

2. See chapter six.

3. Honaker to Secretary of State, January 19, 1938, RG 59, 150.626J/356, NARA.

4. Shapiro, "German-Born U.S. Soldier."

5. Shapiro, "German-Born U.S. Soldier."

6. This is a very inadequate summary of material in Herbert, *Best*, 403–521.

7. Anna Geist in Memoriam, Raymond Geist Papers, Franklin D. Roosevelt Library.

8. Commissioner of Immigration and Naturalization to Circuit Court Montgomery County, Rockville, Maryland, January 15, 1945, and Citizenship Petition, USCIS FOIA GEN2018002206.

9. Dated July 28, 1945, Raymond Geist Papers, Franklin D. Roosevelt Library.

10. Information from Susan Cooper and John Maller.

11. The key contemporary source is Wall to Director FBI, May 2, 1945, RG 65, Entry A1-112, box 2, classification 64, folder 64-175-232, section 5, serials 312–366, NARA. In support of this, Nathaniel Davis memo re Geist, July 2, 1945, OPF, NARA-SL: "Messersmith has it in mind to become the chief American representative on the German Control Council when it is changed from military to civilian control and has told Geist that he expects to have him with him." On Geist's exhilaration, Memorandum of conversation with Mr. Geist, July 27 and August 2, 1946, copy in OPF, NARA-SL.

12. Affidavit of August 26, 1945, *Nazi Conspiracy and Aggression*, vol. 4, 1759-PS.

13. Stiller, *George S. Messersmith*, 269–270.

14. Geist to Cecil Gray, March 29, 1946, copy in OPF, NARA-SL.

15. Messersmith to Donald Russell, May 15, 1946; Geist to Cecil Gray, June 10, 1946; Memorandum of conversation with Ambassador Thurston, July 25 and August 1, 1946, copy in OPF, NARA-SL.

16. Memorandum of conversation with Mr. Geist, July 27 and August 2, 1946, copy in OPF, NARA-SL.

17. Memorandum of conversation with Mr. Geist, July 27 and August 2, 1946, copy in OPF, NARA-SL.

18. HST to CWG, undated, note in OPF, NARA-SL.

19. See Norman J.W. Goda, Richard Breitman, Barbara McDonald Stewart, and Severin Hochberg, eds., *To the Gates of Jerusalem: The Diaries and Papers of James G. McDonald, 1945–1947* (Bloomington: Indiana University Press in association with the United States Holocaust Memorial Museum, 2015), 13, 21–23, 228–229.

20. Geist to Peurifoy, June 9, 1948; Geist to Armour, June 9, 1948; Armour to Geist, July 2, 1948: copies in OPF, NARA-SL.

21. Hening to Dr. George P. Biggs, October 6, 1948, copy in OPF, NARA-SL.

22. Marshall to Geist, November 26, 1948, OPF, NARA-SL. Biggs to State Department, October 4, 1948, and Hening to Biggs, October 6, 1948, OPF, NARA-SL. Biggs's first letter to Geist was returned to the State Department, which suggested he contact Geist at Edgemoor Lane in Bethesda.

23. Details in OPF, NARA-SL.

24. Kopp to Geist, December 2, 1954, Raymond Geist Papers, Franklin D. Roosevelt Library. "Ex-U.S. Attaché in Berlin Gets German Medal," *Los Angeles Times*, December 9, 1954.

25. "Kündigungsschreiben der Landesjustizverwaltung an den Richter Dr. Franz Bunzel (1896-1973)" [Letter of resignation of the regional justice administration to the judge Franz Bunzel (1896–1973)], July 24, 1933, paper, 29.8 x 21 cm, Jewish Museum Berlin, http://objekte.jmberlin.de/object /jmb-obj-499488;jsessionid=303403F94DB86C3486F296BF5603D78C.

26. "Hedwig Münden (née Salomon) * 1879," Stolpersteine Hamburg, Hamburg.de, http://stolpersteine-hamburg.de/en.php?MAIN_ID=7&BIO _ID=2700.

27. Vorschlagsliste Nr. 266, Auswärtiges Amt, September 11, 1954, attached to G. Pfeiffer to Breitman, December 10, 1982.

28. Lochner Diary, May 20, 1939, Louis B. Lochner Papers, box 11, diaries folder, Wisconsin Historical Society.

INDEX

Credit: Carol Breitman

Richard Breitman is distinguished professor emeritus in history at American University and the author or coauthor of twelve books and many articles in German history, US history, and the Holocaust. Apart from his book *FDR and the Jews*, coauthored with Allan J. Lichtman, he is best known for *The Architect of Genocide: Himmler and the Final Solution* and *Official Secrets: What the Nazis Planned, What the British and Americans Knew*. He lives in the DC metro area.

PublicAffairs is a publishing house founded in 1997. It is a tribute to the standards, values, and flair of three persons who have served as mentors to countless reporters, writers, editors, and book people of all kinds, including me.

I. F. STONE, proprietor of *I. F. Stone's Weekly*, combined a commitment to the First Amendment with entrepreneurial zeal and reporting skill and became one of the great independent journalists in American history. At the age of eighty, Izzy published *The Trial of Socrates*, which was a national bestseller. He wrote the book after he taught himself ancient Greek.

BENJAMIN C. BRADLEE was for nearly thirty years the charismatic editorial leader of *The Washington Post*. It was Ben who gave the *Post* the range and courage to pursue such historic issues as Watergate. He supported his reporters with a tenacity that made them fearless and it is no accident that so many became authors of influential, best-selling books.

ROBERT L. BERNSTEIN, the chief executive of Random House for more than a quarter century, guided one of the nation's premier publishing houses. Bob was personally responsible for many books of political dissent and argument that challenged tyranny around the globe. He is also the founder and longtime chair of Human Rights Watch, one of the most respected human rights organizations in the world.

·　　·　　·

For fifty years, the banner of Public Affairs Press was carried by its owner Morris B. Schnapper, who published Gandhi, Nasser, Toynbee, Truman, and about 1,500 other authors. In 1983, Schnapper was described by *The Washington Post* as "a redoubtable gadfly." His legacy will endure in the books to come.

Peter Osnos, *Founder*